'Since at l[and Other Postmodernist Myths

M. J. Devaney

First published in Great Britain 1997 by
MACMILLAN PRESS LTD
Houndmills, Basingstoke, Hampshire RG21 6XS and London
Companies and representatives throughout the world

A catalogue record for this book is available from the British Library.

ISBN 0–333–68164–9

First published in the United States of America 1997 by
ST. MARTIN'S PRESS, INC.,
Scholarly and Reference Division,
175 Fifth Avenue, New York, N.Y. 10010

ISBN 0–312–17511–6

Library of Congress Cataloging-in-Publication Data
Devaney, M. J., 1964–
"Since at least Plato" and other postmodernist myths / M.J. Devaney.
p.   cm.
Originally presented as the author's thesis (doctoral)—University
of Virginia, 1994.
Includes bibliographical references and index.
ISBN 0–312–17511–6
1. Postmodernism—Controversial literature.   I. Title.
B831.2.D48 1997
149'.97—dc21   97–7781
                                                          CIP

© M. J. Devaney 1997

This book is printed on paper suitable for recycling and made from fully managed and sustained forest sources.

10   9   8   7   6   5   4   3   2   1
06   05   04   03   02   01   00   99   98   97

Printed and bound by
Antony Rowe Ltd, Chippenham, Wiltshire

'SINCE AT LEAST PLATO . . .'
AND OTHER POSTMODERNIST MYTHS

To my mother, my father, and Charles

Contents

Acknowledgments

This book orginated as my doctoral dissertation, written at the University of Virginia under the direction of Micahel Levenson, and benefitted in the early stages of its transition from dissertation to book from his advice, as well as from the valuable suggestions of Rita Felski and Richard Rorty. Raymond Tallis was instrumental in both providing me with guidance on how to improve the manuscript, and directing Macmillan's attention to it, and I am very grateful to him for all his help and time. The participants on alt.postmodern, especially 'moggin,' engaged in lively, at times heated, dialogue with me and helped me to see the weaknesses in my arguments. Discussions with a number of people over the past several years, including Phil Novak, Julie Grossman, and Jimmy Doyle, have improved the book in all sorts of ways. I would also like to acknowledge Charmian Hearne, my editor at Macmillan, for her role in seeing the book through all the stages of the publishing process. Finally, I would like to offer my deepest thanks to my parents, for all the love and support they have given me, and my husband, Charles Palermo, whose patience and encouragement during the long process of writing a dissertation and publishing a book have been abundant.

Introduction

In her recent *Risking Who One Is: Encounters with Contemporary Art and Literature*, Susan Rubin Suleiman provides the contours of the 'debate over postmodernism' (a phrase that by now has become as much of a critical commonplace as 'the quarrel between the ancients and the moderns' used to be) via what she calls a 'brief bedtime story':

> Once upon a time, not so long ago, there existed in the world of intellectuals a 'debate over postmodernism' . . . In philosophy, postmodernism was identified as a self-styled mode of 'weak thought,' prizing playfulness above logic, irony above absolutes, paradoxes above resolutions, doubt above demonstration. Some intellectuals found this dance of ideas liberating; to others, it appeared irresponsible, a dangerous nihilism. In the arts – literature, photography, architecture, film, performance, painting – postmodernism was identified with a freewheeling use of pastiche, quotation, and collage, methods that some intellectuals saw as innovative and critical, having the potential to undo (or at least put into question) received ideas and established ideologies. Other intellectuals voiced their disapproval or despair; for them, the loose eclecticism of postmodernist art, mixing up historical styles, ignoring boundaries between genres, scrambling distinctions between 'high' art and 'low,' between original and copy, was of a piece with the laxness of postmodernist philosophizing, a sign of the cultural exhaustion of capitalism, or of the decay produced by the proliferation of mass culture.
>
> (1994: 223)

There is, however, a third possibility here – that is, one's options with respect to the debate over postmodernism are not limited to regarding the ideas Suleiman refers to as either liberating or dangerous. Rather, one might question the assumption that informs both judgments, namely, that these ideas are indeed critical, provocative, and innovative. What I maintain in the following chapters is that the ideas promulgated by those whom Sulieman calls 'pro-postmodernists' and widely drawn upon by other contemporary

1

theorists and critics are either (a) trite (as is the case with the prizing of paradoxes over resolutions, since 'pro-postmodernists' tend to mistake false oppositions for paradoxes), (b) uncritical, or (c) as old as Plato.[1]

Consider, for example, Suleiman's claim that

> It appears to be a truth universally accepted, by the modernist critics of postmodernism, that postmodernist theory is incapable of furnishing an ethics or a politics. By arguing against a unified (rational) subject and (his) universal values, this theory, according to its critics, is unable 'to take any principled oppositional stance,' be it as concerns individual action or 'local or world politics.'
>
> (231, quoting Christopher Norris)

'I find it astonishing,' she concludes,

> that this argument is still current (witness its being made, in 1992, by Norris), despite the fact that it has been answered again and again by postmodernist theorists of contingency – who argue, in brief, that values are not universal but context-bound, not discovered in some Platonic sky but fashioned by historically situated human beings, and are for that reason subject to change. . . . The universalist (or, if you will, modernist) claim is that only by ascribing universal validity to one's ethical beliefs is one able to act ethically. A postmodernist ethics refuses to take this step, arguing that such ascriptions merely elevate one set of contingent beliefs to 'universal' status and that too many horrors have been inflicted by some human beings on others in the name of *their* universal values.
>
> (231–2; her emphasis)

Since, however, arguments for both relativism and absolutism have been propounded simultaneously and continuously throughout the history of western philosophy[2] this is not a debate the parties to which can be labeled 'pro-modernist' and 'pro-postmodernist.' The problem in this case, then, with the 'pro-postmodernist' position as Suleiman outlines it, is not that the apologists for it deny the existence of absolute values, and so, as Suleiman's 'pro-modernists' would have it, render principled moral and political action impossible. Rather, the problem is that both parties seem to assume that the idea that values are relative is innovative, or at least, as Suleiman describes it, anti-modernist.

To be sure, a number of theorists of postmodernism have objected to the notion that the term 'postmodernism' is meant to denote a set of new ideas. Judith Butler, for example, after having suggested that 'if the term postmodernism has some force or meaning within social theory, or feminist social theory in particular, perhaps it can be found in the critical exercise that seeks to show how theory, how philosophy, is always imbricated in power,' claims that 'that the philosophical apparatus in its various conceptual refinements is always engaged in exercising power is not a new insight, but then again the postmodern ought not to be confused with the new.' 'After all,' she concludes, 'the pursuit of the "new" is the preoccupation of high modernism; if anything, the postmodern casts doubt upon the possibility of a "new" that is not in some way already implicated in the old' (1995: 216). The irony, however, is that Butler here proposes as itself a new notion the rejection of the notion of a 'new' that is not in some way imbricated in the old. And it is only by positing a strawman – 'high modernists' believed that the 'new' was generated *in vacuo* (has Butler read 'Tradition and the Individual Talent'?) – that she is able to represent the trite observation that the new is always implicated in the old as 'postmodern.' (Moreover, she makes this observation about 'high modernism' after she has also suggested that part of what she understands to be the 'project of postmodernism' is 'to call into question the ways in which . . . "examples" and "paradigms" serve to subordinate and erase that which they seek to explain' (215).)

Other theorists of postmodernism have also proposed that what renders an idea 'postmodern' is not that it's new; rather, they suggest, what makes it 'postmodern' is that it is now widely accepted. Steinar Kvale, for one, argues that

It is debatable whether postmodernity is actually a break with modernity, or merely its continuation. Postmodern writers may prefer to write history so that their own ideas appear radically new. Postmodern themes were present in the romanticism of the last century, in Nietzsche's philosophy at the turn of the century, with the surrealists and in literature, for instance, in Blixen and Borges. What is new today is the pervasiveness of postmodern themes in culture at large.

(1995: 19)

However, Kvale offers no evidence that 'a loss of belief in an object-ive world and an incredulity toward meta-narratives of legitima-tion' (19) – which he claims 'postmodern thought is characterized by' (19) – are pervasive in the culture at large, and indeed, I see no evidence of wide agreement among people today with respect to the question of the nature of reality or with respect to the believability of metanarratives of legitimation. Nor do I see that there has ever been any such consensus, which is to say that the terms 'modern-ity,' 'modernism,' and 'modernist,' as explicated by many theorists of postmodernism – e.g., 'modernist' thought is characterized by a belief in an objective world – are as problematic as 'postmodernity,' 'postmodernism,' and 'postmodernist.'

In suggesting that '[i]t's not the world that is postmodern . . . [but] the perspective from which that world is seen that is postmodern' (1995: 9), Hans Bertens acknowledges the problem with propos-ing that the term 'postmodern' has force because it describes a post-war *Zeitgeist*. 'Although the omnipresence of the postmodern and its advocates would seem to suggest otherwise,' he continues, 'not everybody subscribes to the view that language constitutes, rather than represents, reality' or that 'the autonomous and stable sub-ject of modernity has been replaced by a postmodern agent whose identity is largely other-determined and always in process' (9). Yet Berten's claim that it is the perspective from which the world is seen rather than the world itself that is 'postmodern' is no more enlightening than Kvale's on the question of what the force of the term is supposed to be. For the argument, for example, that lan-guage constitutes reality amounts, as some postmodernists articulate it, to an espousal of idealism (i.e., the belief that reality does not exist independently of our minds, languages, or conceptual schemes), which has long been a staple of western philosophical thought, or, as other postmodernists have articulated it, to the claim that our experience of reality is mediated by language, which is trite.[3]

It is worth noting, moreover, that both the claim that language constitutes rather than represents reality and the claim that the auto-nomous and stable subject of modernity has been replaced by a postmodern agent whose identity is largely other-determimed and always in process – among what Bertens refers to as 'some of the more familiar postmodern tenets' (10) – pose false oppositions. It doesn't follow that if language constructs reality, it can't represent it, especially if the claim that language constructs reality is glossed as meaning that language mediates our experience of reality. (Witness

Bertens' description of 'the Derridean reading according to which representation has always been an illusion since experience is inevitably mediated by language, and thus always coded' (86). What this implies is that the only way representation could be 'real' is if experience weren't mediated by language, and yet representation just *is* experience, whether linguistically constructed or not, mediated by language – that is, representation is not an illusion even if representation is a representation of a representation, since it's still, well, representation.) Nor does it follow that if subjects are largely other-determined and always in process, they can't be autonomous and stable. That is, it doesn't follow that if the subject is determined 'within and constituted by language' (6) (this is how Berten's defines 'other-determined'), it lacks free will (one would have to make an argument to the effect that the fact that subjectivity is constituted in and by language proves that determinism is true). Nor does it follow that if the subject is always in process, it doesn't persist over time; indeed, the idea that the subject is always in process entails just the opposite, for the very idea of something being always in process requires that there is a something that is always in process – that is, requires stability. (So I shouldn't really be describing subject-as-stable-entity/subject-as-an-entity-that-is-always-in-process as a false opposition because it's not simply the case that the subject *could* be both always in process and stable; rather, it *has* to be stable to be always in process.) This kind of sloppy thinking is one example (another would be Suleiman's implying that if values are context-bound or contingent, they can't be universal) of the uncritical quality of theories of the postmodern that I address throughout what follows, and that, in large part, has motivated this project.

It is the fact that these theories are critically wanting that renders the alarmist sentiments – to the effect that they presage the downfall of western civilization – of a number of critics of postmodernist theory unwarranted and their criticism misplaced. Lynne Cheney, for example, in her recent *Telling the Truth*, states that her mission in her book is 'to consider the distortions and divisions being wrought by a kind of thinking that denies there is truth and to examine how it is that this postmodern approach has become entrenched and powerful' (1995: 21), and claims that 'so much that follows from denying the idea of truth is deeply unsettling' (19). But if indeed the postmodern approach involves a kind of thinking that denies there is truth, then, since the denial of truth is, on the face of it, a truth-claim, Cheney's criticism of this attack on truth is misdirected. Rather than dramatically claim, as she does, that the answer to the question of 'whether we as a society find the will to live in truth' may 'very well determine whether we survive' (206), she ought to be asking whether any of 'the growing number of academics' she claims subscribe to the view that 'the truth is not merely irrelevant, [but] . . . no longer exist[s]' (16) have succeeded in denying the existence of truth without pragmatically self-refuting themselves. The reason she doesn't pursue this issue, as becomes clear, is that she is not in fact interested in it; rather, she merely uses the idea that the 'postmodern approach' involves a kind of thinking that denies the existence of truth as a means of making her opponents – leftists, as it turns out – look 'dangerous,' and as a smoke screen for passing off her own reactionary views as self-evident truths. Consider, for example, the following remarks she makes about Foucault:

> His ideas were nothing less than an assault on Western civiliza-
> tion. In rejecting an independent reality, an externally verifiable
> truth, and even reason itself, he was rejecting the foundational
> principles of the West. This was revolution by other means, and
> in the voice of those who took up the call, one hears the thrill of
> being part of a subversive movement, the excitement of particip-
> ating in forbidden acts.
>
> (91)

The idea that to reject, say, the existence of a mind- or language-independent reality, is to participate in a forbidden act is laughable; indeed, anti-realism is as much of a foundational principle in western philosophy as realism is. That theorists of postmodernism (and by 'theorists of postmodernism' I don't mean, as I explain below, Foucault, Derrida, Lacan, etc.) argue that the idea that reality does not exist independently of language is subversive I do not deny; that Cheney allows the argument to stand, however, demonstrates that her criticism is not only misguided, but weak. She provides no arguments to defend realism; rather she seems to assume that to denounce anti-realism as an 'assault on Western civilization' is enough to secure the truth of realism. Moreover, like many theorists of postmodernism, she fallaciously assumes that a belief in metaphysical anti-realism entails a commitment to a leftist politics and that a belief in metaphysical realism entails a commitment to a conservative politics. Cheney complains about what she identifies as 'one of the characteristics of postmodern thought' – that its claims are 'usually asserted rather than argued, reasoned argument having been rejected as one of the tools of the white male elite' (18) – but the claims she makes in her own book amount to little more than unargued opinion masquerading as self-evident truth.

My critique of theories of the postmodern centers on two *topoi* I have found to be widely present in them. In Part I, I examine the claim commonly made by theorists of the postmodern to have replaced something they call 'the logic of either/or,' alleged to structure 'western metaphysics,' with something else they call 'the logic of both/and,' alleged to violate the law of noncontradiction. The problem with this claim, as I try to show, has nothing to do with the question of whether there are true contradictions – that is, I don't argue that the idea that there could be true contradictions is prima facie absurd, and that therefore 'the logic of both/and' is absurd because its sponsors assume the existence of true contradictions. Rather, the problem – to which I have already alluded in suggesting that when 'pro-postmodernists' prize paradoxes over resolutions, they are typically mistaking false oppositions for contradictions – is that the arguments these theorists make on behalf of 'the logic of both/and' betray the fact that they don't know what a contradiction is or what would count as a true one, and that they harbor serious misconceptions about classical logic in general and its bearing on the so-called western metaphysical tradition. In addition to examining a host of general, theoretical claims advanced about 'the logic of both/and,' I also examine the attempts of a number of theorists and critics to practically apply this 'logic' to the analysis of literary texts.

In Part II, I take up the accounts that theorists of postmodernism have offered of both realist fiction and the fiction they associate with 'postmodernism.' Those theorists who address the subject of literary history tend to figure realist fiction and the fiction they want to claim marks a radical departure from it (as well as from 'modernist' fiction) as the repository of certain epistemological, metaphysical, moral, and political beliefs, as the expression of *Zeitgeister*, epistemes, paradigms, or *Weltanschauungen* termed 'modernity' (or 'the western metaphysical tradition' or 'Enlightenment thought') and 'postmodernity.' The problems here are numerous, and are in large part the product of misapprehensions about the history of western thought over the last three hundred years: they include, *inter alia*, the assumption that eighteenth- and nineteenth-century realist fiction unthinkingly reflects the idea that reality exists independently of beliefs about it because that was the 'idea of the time' back then, and the assumption that postmodernist fiction, by contrast, radically questions the nature of reality by positing that reality is a linguistic construct – the latter being presented not only as the 'idea of the time' in the late-twentieth century, but also as the truth about the nature of reality.

Theorists of postmodernism effect this reductive schematization in a number of ways, one of which I discuss at length – one wherein Newtonian and post-Newtonian physics are represented as having certain metaphysical, epistemological, moral, and political implications that are 'reflected' in realist and postmodernist fiction (e.g., Newton's theory of absolute space and time 'implies' a commitment to an absolutist epistemology that is definitive of 'Enlightenment thought' and that is mirrored in the realist fiction not only of the eighteenth and nineteenth centuries, but also in the 'outmoded' realist fiction of the twentieth century, while Einstein's theory of relative space-time 'implies' the truth of cognitive relativism, which describes a postmodernist epistemology that is reflected in postmodernist fiction).

A word is in order about whose work it is that I am proposing to critique. It is not primarily Derrida's, Foucault's, etc. Since it is widely assumed that the French *philosophes* are quintessentially 'postmodernist,' an explanation is warranted as to why they don't figure largely in what follows. There are two related reasons why they don't. First, my concern is with the theorization of postmodernism and with the appropriation of ideas associated with this theorization by many contemporary theorists and critics, and, as Bertens observes, 'no matter how we evaluate the significance of [Derrida et al.'s] contributions to that ever expanding intellectual/artistic complex that is postmodernism, they have not involved themselves in . . . attempts to define and theorize the postmodern' (17).

The exception, of course, to this, is, as Bertens notes, Lyotard (17). I regard Lyotard's claims as skeptically as I do that of other theorists of postmodernism. His notorious definition of the postmodern as an incredulity toward metanarratives is, if taken to be positing the existence of a late-twentieth century sensibility, belied not only by the millions of people who still seek legitimation for their beliefs in the metanarratives provided by a whole host of religions, but also by theorists of postmodernism – including Lyotard himself, under this interpretation of his definition – who seek to legitimate their claims about postmodernism by reference to epistemes, paradigm shifts, etc. If, on the other hand, Lyotard's definition is interpreted not as positing the existence of late-twentieth century sensibility, but rather as positing the existence of a transhistorical *mentalité* (an interpretation suggested by his claim in 'Answering the Question: What is Postmodernism?' that postmodernism is modernism in its nascent state), then why call it 'postmodern'? To do so is not only misleading (the term, after all, implies 'after the modern') but arbitrary (one might as well define the postmodern as a credulity towards metanararatives and the modern as an incredulity toward metanarratives). That said, however, Lyotard has not contributed in a significant way to the arguments that assert the existence of a contradictory postmodernist logic or to the arguments that propose regarding eighteenth- and nineteenth-century art in terms of a reflection of 'Enlightenment thought' and late twentieth-century art in terms of a reflection of 'post-Enlightenment thought' – he makes remarks here and there that are relevant to these arguments, and where he does, I take note, but he has not substantively engaged with them.

Second, since my purpose in criticizing theories of postmodernism is not to argue against the ontology, metaphysics, or epistemology that informs the ideas its apologists advance about reality, language, knowledge, truth, logic, or self, but to expose the uninformed and uncritical thinking that gives rise to the belief that these ideas warrant the designation 'postmodernist,' and since those postwar French philosophers most often invoked as the 'fathers' of postmodernism don't claim to be advancing an ontology, metaphysics, or epistemology that is characteristic of or particular to a new epoch in the history of cultural production, there are no grounds for me to criticize them *as postmodernists*. That is, the idealism, for example, implied by the way any number of theorists of postmodernism gloss the claim that language constructs reality might well be manifest in, e.g., Derrida's 'Il n'y a pas de hors-text,' but Derrida, whether or not he espouses the linguistic idealism often attributed to him, does not represent the idea that there is no outside-text as being a new account of the nature of reality. If I were writing a defense of metaphysical realism and if I believed Derrida was espousing linguistic idealism, I might object to his work on the grounds that it is idealist. But since I am not writing defense of metaphysical realism or of any philosophical theory, but rather am criticizing the sloppy thinking that characterizes theorizations of postmodernism and its progeny, I am not in position to object to his work on the grounds that it is postmodernist. That Derrida himself rejects the term 'postmodernist' is not to the point; his work could still be in line with the idea of the postmodern as it is conceptualized by theorists of postmodernism even though he refuses the label. However, my suggestion is that it isn't, that indeed his philosophical disposition is at odds with the idea of periodization that postmodernism depends on (as Ingeborg Hoesterey puts it, 'the teleological linearity of a modernism/postmodernism dialetic is not in the interest of the deconstructive operation' (1991: xii)).

That said, there can be no doubt that the work, or at least interpretations of the work, of a number of postwar French philosophers who have not theorized the postmodern has played a part in the development of theories of postmodernism, and to the extent that their work or interpretations of it bear on the subjects I explore here, I address them. Because, for example, Derrida is credited by a number of theorists as being the 'inventor' of the 'contradictory' logic of 'both/and,' I examine what grounds there might be to this attribution. There are, I suggest, problems with some of Derrida's assertions about logic, but he does not, unlike those theorists of postmodernism who have drawn on his work in an effort to support their claims for the existence of a contradictory postmodernist logic, persist in arguing for the existence of a logic that violates the law of noncontradiction that is based in a fundamental misapprehension of what constitutes a contradiction. Theorists of postmodernism who believe that Derrida's remarks support their own claims to the existence of a logic that violates the law of noncontradiction are not, I think, wholly unwarranted in their belief – however, they not only fail to cast a critical eye on what Derrida says; they also go on to reify what he himself does not.

Since I don't believe that the ideas that, as a result of the efforts of a multitude of primarily English-speaking theorists and critics, have come to be associated with postmodernism threaten western civilization, or even academe, then why have I bothered to issue a critique of them? I've bothered because I believe that the bulk of the work that embraces these ideas is third-rate – which is to say that I think there is no better reason for critiquing a school of thought that has achieved the prominence that postmodernism has achieved than that one believes that the bulk of the work produced in its name is third-rate. Clearly this work would not be as well-regarded as it is nor would it be proliferating as it is if more members of the academic community agreed with my estimation of it. I've undertaken this project in the hope of persuading more of them to regard the very idea of postmodernism skeptically.

Part I
Postmodernism and the Innocuous Logic of 'Both/And'

1
The Rhetoric of the Logic of Both/And

The prevalence of the logic of contradiction in postmodern thought is perhaps so obvious as to escape notice. Certainly the continental propensity to accept contradiction explains much of the oft-commented upon failure for a dialogue to develop between continental and Anglo-American philosophy. Marxism, structuralism, poststructuralism, and other derivatives of Hegelianism (including psychoanalysis) all render visible contradictions that are somehow both immanent and hard to discern. Marx and Freud still retain (in the notions of a communist society and in the cure) some hope for eventual overcoming of contradiction, but structuralism and poststructuralism find in contradiction (binary oppositions or the antinomies revealed by a deconstructive reading) both beginning and end.

(McGowan, 1991: 49)

Ps and Qs

Against McGowan, it could be argued that the 'oft-commented upon failure for a dialogue to develop between continental and Anglo-American philosophy' is not the result of something as ill-defined as a postmodernist 'propensity' to accept contradictions. Nor, it could be argued, is this failure the consequence of a more specific disagreement – the result, say, of a disagreement between postmodernists and analytic philosophers who accept classical logic over the question of whether the Liar sentence ('This sentence is false') is a true contradiction. After all, there is dialogue between classical logicians who suggest that the sentence is not a true contradiction and dialetheists who claim that it is.[1] And so if postmodernists did make a provocative case for why the Liar sentence ought to be regarded as a true contradiction, one would expect to find classical logicians engaging them just as they engage dialetheists.

I likewise question David Roochnik's suggestion – made in

15

response to calls from John Smith and Alan Montefiore for ser-ious dialogue and mutual respect between analytic and continental philosophers – that the 'proposed dialogue . . . between contempor-ary French and Anglo-American philosophy [is not] a realistic and viable expectation' because the former reject and the latter accept the law of noncontradiction (1986: 148). He argues that a 'philosophical dialogue implies disagreement or controversy' (148) and that, on the one hand, such a dialogue can only take place if there is agree-ment about fundamental issues. On the other, he claims that '[i]f there is no disagreement a conversation can still occur, but it will not be a dialogue' because 'it will be [something] that is grounded upon some fundamental agreement' (148). So he implies that philo-sophical dialogue may well be impossible as such.[2] If this is the case, then all that is possible between philosophers is 'conversation' (this includes instruction and didactic persuasion, both of which Roochnik thinks are 'highly desirable,' but neither of which yield a dialogue as he defines it), and so I suggest that if 'conversation' could occur between Anglo-American philosophers and 'post-Nietzschean continental philosoph[ers]' (159), we would have all we could hope for. Since Roochnik admits that it is conversation – 'an exchange culminating in a moment of learning' – that appears 'to be the hope of Smith [and] Montefiore' (153), what he really needs to show in order to demonstrate that their hope is unrealistic is that conversa-tion, as he defines it, cannot occur between them. As I've indicated, however, such exchanges do in fact occur between dialetheists and classical logicians (which suggests that if Roochnik is right in claim-ing that some fundamental agreement is required for conversation to occur, disagreement about the truth of the law of noncontradiction does not constitute a fundamental disagreement).

Nor, finally, do I think that, as Richard Freadman and Lloyd Reinhardt put it, 'significant *rapprochement* between the "analytic" (and associated aesthetico-humanist) paradigm and the "contin-ental" one is not possible' because, 'as some would say of Derrida and Searle, they are simply talking different languages' (1992: 7; Freadman and Reinhardt aren't themselves claiming that no *rap-prochement* is possible). For if theorists of postmodernism – who often represent postmodernism as an outgrowth of contemporary continental thought – and analytic philosophers who accept clas-sical logic were simply talking different languages, then the idea that postmodernist thought 'subverts' classical logic would be unintel-ligible. I suggest, rather, that theorists of postmodernism who argue that postmodernist thought has replaced 'the logic of either/or' with 'the logic of both/and' believe that this logic poses a challenge to the law of noncontradiction of classical logic, but that because these theorists have a muddled conception of this law, and of classical logic in general, the challenge they suggest is posed by 'the logic of both/and' never gets off the ground. So I think that there has been no impetus for those in the analytic camp who are committed to classical logic to engage the postmodernist one. Dialogue is at least possible between classical and other sorts of logicians – paraconsistents, relevantists, situationists, intuitionists, all of whom find classical logic to be inadequate in certain respects – because these revisionist logicians, unlike their postmodernist counterparts, are thoroughly familiar with classical logic.

'Binary logic operates within the limits of an exclusive disjunction ("either ... or ...")': On the contrary

A representative account of the logic – often asserted to be the brainchild of Derrida[3] – that 'problematizes' the law of noncontradiction of classical logic is provided by Alan Schrift in 'The Becoming-Postmodern of Philosophy':

> When marking the interval between philosophy's classical hierarchical oppositions and the undecidables, Derrida marks the limits of the binary logic that guides the history of metaphysics. In so doing, he displays another sort of logic that he calls the 'logic of supplementarity.' This 'other' logic has been repressed and excluded by the history of philosophy. Whereas binary logic operates within the limits of an exclusive disjunction ('either ... or ...'), Derrida's undecidable logic of supplementarity is a logic of 'both ... and ...' that resists and disorganizes classical binary thinking. The fundamental laws of binary logic are the principles of identity ($A = A$) and noncontradiction (not [A and not-A]). The movement of the undecidables exhibits a different principle: the nonexclusive conjunction *both* A *and* not-A. The *pharmakon*, for example, 'acts as both remedy and poison. . . .' *Pharmakon* plays between the poles of remedy and poison, and to render it as either 'remedy' or 'poison,' as the binary thinking of the history of metaphysics is prone to do, cancels the resources of signification reserved in that sign[.]
>
> (1990: 104)

Classical logic does not, however, as Schrift puts it, 'operate[ ] within the limits of an exclusive disjunction ("either . . . or . . .").' That it doesn't is indicated by the fact that the symbol standardly used to signify disjunction in formal logic is '∨' – which derives from the Latin 'vel,' meaning 'either . . . or . . . or maybe both,' as distinct from 'aut,' meaning 'either . . . or . . . but not both.' As far as I know, the exclusive sense of 'or' has no standard operator of its own, but it can be expressed in the propositional calculus as ([P ∨ Q] & [~P ∨ ~Q]).[4]

Classically, of course, a disjunction of the form (P ∨ ~P) – as distinct from that of the form (P ∨ Q) – is exclusive by virtue of the fact that its disjuncts are contradictories. I suggest that Schrift, in claiming that classical logic operates within the limits of an exclusive disjunction (either . . . or . . .), in effect reduces all disjunctions to the tautology (P ∨ ~P) – that is, he conflates (P ∨ ~P) and (P ∨ Q). Likewise, he conflates (P & ~P) and (P & Q). He assumes that to assert that the *pharmakon*[5] is either a remedy or a poison is formally equivalent to asserting (P ∨ ~P). And so he arrives at the mistaken conclusion that to state that it is both a poison and remedy is formally equivalent to asserting (P & ~P). If Schrift were to claim that the *pharmakon* was both a remedy and not a remedy, or both a poison and not a poison, at the same time and in the same sense, then that *would* amount to a contradiction by the lights of classical logic, for, by it, if the *pharmakon* is a remedy it cannot *not* be a remedy at the same time and in the same respect, and if it is a poison, it cannot *not* be a poison at the same time and in the same respect. That is, as far as classical logic is concerned, there would be no contradiction if the *pharmakon* were a remedy and not a remedy at the same time but in different senses or different respects, or were a remedy and not a remedy in the same sense but at different times. Suppressing mention of these stipulations is one of the oldest sophistic tricks in the book. As the Socrates of *The Republic* cautions after having asked Glaucon whether 'the same thing [can] both stand still and move in the same part at the same time' and having received the answer 'Impossible' from him,

'Let us be even more exact or we may have a dispute somewhere before we go on. Suppose a man is standing still, but moving hands and head; if someone were to say the same man is standing still and moving at the same time, we should not allow that to be right, but we should say part of him stands still and part moves. Isn't that right?'

'It is.'

'The speaker might go further in this and refine upon it with quite a bit of pretty wit. He might say of a spinning top that the whole thing stands still and turns at the same time, when it fixes the peg in one spot and goes round and round upon it, and so also anything else does this that goes round in a circle in the same place, but we should not accept that. We should say that such things are not resting and revolving in the same parts of themselves, but they have a straight part (the axis) and a circling part (the periphery); in the straight part it moves round; and when it leans the perpendicular to right or left or front or back while it revolves, then it does not stand still anywhere.'

'Yes,' [Glaucon says], 'they are opposites.'

'So such a saying will not dismay us, and it will never convince us that the same thing in the same place towards the same thing could sometimes be or do or suffer two opposites.'

(1956: 235–6)

Schrift does not claim that the *pharmakon* is a poison and not a poison, or a remedy and not a remedy, at the same time and in the same respect. Rather, he points out that it is a poison (because it robs Socrates of his mortal existence) as well as a remedy (because Socrates believes, as Shrift notes, that 'we have reason to hope that death is a good that a virtuous man need not fear' (104)). His claim that the *pharmakon* is both a remedy and a poison, then, is not an instantiation of a 'different principle' – a true conjunction of the form (P & ~P). Rather, in terms of the propositional calculus, it could at best be regarded as formally equivalent to (P & Q) – a conjunction that would be true just in case both of its conjuncts were true.

The idea that the *pharmakon*'s being both a remedy and poison amounts to a contradiction has become something of a critical commonplace in the commentary on it. Brayton Polka, for one, remarking on 'Derrida's splendid[ ] depict[ion] of the contradictory logic' of Plato's dialogues – the 'written laws of Athens' that have unjustly condemned Socrates, he notes, 'are the *pharmakon*, the drug, the hemlock, both poison (for the body) and cure (for the soul) (1993: 36) – argues that though 'Derrida knows that it is foolish to rush to the conclusion that Plato, the incomparable master of logic, simply contradicts himself,' he 'does not know – it appears – that it is equally foolish to impale yourself on the opposite horn of the dilemma, that of proposing that Plato can escape contradiction' (36–7). This, Polka claims, 'is the solution that Derrida adopts in arguing that the *pharmakon*, by exceeding the oppositions structuring the discourse of Plato, as of all Greek discourse, bears the logic of the supplement' (37). Polka thinks that 'Greek scription *is* (without supplement) contra-diction, the *pharmakon*, the scapegoat which is both inside and outside, both poison and remedy, without relief (*relève*)' (38). That is, Polka thinks that Derrida tries to resolve, via the logic of the supplement, what is not resolvable within Greek discourse – 'Greek literature and philosophy' is, Polka claims, 'subject to the law of contradiction' (23) – that Derrida 'exceed[s], historically . . . the logic not only of the *Phaedrus* but also the *Parmenides* and the *Sophist* and all the rest of Plato's dialogues' (37). But again, since the *pharmakon*'s meaning or being, as Polka himself describes it, both a remedy (for the soul) and poison (for the body) doesn't violate the law of noncontradiction in the first place, there is nothing in this case for Derrida's logic of the supplement to resolve, and nothing in this case for Polka to claim is unresolvable within Greek discourse.

Steve Shankman, for another, argues in 'Plato and Postmodernism' that what Derrida implies in 'Plato's Pharmacy' is that

> [i]f Plato knew what he was doing, if he was in control of his language rather than being in the inevitable position of having his language control him . . . he would have made sure that the word *pharmakon* everywhere and unambiguously referred to the same specific thing: he could not have allowed it to mean both remedy *and* poison at the same time. Derrida's impressively learned, agile, but overly long and meandering essay then consists – to a large degree – of a relentless scholasticism that points out the often contradictory nature of the various things referred to chiefly by the word *pharmakon* and its cognates as Derrida ultimately argues that 'La pharmacie n'a pas de fond.'
>
> (1994: 8; his emphasis)

However, Shankman concludes, Derrida

appears to be confusing the philosopher Plato's views about language with the views of the ideologist Cratylus. The philosopher knows that words need not always mean the same thing, that ambiguity is intrinsic to the linguistic process. It is not Plato's pharmacy that has no foundation. It is rather Derrida's reading of Plato's pharmacy that has no foundation, because Derrida has made the fundamental mistake of assuming that for Plato, being a philosopher means, above all, achieving a systematic terminological consistency.

(18)

It may be that Derrida has made a fundamental mistake – not one of assuming that for Plato, being a philosopher means achieving a systematic terminological consistency, but rather one of assuming that there is necessarily a terminological inconsistency if an instance of the word *pharmakon* in Plato's text can be shown to mean both remedy and poison at the same time (I suggest below that Derrida does fail in places to acknowledge the distinction between exclusive and inclusive disjunctions). But Derrida aside, Shankman does make such a mistake. Shankman's argument is that Plato would not have been disturbed by the possibility of the word *pharmakon* meaning both remedy and poison at the same time because Plato accepted 'the inherently ambiguous and analogical nature of language' (8). Reality, according to Shankman, is paradoxical, and so '[l]anguage that is truly philosophical, such as Plato's in the *Phaedrus*, [has to] openly acknowledge its own paradoxical nature if it is to be true to the paradoxical nature of reality' (10). My argument is that Plato would not have been disturbed by the possibility of the word *pharmakon* meaning both remedy and poison at the same time because there is nothing necessarily contradictory about it meaning both at the same time.[6]

A misunderstanding of the law of the excluded middle – in particular, of the middle it excludes – seems in part to be the source of the misunderstanding of the law of noncontradiction evident in theories of postmodernism. Schrift erroneously takes the compound statement 'the *pharmakon* is either a poison or remedy' to be an instantiation of the law of the excluded middle ($P \lor \sim P$), and therefore apparently thinks that, in judging it to be false, he is rejecting the law of the excluded middle. In the course of denying that Nietzsche (the 'father' of postmodern philosophy on his view) is 'offering another privileged binary opposition' in 'resorting to the language of life-affirmation and life-negation or healthy and decadent will to power' (107), he further argues that:

An interpretation of healthy and decadent will to power in a nonoppositional sense is possible in terms of viewing 'health and disease' or 'affirmation and negation' as two poles of a single continuum that is will to power. Such an interpretation does not posit two mutually exclusive alternatives that call for some choice as is the case with the classical binary oppositions. Instead, the affirmation and negation of life are the normative limits of an open-ended continuum of will to power that admits only of 'degrees of gradation.'

(108)

He seems to be suggesting that 'X is healthy or X is diseased' amounts, classically speaking, to an instantiation of the law of the excluded middle – a compound statement that posits two mutually exclusive alternatives and that calls for some choice. However, 'X is healthy' and 'X is diseased,' where 'healthy' and 'diseased' are two poles of a single continuum, would be regarded by classical logicians as contraries, not contradictories – that is, as statements that don't necessarily call for some choice because both could be false.[7]

His pointing out that the word *pharmakon* plays between the poles of remedy and poison also suggests that what he believes is excluded by the law of the excluded middle are all the gradations that exist between two extremes. However, since the law states that for any proposition, either it or its negation is true, what it excludes is the possibility that neither P nor ~P is true – e.g., it cannot be the case that neither 'it is raining' nor 'it is not raining' is true. Nor can it be that both are false. It could, however, be that both 'it is drizzling' and 'it is pouring' are false because there are alternatives between these two extremes – the rain could be light but more than a drizzle or the rain could be hard but less than a downpour. There is no third possibility between 'it is raining' and 'it is not raining,' but there are a range of possibilities between 'it is drizzling' and 'it is pouring.' However, to accept that the statement 'either it is raining or not raining' is true does not mean one has to exclude the possibility that it is drizzling or pouring, for if it is drizzling or pouring, it is, of course, raining.

'It is raining' and 'it is not raining' are contradictories, meaning they are necessarily opposed with respect to truth and falsity – if 'it is raining' is true, then 'it is not raining' (at same time, in the same place, and in the same sense) is false, and vice versa: they can't both be true and they can't both be false. 'It is drizzling' and 'it is pouring' are contraries, meaning it is impossible for both to be true at the same time, in the same place, and in the same sense, but both may be false. 'The *pharmakon* is a poison' and 'The *pharmakon* is a remedy' are not contradictories because they are not necessarily opposed with respect to truth and falsity; neither are they contraries because, on Schrift's construal, the *pharmakon* is a poison in one respect and a remedy in another respect, and so it *is* possible within the terms of classical logic for both to be true at the same time.

One might note that hemlock, in a certain dose, will not kill human beings and can be used to remedy bodily pain – that is, with respect to the body, it can be, depending on dosage, either poisonous or remedial. Thus, 'Hemlock is a poison' and 'Hemlock is a remedy' could be contraries where 'poison' and 'remedy' were being used in the same sense – with respect to the body – and both, construed absolutely, would be false since hemlock is neither absolutely a remedy nor absolutely a poison with respect to the human body. The point is that the terms of what theorists of postmodernism call a 'binary opposition' may (depending on what the terms in question are) be predicated of a subject in such a way as to produce contrary assertions about it, both of which could be false, or they may be predicated of a subject in such a way as to produce assertions that are not contraries, both of which could be true.

For example, 'X is rich' and 'X is poor' will be contraries where 'rich' and 'poor' are being used in the same sense – e.g., rich or poor with respect to monetary wealth – in which case it will be impossible for both to be true, but both could be false (X may be neither rich nor poor but moderately well off). However, these assertions will not be contraries where 'rich' and 'poor' are being used in different senses – e.g., rich in a material sense and poor in a spiritual sense – in which case both could be true. This distinction is important if only because theorists of postmodernism sometimes seem to be accusing 'the western philosophical tradition' of denying that contrary assertions may both be false of something (the source of this accusation typically being a conflation of contradictories and contraries), and sometimes seem to be accusing it of 'repressing' the possibility of predicating both terms of a 'binary opposition' of something. Schrift makes both accusations – he claims that this tradition interprets 'classical binary oppositions' as 'posit[ing] two mutually exclusive alternatives that call for some choice' (and so, on his account, this tradition would force a choice between 'X is rich' and 'X is poor,' where 'rich' and 'poor' are being used in the same sense), and he argues that it has repressed the possibility of regarding the *pharmakon* as being both a remedy (in one sense) and a poison (in another sense).

Schrift also seems to imply that to reject the law of the excluded middle entails rejecting the law of noncontradiction. But this is not so. Intuitionist logic, for example, challenges the law of the excluded middle on the grounds that truth is not a predicate that, as Michael Dummett puts it, 'may attach to [a statement] even when we have no means of recognizing the fact' (1977: 7), but it does not reject the law of noncontradiction. From an intuitionist standpoint, an unproven mathematical statement, for instance, cannot be asserted to have a determinate truth-value independently of our capacity, at least in principle, of proving or disproving it:

> *We no longer explain the sense of a statement by stipulating its truth-value in terms of the truth-values of its constituents, but by stipulating when it may be asserted in terms of the conditions under which its constituents may be asserted.* The justification for this change is that this is how we in fact learn to use these statements: furthermore, the notions of truth and falsity cannot be satisfactorily explained so as to form a basis for an account of meaning once we leave the realm of effectively decidable statements. One result of this shift in our account of meaning is that, unless we are dealing only with effectively decidable statements, certain formulas which appeared in the two-valued logic to be logical laws no longer rank as such, in particular the law of the excluded middle: this is rejected, not on the ground that there is middle truth-value, but because meaning, and hence validity, is no longer to be explained in terms of truth-values.
>
> (1978: 18)

As an example, Dummett considers a dispute over the logical validity of the statement 'Jones was either brave or not brave':

> A imagines Jones to be a man, now dead, who never encountered danger in his life. B retorts that it could still be true that Jones was brave, namely if it is true that if Jones *had* encountered danger, he would have acted bravely. A agrees with this, but still maintains that it does not need to be the case that either 'Jones was brave' = 'If Jones had encountered danger, he would have acted bravely'

nor [*sic*] 'Jones was not brave' = 'If Jones had encountered danger, he would not have acted bravely' is true. For, he argues, it might be the case that however many facts we knew of the kind which we should normally regard as grounds for asserting such counterfactual conditionals, we should still know nothing which would be a ground for asserting either. It is clear that B cannot agree that this is a possibility and yet continue to insist that 'Jones was brave' or 'Jones was not brave' is true; for he would then be committed to holding that a statement may be true even though there is nothing whatever such that, if we knew of it, we should count as evidence or as a ground for the truth of the statement, and this is absurd.

(15)

If B still wants to insist on the logical necessity of 'Jones was either brave or not,' Dummett continues, he will have to argue either that there is some fact of the kind we typically appeal to in asserting counterfactuals, which, if we knew of it, would decide us in favor of one or the other, or that there is a fact of some kind which perhaps God might know of, but which we never could directly – *viz.*, that Jones either had the quality of courage within him or didn't, so that if he had encountered danger, and he had had this quality, then it would have been revealed in his actions: '[a]nyone of a sufficient degree of sophistication,' Dummett argues, 'will reject B's belief in a spiritual mechanism; either he will be a materialist and substitute for it an equally blind belief in a physiological mechanism, or he will accept A's conclusion that "Either Jones was brave or was not" is not logically necessary' (15–16).

Whatever one may think of this as a challenge to the logical necessity of $(P \lor \sim P)$, it does not amount to a denial of the logical necessity of $\sim(P \ \& \ \sim P)$. To claim that a statement is neither true nor false is not the same as claiming that it is both true and false, nor does it follow from asserting the former that one must commit oneself to the latter – indeed, a number of logicians have tried to use a denial of the law of the excluded middle to block the reasoning that leads to paradoxes like the Liar, though Graham Priest, among others, argues that this truth-value gap approach to the logical paradoxes does not work (1987: 15–20). (On the other hand, one might, like Priest, question the plausibility of a statement being neither true nor false, but accept the possibility of it being both true and false.)[8]

Derridean derivations

Whether Derrida thinks of his 'logic of supplementarity' as a contradictory logic of both/and is debatable, as is the question of whether this is what he means by calling the *pharmakon* an 'undecidable.' In *Positions*, he argues that

> [i]t has been necessary to analyze, to set to work, *within* the text of the history of philosophy, as well as *within* the so-called literary text . . . certain marks . . . that by *analogy* . . . I have called undecidables, that is, unities of simulacrum, 'false' verbal properties (nominal or semantic) that can no loger be included within philosophical (binary) opposition, resisting and disorganizing it, *without ever* constituting a third term, without ever leaving room for a solution in the form of speculative dialectics (the *pharmakon* is neither remedy nor poison, neither good nor evil, neither the inside nor the outside, neither speech nor writing; the *supplement* is neither a plus or a minus, neither an outside nor a complement of an inside, neither accident nor essence, etc.; the *hymen* is neither confusion nor distinction, neither identity nor difference, neither consummation nor virginity, neither the veil nor the unveiling, neither the inside nor the outside, etc. . . . Neither/nor, that is, *simultaneously*, either *or*).
>
> (1981b: 42–3)

This would appear to throw doubt at least on the idea that by Derrida's logic of supplementarity, the *pharmakon* is both a remedy and not a remedy, or both a poison and not a poison, at the same time and in the same sense. On the other hand, however, Derrida does suggest that the 'undecidable' is a contradiction – not a 'contradiction in the Hegelian form of contradiction,' he claims, because 'the Hegelian concept of contradiction (*Widerspruch*) . . . as its name indicates . . . is constructed in such a way as to permit its resolution within dialectical *discourse*' (101, n. 13). Rather, the 'undecidable' 'situates, in a rigorously Freudian sense, the *unconscious* of philosophical contradiction, the unconscious which ignores contradiction to the extent that contradiction belongs to the logic of speech, discourse, consciousness, presence, truth, etc.' (101, n. 13). He attempts, he says, 'to bring the critical operation to bear against the unceasing reappropriation of [the] work of the simulacrum by a dialectics of the Hegelian type . . . for Hegelian idealism consists precisely of a . . . resolution of contradiction into a third term' (43).

How does he do this? Well, according to McGowan, he takes an 'oppositional pair between which a text (or a society) asks us to choose (which term is worth more or should be granted priority either logically or temporally) and . . . declares that the choice is "undecidable" ' (105):

> In place of the hierarchical resolution of the contrast, a resolution that places one term above the other, the Derridean (non)solution places them in tensional play with one another, an oscillation that is not resolved in favor of one or the other. . . . To let the play continue would be to let differences bloom and contradictions remain in tension, as opposed to the recuperation of the other into the same that is always imposed as the end (telos) of a traditional philosophy. Play, then, might be characterized as what results from irresolvable contradictions.
>
> (1991: 105–6)

That this opposition to 'the recuperation of the other into the same' is a part of Derrida's strategy is suggested by his discussion of the *pharmakon* in 'Plato's Pharmacy.' The *pharmakon* has 'no stable essence, no "proper" characteristics'; it is 'an element that is *in itself*, if one can still say so, *undecidable*' (1981a: 125, 138; his emphasis). It 'has no ideal identity' (126) – it 'cannot be handled with complete security, neither in its being, since it has none, nor in its effects, the sense of which is always capable of changing' (126). The idea would seem to be that it has no one 'essential' meaning – rather, it has several (including 'remedy' and 'poison'), none of which is its 'true' one. Derrida maintains that Plato was, on the one hand, 'suspicious of the *pharmakon* in general, even in the case of drugs used exclusively for therapeutic ends' (99). That is, Plato regarded *pharmakon* as 'really' meaning 'poison,' reduced its sense as 'remedy' to 'poison' in considering pharmaceuticals to be, according to Derrida, 'essentially harmful because . . . artificial' (99). On the other hand, Derrida seems to suggest that the *pharmakon* emerges in the *Phaedo* as 'essentially' a remedy – it 'is presented to Socrates as a poison; yet it is transformed, through the effects of the Socratic *logos* and of the philosophical demonstration in the *Phaedo*, into a means of deliverance, a way toward salvation, a cathartic power' (126). Derrida's argument thus appears to be that Plato, resisting the idea that the *pharmakon* is not 'anything in itself,' is compelled to reduce it to one of its two 'poles' in any given context. 'Plato decides in favor of a logic that does not tolerate ... passages between opposing senses of the same word' (99), and, 'no doubt it could be shown ... that [the] blockage of the passage of opposing values [in translations] is itself already an effect of "Platonism," the consequence of something already at work in the translated text' (98):

> All translations into languages that are heirs and depositories of Western metaphysics ... produce on the *pharmakon* an *effect of analysis* that violently destroys it, reduces it to one of its simple elements by interpreting it, paradoxically enough, in light of the ulterior developments it itself has made possible. Such an interpretative translation is thus as violent as it is impotent: it destroys the *pharmakon* but at the same time forbids access to it, leaving it untouched in its reserve.
>
> (99; his emphasis)

However, though Plato himself 'decides in favor of a logic that does not tolerate opposing passages of the same word,' his use of the word in his dialogues, Derrida claims, works against his decision; translations into languages that are the 'heirs and depositories of Western metaphysics' counteract this 'textuality of the text,' thus restoring the 'Platonism' to Plato's work in those places where it has been undermined by Plato's language:

> When a word inscribes itself as the citation of another sense of the same word, when the textual center-stage of the word *pharmakon*, even while it means *remedy*, cites, re-cites, and makes legible that which *in the same word* signifies, in another spot and a different level of the stage, *poison* (for example, since that is not the only other thing *pharmakon* means), the choice of only one of these renditions by the translator has as its first effect the neutralization of the citational play, of the 'anagram,' and, in the end, of the very textuality of the text itself.
>
> (98)

So the *pharmakon* is not 'really' both a remedy and a poison, but its 'effect' is always as (at least) both. Although Derrida does not imply in this passage that the *pharmakon*'s meaning both remedy and poison at the same time is a contradiction (indeed, the fact that he notes that poison is 'not the only other thing *pharmakon* means' could be read as indicating less of an interest in the idea of a word having ostensibly opposed meanings at the same time than with the idea a word just having several meanings, ostensibly opposed or not, at the same time), he does go on to argue that the passage between opposing senses of the same word is 'something quite different from . . . the dialectic of opposites' (99), and so Schrift's interpretation seems not entirely unfounded. If Schrift's interpretation is close to the mark, however, then Derrida is right to suggest that the passage between opposing senses of the same word is something quite different from the dialectic of opposites, but only because the same word having two (or more) meanings at the same time doesn't necessarily constitute a contradiction in the first place, and so a resolution might not be called for.

If Schrift's interpretation is right, however – if Derrida is suggesting that *pharmakon*, for example, always has at least two meanings – the question still remains how this makes it undecidable. Another interpretation is possible – it could be that Derrida believes that the word *pharmakon*, having no one 'true' meaning, could mean 'remedy,' could mean 'poison,' depending on context, and, as such, the alleged contradiction between its sense as poison and its sense as remedy can't be 'resolved' by reducing it, in the abstract, to one or the other of its 'poles.' This seems to be along the lines of how McGowan reads Derrida: '[i]n place of the hierarchical resolution of the contrast, a resolution that places one term above the other, the Derridean (non)solution places them in tensional play with one another, an oscillation that is not resolved in favor of one or the other' (105–6).[9] So the meaning of the word oscillates between 'remedy' and 'poison,' and this is what renders it undecidable – i.e., it's impossible to say that its 'true' meaning is either 'remedy' or 'poison.'

One can label *pharmakon* 'undecidable' on these grounds if one wants – 'undecidable' in this sense does not amount, as Derrida insists in the afterword to *Limited Inc.*, to 'some vague "indeterminacy"' ('I do not believe I have ever spoken of "indeterminacy," whether in regard to "meaning" or anything else. Undecidability is something else again. . . . [U]ndecidability is always a *determinate* oscillation between possibilities (for example, of meaning, but also of acts). These possibilities are themselves highly *determined* in strictly *defined* situations' (1988: 148)). But again, since logic does not compel us to make a choice between the two (or more) meanings of, e.g., *pharmakon* in the first place, no 'irresolvable contradiction' is generated if one refuses to favor one of its meanings over the other(s).

I don't really know, in the end, what Derrida is calling for when he calls for 'another "logic," ' a 'logic' that, he says, 'doubtless takes into account the conditions of . . . classical and binary logic, but . . . no longer depends entirely on it' (117). Specifically, I don't know whether this 'other' logic is one that rejects the law of noncontradiction. Consider, however, his rejoinder to Gerald Graff's remark that 'some American critics of your work (Searle among them) accuse you of setting up a kind of "all or nothing" choice between pure realization or self-presence and complete freeplay or undecidability' (114):[10] 'the "all or nothing choice" was not "set up" by me,' Derrida claims; rather, he argues, it is 'implied in every distinction or every opposition of concepts' (120):

> The discourse [speech-act theory] that seems problematic to me . . . neither can nor should avoid saying: it's either serious *or* non-serious, ironical *or* nonironical, present *or* nonpresent, metaphorical *or* nonmetaphorical, intentional *or* nonintentional, parasitic *or* nonparasitic, citational *or* noncitational, promissive *or* nonpromissive, etc. To this oppositional logic, which is necessarily, legitimately a logic of 'all or nothing' and without which the distinction and limits of a concept would have no chance, I oppose nothing, least of all a logic of *approximation*, a simple empiricism of difference of degree; rather I add a supplementary complication that calls for other concepts[.]
>
> (117; his emphasis)

' "Either . . . or," "yes or no," "all or nothing," ' a 'logic' that, Derrida says, 'one has to accept' (120, 117):

> I always try to do this and I believe that it always has to be done, at any rate in a theoretical-philosophical discussion of concepts and things conceptualizable. Whenever one feels obliged to stop doing this (as happens to me when I speak of *différance*, of mark, of supplement, of iterability and of all they entail), it is *better* to make explicit in the most conceptual, rigorous, formalizing and pedagogical manner possible the reasons one has for doing so, for thus changing the rules and the context of discourse.
>
> (117; his emphasis)

What it is that Derrida does when he feels obliged to stop thinking of 'things conceptualizable' according to the 'logic of all or nothing' is not clear. A speech-act is, he insists, either literal or not, for example, and not a 'little' literal or 'more or less' literal. Derrida here is responding not just to the general question raised by Graff but to a specific point made by Searle in his *New York Review of Books* article, 'The World Turned Upside Down.' Searle claims that in lecturing to literary critics he has found 'two persuasive presuppositions ... both oddly enough derived from logical positivism,' the first of which is 'that unless a distinction can be made rigorous and precise it isn't really a distinction at all' (quoted in *Limited Inc.*, 'Afterword,' 123). Derrida, taking this remark to be an attack on him, is outraged by it:

> How can one dare, resorting to such a worn-out rhetorical procedure, to make the pretense of attributing the demand for 'rigorous and precise distinctions' to a philosophical doctrine or tendency ('logical positivism') which one ostensibly holds to be very circumscribed, even outmoded, and in any case without any presumed relationship to my philosophical 'style,' all this in order to discredit the logic of my objections?
>
> (123)

Derrida knows, however, that Searle is not suggesting that 'phrases can be *just a little* literal or *more or less* metaphorical' (even though, *pace* Derrida, who asks what logician since there were logicians has ever renounced the axiom that when a distinction cannot be made rigorous and precise it is not a distinction at all, there are degrees of truth theorists who, as the name suggests, do speak of propositions as being a 'little' true, 'more or less true,' 'mostly true,' etc ...). He thinks, rather, that Searle is just resorting to 'journalistic polemics,' pretending 'to have renounced trenchant distinction' (124). So he fails to address what it is that Searle in part is suggesting: that 'the fact that an expression can be both *used* and *mentioned* in the same sentence' does not weaken 'the distinction that philosophers and logicians make between the *use* and the *mention* of expression,' and 'the fact that a single utterance might express a conscious speech act of one type and an unconscious one of another type' is not 'a serious problem for the theory of speech acts' (1983: 78; his emphasis). Whether Derrida's 'supplementary complication' entails that a given speech-act may also be both literal and not literal at the same time and in the same sense, again, I do not know. What I can say, however, is that I think Derrida avails himself of the interpretation that Schrift, among others,[11] puts on him – that predicating both terms of a dualism of something amounts to a paradox.

In his remarks on 'the logic of all or nothing,' Derrida does not, for example, acknowledge the difference between predicates that are formally equivalent to A and not-A and predicates formally equivalent to A and B: within the terms of classical logic, either something is or isn't A (a statement is either literal or not, and, again, not a *'just a little* literal,' etc.), but it isn't necessarily the case that something is either A or B, one or the other – it could be both or it could be neither (a statement could be both literal and metaphorical, and it could be neither (e.g., 'Julius Caesar is a prime number' used as an example of mispredication)). Given that he doesn't, it isn't so suprising to find Susan Hekman, for one, arguing that

> [Derrida] challenges the metaphysics of presence, an epistemology organized in terms of dualisms and hierarchies, with his notion of *différance*. The metaphysics of presence casts *all distinctions in black and white terms*; all dichotomies are *hierarchial and absolute* and thus end up repressing or denying difference rather than expressing it.
>
> (1990: 110; my emphasis)

Hekman, however, goes on to construe *différance* in a way that Derrida's unequivocal condemnation of what he refers to as 'empiricist confusion' suggests he would have no truck with:

> Derrida's thesis of *différance*, on the other hand, encourages us to think of the differences between men and women not in terms of absolute hierarchies but in terms of shadings rather than absolute oppositions. *Différance* thus offers us a way of talking about sexual difference that displaces the oppositions of the metaphysics of presence without denying the differences between the sexes. It offers a way of talking about sexual differences in terms of multiplicity and plurality rather than hierarchy.
>
> (110)

So a person could be more or less female, just a little bit male, female up to certain point, mostly male, etc. – Derrida would, I think, be right to question this kind of talk, if only because 'male' and 'female' are not obviously vague predicates (such as, say, 'bald' is thought to be). But he would be wrong if he thought that something must be either male or female, all or nothing. Some babies, for example, are born with external male sex organs and female internal sex organs (as a result of a rare, inherited disease – adrenal hyperplasia – transmitted to the fetus). Such babies, then, are not, in some vague and nonspecifiable way, 'a little bit' female and 'a little bit' male; rather, they are male in one quite specific respect and female in another. Derrida's claim that one 'has to accept' what he calls the logic of either/or, his failure to make a distinction between exclusive and nonexclusive disjunctions, then, may well be the ground of Hekman's typically postmodernist assertion that the 'metaphysics of presence casts all distinctions in black and white terms.'

Barbara Johnson, for another, in the introduction to her translation of *Dissemination*, argues that '[i]n its deconstruction of the either/or logic of noncontradiction, Derrida's writing attempts to elaborate an "other" logic' (xvii):

> It can be said that everything in Derrida's discussion of the *Phaedrus* hinges on the translation of a single word: the word *pharmakon*, which in Greek can mean *both* 'remedy' and 'poison.' In referring to writing as a *pharmakon*, Plato is thus not making a *simple* value judgment. Yet translators, by choosing to render the word sometimes by 'remedy' and sometimes by 'poison,' have consistently *decided* what in Plato remains undecidable, and thus influenced the course of the entire history of 'Platonism.' When one recalls the means of Socrates' death, one begins to see just how crucial the undecidability between remedy and poison might be.
>
> (xxiv–xxv, her emphasis)

Johnson's assumption here is not only that translators, in rendering *pharmakon* as either 'remedy' or 'poison,' must be committed to the idea that the *pharmakon* is *absolutely* a poison or *absolutely* a remedy, but also that they somehow manage to convey this absolutism by their merely translating the word as either 'poison' or 'remedy.' She also assumes that since the *pharmakon* is not absolutely a poison or absolutely a remedy, it 'deconstructs' the 'either/or logic of noncontradiction.' And, again, Derrida's categorical assertions about 'either/or,' 'yes or no,' 'all or nothing,' may well be the source of both these assumptions.

Johnson also cites Derrida's claim in *Dissemination* that 'It is . . . not simply false to say that Mallarmé is a Platonist or a Hegelian. But it is above all not true. And vice versa', and remarks:

Instead of a simple either/or structure, deconstruction attempts to elaborate a discourse that says *neither* 'either/or,' *nor* 'both/ and' nor even 'neither/nor,' while at the same time not totally abandoning these logics either.

(xvii; her emphasis)

As John Ellis points out, however, 'surely [this] is not . . . a real alternative logic':

> Presumably, one could pursue a serious and subtle inquiry into the particular ways in which Mallarmé shares common features with, or is indebted to, Plato or Hegel and the ways in which he is not. No one would approach this inquiry thinking that the key question here is whether Mallarmé is, or is not, identical in all respects with Plato. . . . [A]nyone who insists on that level of generality will only seem to be interrupting something that has gone well beyond this elementary level of analysis. Derrida's statement that it is neither true nor false to say that Mallarmé is a Platonist works only on that level of generality and is therefore devoid of substantial content. To do no more than contemplate the extremes of Mallarmé's being either totally Platonist or not in any way Platonist adds nothing to the inquiry beyond two simple and equally unpromising positions and the implication (for is there anything else implied here?) that the truth is somewhere between them. But where else could it be?

(1989: 6–7)

Johnson's suggestion that, by the 'logic' of deconstruction, Mallarmé is not either a Platonist or a Hegelian, is not both a Platonist and Hegelian, and is not neither a Platonist nor a Hegelian, is an instance of the fallacy *secundum quid et simpliciter*, which arises, as Keith Simmons notes, when 'an expression used in a restricted way is taken as if it were unrestricted. A leading example of Aristotle's is the inference from "The Ethiopian is white, with respect to his teeth and eyeballs" to "The Ethiopian is white, absolutely"' (1993: 89). Johnson suppresses mention of the qualifications that render all the possibilities she mentions true *secundum quid* – that is, she represents them as if they were true *simpliciter* in order to create the impression that the 'logic' of deconstruction is paradoxical. If one were to make those tacit qualifications explicit, then, with respect to Mallarmé, what one would be left with is the perfectly innocuous assertion that it isn't the case that Mallarmé is not, in any respect, either a Platonist or a Hegelian, nor is he either wholly a Platonist or wholly a Hegelian, nor he is both wholly a Platonist and wholly a Hegelian. Rather, he is a Platonist in some respects and a Hegelian in other respects.

Examples of this fallacy abound in postmodernist theory. Richard Kearney, for example, asserts that one of 'the main conclusions to be drawn from Derrida's deconstruction of the metaphysical distinction between the imaginary and the real' is that '[l]iterature is *both* true *and* false. And following the deconstructive logic of undecidability this also means it is *neither* true *nor* false' (1989: 290). Kearney commits the fallacy twice. On the one hand, he argues from literature is 'true' in one respect (in 'copying' reality) and 'false' in another (because in 'copying' reality it is only copying a copy), to 'literature is *both* true *and* false,' the implication of the latter being that literature is true absolutely and false absolutely – that is, he illicitly treats a restricted expression as if it were unrestricted in order to lend it the air of paradox. On the other, he argues from 'literature is *both* true *and* false' – true in one respect and false in another – to '[a]nd following the deconstructive logic of undecidability this also means it is *neither* true *nor* false,' the implication of the latter being that literature is not true in any respect or false in any respect – again, in order to lend his claim the air of paradox, he represents 'literature is *neither* true *nor* false' as if were an unrestricted expression.

Considering both Derrida's categorical assertions about the necessity of all-or-nothing distinctions and the fact that he makes sophistic claims like 'It is simply false to say that Mallarmé is a Platonist or a Hegelian. But it is above all not true. And vice versa,' one can allow the following: that for theorists of postmodernism to come to the conclusion that what Derrida is suggesting is that 'the binary thinking of the history of metaphysics' dictates that *pharmakon* has to be rendered as either 'remedy' or 'poison' because to allow that the word could have both meanings at the same time would be contradictory, or dictates that Mallarmé has to be seen as either a Hegelian or a Platonist because to regard him as being both would be paradoxical, and so on, is not entirely unreasonable.

The logic of Both/And: No Apocalypse Now

Whatever the source, theorists of postmodernism harbor misconceptions about classical logic. They reject something called 'either/

or thinking,' which they often appear to associate with the law of the excluded middle, and affirm instead something they call 'both/and thinking,' which they suggest violates the law of noncontradiction, and which they are wont to argue renders things 'undecidable,' 'indeterminate,' or 'ambivalent':

> One of the most influential of postmodern theorists, Ihab Hassan, is fond of creating parallel columns that place characteristics of [the modern] next to their opposite characteristics in [the postmodern], usually making clear his preference for the postmodern. But this 'either/or thinking' suggests a resolution of what I see as the unresolvable contradictions within postmodernism. For example I would see it less as a case of postmodern play versus modernist purpose, as Hassam claims (1982, 267–8), than a case of play with purpose . . . [T]he postmodern partakes of a logic of 'both/and,' not one of 'either/or.' And, not surprisingly, those who privilege the modernist over the postmodernist also work in similar oppositional binary terms. . . . [T]he major danger in setting up this kind of structure is that of creating a 'strawman' in order to make one's point more clearly. . . . No matter which 'ism' is preferred, both it and its antagonist run the risk of . . . reduction.
>
> (Hutcheon, 1988: 49)

> [W]hat is so striking about postmodernist humor . . . is its refusal to see truth as something that exists along an either-or axis. Consequently, postmodernist humor at the same time becomes *both* a negative *and* a positive perspective on the world. . . . [I]t does not represent a destructive or constructive thrust, but, paradoxically, both at once.
>
> (Olsen, 1990: 19)

> [The garden in Christopher Bruce's and Lindsay Kemp's ballet *Cruel Garden*] is simultaneously two things: the site of blood or of death and cruelty, and the site of growth or development. . . . In the Renaissance and its aftermath, the ritual space of the garden was clearly *identifiable*. . . . In the postmodern condition, the 'identity' of such a garden is no longer available; the postmodern garden or space is typically ambivalent or disjunctive, self-contradictory. . . . [I]ts 'identity' is founded upon the ways in which it actually differs from itself in its paradoxical ambiguity or ambivalence, as a site of blood or of flowers.
>
> (Docherty, 1990: 20)

[Calvino's] *Invisible Cities* . . . questions the binary either/or way of thinking characteristic of the modernist perception of space and the place of the subject as an observer from a privileged perspective . . . Brian McHale has noted how Calvino's cities echo Foucault's idea of *heterotopia*, a space which makes the drawing of definite boundaries impossible. It is not capable of conceptualization in binary terms, it is both/and rather than either/or. This is the space of paradox, which truly undermines modernist methods of reasoning, even undermines language itself by making the specific naming of places in space impossible.

(Cooke, 1990: 99–100)

Can we speak of *impossible* worlds? Umberto Eco thinks not. He excludes logical impossibility from the propositions that constitute worlds: every proposition must be *either* true or false of a possible world, it cannot be *both* true *and* false. This is to say that possible worlds, according to Eco, obey the law of the excluded middle. Worlds which violate the law of the excluded middle, about which, in other words, certain propositions are both true and false, Eco refuses to regard as full-fledged, self-sustaining worlds.

* * *

Radically discontinuous and inconsistent, [the empire of Calvino's Great Khan] juxtaposes worlds of incompatible structure. It violates the law of the excluded middle: logically, *either* Trude is everywhere *or* Cecilia is everywhere; in the Empire of *Invisible Cities*, both are everywhere, and so are Penthesilea and the other continuous cities as well.

(McHale, 1987: 33; 44)

The conflation here of the law of the excluded middle and the law of noncontradiction aside, if the empire is radically *discontinuous*, and if indeed Cecilia, Trude, etc., are different possible *worlds*, no contradiction is generated if Trude is everywhere in its world and Cecilia is everywhere in its: for a proposition and its negation to be a contradiction, they both have to be affirmed of the *same* world (McHale demarcates the postmodern from the modern by suggesting that the latter presents a number of different perspectives on the same world and that the former presents a number of different worlds – on his argument, then, if contradictions were to be found anywhere, they would more likely be found in what he identifies as modernist fiction). Logically, either Trude is everywhere or Cecilia is everywhere only if they are part of the same continuous world; since, by McHale's account they are 'incommensurable and mutually exclusive worlds' (44) (or different 'levels of reality' (1986: 101), as Calvino himself might call them), they can both be everywhere without paradox. The empire, then, in being radically discontinuous, is not inconsistent, nor are Trude or Cecilia in themselves inconsistent: Trude itself, for instance, is not a world in which the proposition that it is everywhere is both true and false; rather it is a world in which the proposition that it is everywhere is true (McHale appears to conflate the notion of inconsistent, impossible worlds in which 'certain propositions are both true and false' with consistent, possible worlds that are incommensurable with other consistent, possible worlds).

If the 'postmodern garden' is simultaneously the site of growth and of death, then how is it disjunctive, much less ambivalent? And if it's disjunctive, then how is it self-contradictory? What, moreover, could possibly be self-contradictory about a garden being both a place of life and death? A clue as to why Docherty might think it to be so is provided by his suggestion that 'its "identity" is founded upon the ways in which it actually differs from itself': his presupposition seems to be that gardens are 'really' sites of growth – that that's their 'true' identity – so that if they are also sites of death, they 'contradict' themselves. This sort of presupposition, odd as it is, especially for a member of a school of thought that claims to reject essentialism of any kind, is, nonetheless, one that I think informs a number of claims made on behalf of the contradictions of postmodernism. However, it is a banal fact, not a true contradiction, that gardens are places of both life and death and that they have, for obvious reasons, often functioned as such symbolically in western art.

What is paradoxical about humor that presents the world in both a positive and negative light? And what has this got to do with the refusal of postmodernist humor to see truth as something that exists along an either/or axis? The idea, perhaps, is that it's true both that there are good things and bad things about the world and that postmodernist humor gives expression to this. But again, like gardens being both sites of life and of death, this is a truism, not a true contradiction.

Art that is both playful and purposeful at the same time is likewise hardly an 'unresolvable contradiction.'[12] Nor is postmodernism itself 'contradictory,' as Hutcheon claims, in being both a break from as well as a continuation of modernism:

> [T]he binary oppositions that are usually set up in the writing on postmodernism – between past and present, modern and post-modern, and so on – should probably be called into question, if only because ... *post*modernism literally names and constitutes its own paradoxical identity, and does so in an uneasy contra-dictory relationship of constant slippage. So much that has been written on this subject has physically taken the form of opposing columns, usually labelled modernist versus postmodernist. But this is a structure that implicitly denies the mixed, plural, and contradictory nature of the postmodernist enterprise.
>
> (20)

Ronald Schleifer likewise argues:

> [T]he postmodern, which has been variously described as con-tinuous with and as a break with the modern, can be understood as metonymically linked to its antecedent. It is inhabited with the same sense of negative materiality that modernist discourse presents, but its relationship to that materiality is not quite – not wholly – the 'same.' If the modern is shocked by its own lan-guage, overwhelmed by the flooding of metonymy, the drumbeat of material death within discourse and history, then for the post-modern, I believe, the shock has subsided. The postmodern is metonymically related to the modern in that complex sense of that term. It is a 'part' of modernism – from one vantage point, its culmination; from another, participating, in a debased form, in the essential crisis of modernism. But, at the same time, it is modernism's 'other,' precisely as death or negative materiality is life's 'other'; it presents to modernism – as death and the materi-ality of discourse present to life and meaning – what Shoshana Felman has called a 'radical negativity' that *escapes the negative/ positive alternative.*
>
> (1990: 15; his emphasis)[13]

Schleifer would have us believe that there is 'a contradiction be-tween death conceived as a synecdochial part of life and as life's metonymic other' (82); likewise, he, along with Hutcheon, would have us think that postmodernism is 'contradictory' in being both a break from and a continuation of modernism, as well as in being both positive and negative. But just as a conception of death as being, in one sense, a part of life is perfectly compatible with a conception of it in another sense as being other to life, so a conception of postmodernism as a continuation of modernism in some respects, and as positive in certain respects, is perfectly compatible with a conception of it as a break with modernism in other respects, and as negative in certain other respects. In claiming that postmodernism 'escapes' the 'negative/positive alternative,' Schleifer seems to imply that the 'western metaphysical tradition' would force us to choose: either postmodernism is a break from modernism or it is a continuation of it; either it is positive or it is negative.[14] Judith Butler makes this point explicit: to 'install the term ["postmodernism"],' she states, 'as that which can be only affirmed or negated is to force it to occupy one position within a binary, and so affirm a logic of noncontradiction over and against some more generative scheme' (1995: 216). It's not just that the 'logic of noncontradiction' doesn't force one to install the term 'postmodernism' as that which can be only affirmed or negated; one could also wholly accept or wholly reject 'postmodernism' without affirming 'the logic of noncontradiction.' That is – and this a point I will return to – it is precisely because it is possible to accept certain aspects of postmodernist theorizing while rejecting others without violating the law of noncontradiction that to wholly affirm or wholly reject postmodernist theorizing would not be a function of an adherence to the 'logic of noncontradiction'; the law of noncontradiction does not compel one to either affirm 'postmodernism' absolutely or to negate it absolutely, and so if one chooses to, say, wholly accept it, that choice is not dictated by the law.

Since postmodernism's being both a break from and a continuation of modernism, as well as both positive and negative and both playful and purposeful, are perfectly compatible states of affairs, the problem with Hassan's parallel columns is not that they try to resolve, via 'either/or thinking,' unresolvable contradictions.[15] The problem with them, rather, is that they are reductive, as well as overgeneral. Pre-WWII literature cannot be generally described as rejecting play for purpose, or as repudiating immanence in favor of transcendence, or as 'metaphysical' rather than ironic, or as embracing design to the exclusion of chance, nor can post-WWII literature be generally described as embracing playfulness to the exclusion of seriousness, or as denying transcendence, or be said, by and large, to reject metaphysics for irony, or to celebrate chance to the exclusion of design. Hassan acknowledges that 'the dichotomies this table represents remain insecure, equivocal. For differences shift, defer, even collapse; concepts in any one vertical column are not all equivalent; and inversions and exceptions, in both modernism and postmodernism abound.' However, he goes on, 'I would submit that rubrics in the right column point to the postmodern tendency, the tendency of indetermanence, and so may bring us closer to its historical and theoretical definition' (1987: 92). I disagree because I think that the concepts in question are too broad and too pervasive in western culture to point to any tendencies in either 'modernism' or 'postmodernism' that could distinguish them from each other or from the tendencies of other periods.

Hutcheon's definition of postmodernism as something that 'partakes of a logic of both/and,' as something that is both playful and purposeful, both 'immanence denying yet yearning for transcendence,' etc., is likewise reductive and overgeneral. 'The contradictions that characterize postmodernism,' Hutcheon writes, 'reject any neat binary opposition that might conceal a secret hierarchy of values' (42–3). It apparently escapes her notice that in *opposing* the alleged 'both/and' of postmodernism to the alleged 'either/or' of modernism, she is positing a neat, hierarchial binary opposition in which 'postmodernism' is most definitely 'privileged' over 'modernism.' If one glosses over the reductivism of both Hassan's and Hutcheon's positions, takes into account the fact that the terms each invokes are too general to be of any use in distinguishing pre- and post-WWII literature from the literature of other periods, and disregards altogether Hutcheon's claim that a novel that is both playful and purposeful, etc., is 'contradictory,'[16] what one is left with is the unenlightening proposition that, like the writing of all the centuries preceding it, some twentieth-century writing is playful but not purposeful, that some is purposeful but not playful, and that some is both, and so on.

The above passages illustrate the form that claims about the contradictory nature of postmodernism generally take in theories of postmodernism. There is, however, one other account of contradiction and postmodernism of which I am aware, one that is more philosophically informed but nonetheless still confused, that warrants examination here. In *Reflexivity: The Post-Modern Predicament*, Hilary Lawson argues that 'the post-modern predicament is indeed one of crisis, a crisis of our truths, our values, our most cherished beliefs' – a crisis, he claims, that 'owes to reflexivity its origin, its necessity, and its force' (1985: 9):

> Reflexivity, as a turning back on oneself, a form of self-awareness, has been part of philosophy from its inception, but reflexive questions have been given their special force in consequence of the recognition of the central role played by language, theory, sign, and text. Our concepts are no longer regarded as transparent – either in reflecting the world or conveying ideas. As a result all our claims about language and the world – and implicitly all our claims in general – are reflexive in a manner which cannot be avoided.
>
> (9)

'Rooted in the modern concern with the sign, as language or theory,' he continues,

> reflexivity has surfaced in divergent fields in superficially different guises. In factual disciplines such as science or history, anthropology or psychology, reflexive questions have been raised because the so-called 'facts' on which such disciplines are based are no longer uncontentious. Empirical observation is questioned on the grounds that it is theory dependent. Common sense is doubted on the grounds of cultural relativism. This questioning, however, has led to views which are unstable. Such claims as 'there are no facts,' 'there are no lessons of history,' 'there are no definitive answers or solutions,' are all reflexively paradoxical. For, is it not a fact that 'there are no facts,' a lesson of history that 'there are no lessons of history,' and a definitive answer that 'there are no definitive answers'? Often these reflexive problems are ignored, as if they were merely irritating details that could be forgotten about; on other occasions *ad hoc* means of escaping the paradox are hastily erected. Indeed, so long as an arena of certainty is retained the problems of reflexivity can remain at the level of entertaining, but essentially trivial, logical puzzles. Historically such certainty has been found in God, in phenomenological experience, in empirical observation, and in the beliefs of common sense. But today, because of the irreducibly textual nature of our beliefs, all arenas of certainty are in question. Our

'certainties' are expressed through texts, through language, through sign systems, which are no longer seen to be neutral.

(9–10)

The problems here are numerous. First, and most importantly, while the statements 'There are no facts,' 'There are no lessons of history,' 'There are no definitive answers or solutions' may be reflexive, they are not paradoxical. Lawson compares them to the Liar's paradox ('This sentence is false'), but they are not the same as it, for, in contrast to them, it indeed seems to be reflexively paradoxical. That is, the Liar sentence not only refers to itself, but appears to be false if true and true if false, and therefore, both true and false, which, by the law of noncontradiction, is a logical impossibility. This is not the case with, for example, 'There are no facts'; it, rather, is an instance of pragmatic self-refutation – a claim that is falsified by its very assertion. There are no circumstances under which the assertion 'There are no facts' yields the truth-value true. It's not that a state of affairs in which there were no facts is logically impossible, but rather that if it were true that there were no facts, the statement 'There are no facts' could not be asserted ('There are no facts,' 'There are no lessons of history,' etc., are similar to 'I do not exist' – again, a state of affairs in which I did not exist is not logically impossible, but if it were true that I did not exist, I could not assert 'I do not exist'). But there *are* circumstances under which 'This sentence is false' seems to yield the truth-value true, namely the circumstance in which 'This sentence is false' is false – for if it is false, then it is how it is says it is, and so it would appear to be true.

That Lawson is confusing instances of pragmatic self-refutation with instances of apparently true contradictions is suggested not only by his referring to 'This sentence is false' and 'I am lying' as recent versions of Epimenides' 'All Cretans are liars' that 'serve merely to provide further examples of a claim that is falsified in the very statement of that claim,' but also by the following:

The paradoxical nature of [general claims about the world that incorporate within them the logical impossibility of their own verification] is more apparent if they are unpacked and simplified into the form 'the world is red and we have no means of determining that it is red' (e.g., the world is seen through language, and we have no means of determining that this is the case). Such assertions are paradoxical because they claim that one knows the world is such and such while at the same time denying that this is possible. Hilary Putnam has recently tried to formalize this paradox using the example 'We are all brains in a vat.' The paradox in this case arises in precisely the same way: if we really were brains in a vat we would be unable to know that we were brains in a vat, for to do so we could not be brains in a vat. Once again, like the liar paradox, 'we are all brains in a vat' is false if it is true.

(27)

It is exactly because 'we are all brains in a vat' is an example of 'a claim that is falsified in the very statement of that claim' that it is not like the Liar's paradox – it can't be false if true and true if false because there are no conditions under which asserting it could yield the truth-value true.

Second, Lawson's account of how philosophers have approached paradoxes like that of the Liar is questionable. His claim, for example, that 'so long as an arena of certainty is retained the problems of reflexivity can remain at the level of entertaining, but essentially trivial, logical puzzles' is problematic not only because without 'an arena of certainty' one would be unable to identify the Liar sentence as a seeming instance of (P & ~P), but also because logicians in the western philosophical tradition have never regarded the Liar sentence as an entertaining, but essentially trivial puzzle – the large body of writing that has been produced about the Liar's paradox over the course of the last couple of millennia attest to the fact that it has been taken very seriously indeed (Tarski notes that the paradox is said to have 'tormented many ancient logicians and caused the premature death of at least one of them, Philetas of Cos' (1969: 66). Nor is it the case, as Lawson implies by claiming that 'often these reflexive problems are ignored, as if they were merely irritating details that could be forgotten about' while 'on other occasions *ad hoc* means of escaping the paradox are hastily erected,' that the only option other than treating paradoxes as 'merely irritating details' is to hastily construct *ad hoc* means of escaping them – that is, Lawson seems to assume that there couldn't be a means of answering the seeming paradoxicality of, say, the Liar sentence, that wouldn't simply be *ad hoc*.

Finally, the grounds upon which Lawson bases his assertion of a 'crisis,' a 'post-modern predicament,' are unfounded. He suggests that 'today,' paradoxes pose a threat to 'our truths, our values, our most cherished beliefs' because of the 'irreducibly textual nature of our beliefs,' because 'our "certainties" are expressed through texts, through language, through sign systems, which are no longer seen to be neutral.' But since beliefs have *always* been expressed through language, paradoxes 'today' pose no more of a threat to 'our truths, our values, our most cherished beliefs' than they ever did. What the consequences would be if, for example, 'This sentence is false' turned out to be a *bona fide* violation of the law of noncontradiction is another question, a question that has been vigorously debated for thousands of years, but the fact that our beliefs are expressed in language, since that has always been the case, does not make for any particular 'post-modern predicament' or 'crisis' with respect to apparently true contradictions.

2

Paradox, Undecidability, and the Novel

Measure for Measure

Abuse and misuse of the terms 'paradox,' 'contradiction,' and 'indeterminacy' is not only rampant in work explicitly devoted to the theorization of the postmodern, but also in work that draws on such theorizations. In *Fiction in the Quantum Universe*, for example, Susan Strehle argues that John Barth

> repudiates the binary logic that divides ideal and real, form and content, elect and preterite. Hoping to transcend these alternatives, both of which privilege one set of artistic values and techniques from different grounds in absolute systems, Barth will recover the excluded middle: the relative, the actual.
>
> (1992: 132)

'Actuality,' she explains, 'seen through the kindred lenses of physics and fiction in our times, is *indeterminate*; its meaning cannot be singly or completely determined, because it contains a paradoxical *complementarity*, a doubled difference, within itself' (219):

> Opposite and contradictory states – say, behavior as particles and as waves – coexist in potential and interfere with each other, making a single determinate meaning impossible to construct. Seen as definitive of the intersection of physics and literature in important recent essays, these intertwined concepts allow, in both physics and fiction, for a richness of possible meanings and for increased complexity in the models of actuality we can construct. Where binary dualities assumed the absolute identity of terms and the absolute difference between opposites, complementarity assumes that each term is relative and contains some potential interference within itself. More important, complementary terms coexist within a both-and structure.
>
> (219)

The alternatives Strehle alludes to, which she claims Barth hopes to transcend, are modernism and realism – realism here being yoked to the real, to content, to the preterite, and modernism to the ideal, to form, and to the elect. Barth, she explains, rejects 'as the proper goal of art either the simple reflection of a Newtonian reality, with the linearity, causality, and objectivity that characterizes realism, *or the retreat from content to pure form*, to the irreal, private, centered labyrinths of modernism' (131–2; my emphasis). Strehle's point, then, would seem to be the following: that, on account of the law of the excluded middle, nineteenth-century and early twentieth-century writers and critics believed that a novel could have, for example, either form or content but not both at the same time, and that in 'recovering' the excluded middle – that is, on Strehle's understanding, in affirming that such 'opposite and contradictory' properties 'coexist within a both-and structure' – postmodern writers and critics embrace a paradox.[1]

In her initial discussion of realist and anti-realist fiction, Strehle implies that it is critics, and not the writers of such fiction, who have effected the division between them: 'the constricting binary logic of realism and anti-realism has,' she claims, 'reduced fiction's double interest in both art and life to a single dimension for many readers and critics'(2). However, because she wants to claim that the nature of postmodernist fiction is fundamentally different from that of both realist and modernist fiction, she ends up schematizing modernist and realist fiction themselves in terms of the form/content, art/life, ideal/real, and elect/preterite distinctions. That is, she wants to claim that postmodernist writers reflect in their fiction what she thinks of as the 'both/and thinking' of quantum physics, and so she is forced, despite her initial suggestion that all fiction is about both art and life, to assert that the *modus operandi* of realist and modernist writers was 'either/or thinking.'

Needless to say, the idea of a novel's having both form and content at the same time challenges neither the law of the excluded middle nor the law of noncontradiction, and indeed, one might find it hard to believe that Strehle could really be arguing that it does (though one might note that the suggestion that form and content are contradictories, and that postmodernism embraces a paradox in affirming both, is really no more outlandish than Hutcheon's suggestion that one of the 'unresolvable contradictions' of postmodernism is that it embraces both play and purpose). One could, I suppose, read her as suggesting that realists were interested in content and modernists in form, i.e., as suggesting that realists and modernists could have evinced an interest in both, but, as a matter of historical record, realism 'privileged' the one and modernism the other. However, to read her this way one would have to ignore the fact that she thinks this alleged division between form and content was effected by the strictures of 'binary logic.'

It's hard, then, to avoid the conclusion that what Strehle is claiming is that realists 'privileged' content to the exclusion of form, and modernists form to the exclusion of content, because classical logic dictates that form and content (real and ideal,[2] etc . . .) mutually exclude each other. That this is indeed what she is claiming is further suggested by the following:

> [a]ctualist fiction allows for both-and thinking in place of either-or; it creates new models of fictive complementarity where seemingly divergent possibilities, voices, plots, outcomes, and perspectives on reality come together in dialogue. Its version of artistic activity differs vastly from the two limiting and exclusive choices identified by Ortega y Gasset with the garden and the glass: one may represent the world, or one may reflect on the processes of artistic creation. Instead, actualism reflects both, in and through each other.
>
> (221)

It is worth noting that Strehle's appeal to Bohr's principle of complementarity and Heisenberg's uncertainty principle is ill-conceived. If, as she argues, actualist fiction both represents the world and reflects on the processes of artistic creation, then it can't be that complementarity is one of the things definitive of the intersection between quantum physics and contemporary literature, since according to Bohr's principle, 'wave' and 'particle,' for instance, are complementary predicates because they exclude each other. Both are essential to the description of quantum phenomena, but it is not possible to predicate both of the same phenomenon at the same time because the experimental arrangements for measuring momentum are mutually exclusive of those for measuring position. The idea that Bohr's principle of complementarity involves a rejection of the law of noncontradiction is common among contemporary literary critics writing about the relationship between twentieth-century science and literature. Adelaide Morris, for one, in an essay on the poetry of H.D., argues in terms similiar to those of Strehle that '[a] number of exciting practices in [H.D.'s] poetry suggest that like Heisenberg and Bohr, H.D. found uncertainty to be intrinsic to our apprehension of the world': among these practices, she claims, is 'an insistence on the simultaneous validity of mutually exclusive statements' (1991: 209–10). But it is precisely the *simultaneous* validity of mutually exclusive statements that Bohr's complementarity denies. Philip Kuberski, for another, argues in *Chaosmos: Literature, Science, and Theory* that

> [a]lthough complementarity as a concept in physical science was proposed to account for such instances where single perspective descriptions could be displaced by other single perspective descriptions, Bohr seemed ready to give the concept more general application, invoking as he did the Taoist emblem of the interanimation of Yin and Yang, darkness and light. The world itself, it could be said, following Bohr's Taoist extension of complementarity, is never adequately described by the logic of noncontradiction.
>
> (1994: 77)

But the notion that 'the world itself . . . is never adequately described by the logic of noncontradiction' is not only no consequence of complementarity 'as a concept in physical science.' It is also no consequence of Bohr's 'Taoist extension of complementarity.' For it doesn't follow from the idea that what the Taoist emblem connotes is the 'interanimation' of darkness and light that there is something that is both light and dark at the same time and in the same sense. That is, Kuberski appears to be confusing an epistemological claim to the effect that in the absence of a concept of darkness we could have no concept of light with a failure of the law of noncontradiction. He claims that his 'objection . . . to utterances taken to be "postmodernist" or to describe "postmodernism" is that they are not sufficiently "after" or "other" to warrant the prefix' (3) and I share his objection. However, I don't see that he has succeeded in his attempt 'to describe elements in twentieth-century literature and science that are' (3), at least not with respect to his account of Bohr's principle of complementarity, since the idea, e.g., that 'the composition of light – that central emblem of rationality illuminating the concept of enlightenment – can only be known through the coincidence, crossing, complementing of opposites' (77) is not one that is or has been disputed by western philosophers.

Given that Strehle claims that actualist fiction 'allows for both-and thinking in place of either-or,' it can't be that indeterminacy is one of the things definitive of the intersection between quantum physics and contemporary literature either, since what Heisenberg's uncertainty principle states is that it is not possible to measure a subatomic entity for, e.g., both precise position and precise momentum at the same time. As Nick Herbert points out, Bohr's and Heisenberg's principles together 'express basic restrictions which nature seems to impose on any measurement act' (1985: 45). Strehle, in claiming that 'behavior as particles and as waves . . . interfere with each other, making a single determinate meaning impossible to construct,' suggests an awareness of these restrictions. However, her assertion that actualist fiction both represents the world and reflects on the processes of artistic creation, amounting as it does to the assertion that the complements in question – 'portrayed life and the means of portrayal' (2) – are both determinate features of actualist fiction simultaneously, is at odds with her apparent understanding of the restrictions that make it impossible to construct a single, determinate 'picture' of a micro entity in any one measurement act. Similarly, Morris's claim that one of H.D.'s practices is 'an insistence on the simultaneous validity of mutually exclusive statements' is at odds with her suggestion that, like Bohr and Heisenberg, H.D. 'found uncertainty to be intrinsic to our apprehension of the world.'

Furthermore, though measurements for position and momentum cannot be made on a micro object at the same time with precision, they can be on a macro object like a baseball. So the analogy that Strehle draws between actualist fiction and quantum reality – *viz.* that what so-called 'either-or thinking' represents as 'divergent possibilities' come together in actualist fiction just as they do in quantum reality – is, in effect, backwards: what aren't divergent possibilities in classical terms are so in quantum mechanical terms. If Strehle thinks that actualist fiction is like quantum phenomena, then what she really should be arguing is that fiction that allows for 'both-and thinking' – that, for example, allows for the possibility of both representing the world and reflecting on the processes of artistic creation at the same time – differs vastly from actualist fiction, which either represents the world (in which case the possibility of its reflecting on the processes of artistic creation at the same time would be excluded) or reflects on the processes of artistic creation (in which case the possibility of its representing the world at the same time would be excluded). The attempts of postmodernist theorists and critics to establish analogies between quantum mechanical principles and contemporary fiction are unconvincing not only because of the inherent weakness of arguments from analogy, but also because such theorists and critics appear, by and large, not to understand the principles they invoke. So one finds Elizabeth Ermarth arguing that 'while physics is beyond the scope of my present argument'

> the quantum universe does offer especially interesting analogies with my argument about language and time . . . in that the doubling activity [of wave and particle] does not involve classical 'identity,' does *not* involve Either/Or choices but instead maintains an improvisatory equilibrium between determinate and indeterminate and, in discursive terms, between meaning and nonsense, symbolic and semiotic, plot and play.
>
> (1992: 170–1)

If, however, '*improvisatory equilibrium* between one state and another incorporates what has been sundered,' and if postmodern narrative 'joins, for example, what Kristeva calls the symbolic and semiotic dispositions of language' (171; her emphasis), then, *pace* Ermarth, postmodern narratives are 'classical,' capable of being described as both symbolic and semiotic at the same time, unlike the entities of the quantum universe, with respect to which quantum physicists have to make 'Either/Or choices' – have to make a choice between, for example, measuring for definite position or measuring for definite momentum.

Where Strehle fails to establish an analogy between quantum physics and fiction, Ortega y Gasset unwittingly succeeds. She argues that Ortega y Gasset's version of artistic activity is such that one cannot simultaneously represent the world and reflect on the processes of artistic creation, a claim that in itself, though patently false, is at least more like the claim one would have to make if one wanted to argue that producing a work of art was like measuring quantum phenomena than the one Strehle herself makes. However, this is a misrepresentation of Ortega y Gasset, a misrepresentation that Strehle is forced to make once she abandons her initial suggestion that it is readers and critics who are beset by either/or thinking for the argument that realist and modernist fiction itself reflects such thinking. For she begins her book with the following passage from Ortega y Gasset's *Dehumanization of Art*:

We have here a very simple optical problem. To see a thing we must adjust our visual apparatus in a certain way. . . . Looking at the garden we adjust our eyes in such a way that the ray of vision travels through the pane. . . . But we can also deliberately disregard the garden and, withdrawing the ray of vision, detain it at the window. We then lose sight of the garden. . . . Hence to see the garden and to see the windowpane are two incompatible operations which exclude one another because they require different adjustments. Similarly a work of art vanishes from sight for a beholder who seeks in it nothing but the moving fate [of the characters]. . . . The portrayed person and his portrait are two entirely different things; we are interested in either one or the other.

(1–2)

By the end of her book, however, Ortega y Gasset is no longer claiming that the beholder cannot apprehend both the garden and the pane. Nor is he even saying other things he actually said that Strehle refers to, *viz.* that realism catered to the masses by minimizing aesthetic elements and that modernism eliminated the human element altogether. The latter is silly but it is not the same as, or as silly as, what Strehle ascribes to him at the end of her book, namely that a work of art can either represent the world or reflect on the processes of artistic creation but not both. The point is that what he actually does say about the beholder and the work of art – that 'to see the garden and to see the windowpane are two incompatible operations which exclude one another other because they require different adjustments' – is, ironically, analogous to what Bohr says about the observer and subatomic entities – that measuring their position and momentum, for example, are two incompatible operations because the experimental arrangements required to perform such measurements are mutually exclusive of each other.

What Ortega y Gasset says about the garden and the pane is at least more plausible than both what Strehle ultimately ascribes to him and what he himself says about realism and modernism. However, Strehle's answer to him – 'surely this is too simple a model of perception[;] [s]urely vision can accommodate awareness of both garden and pane; surely reading encompasses interests in both portrayed life and the means of portrayal' (2) – is, I think, right. As Robert Kiely notes:

In optical terms the analogy is suggestive, but the dogmatism about the 'exclusivities' of perception is unconvincing precisely because the human eye is capable of and accustomed to continual and finely calibrated adjustments of focus that can send to the brain virtually simultaneous images of garden and window, mediated object and objectified medium.

(1993: 14)

Since, according to Heinz Pagels, Bohr 'liked to extend his complementary principle to other than problems of atomic physics' (1984: 75) he himself might have considered Ortega y Gasset's garden/ pane analogy to be an example of it. He would, however, have been wrong if he had, just as, as Pagels points out, he was wrong to think that 'the principle of complementarity applied to the problem of determining the material structure of living organisms' (75):

We could either kill an organism and determine its molecular structure, in which case we would know the structure of a dead thing, or we could have a living organism but sacrifice knowledge of its structure. The experimental act of determining the structure also kills the organism. Of course, this latter idea is completely wrong, as molecular biologists have shown in establishing the molecular basis of life. I cite this example because it shows that even if you are as smart as Bohr, extending principles of science beyond their usual domain of application may lead to spurious conclusions.

(75–6)

Reading a work of fiction is not like trying to measure simultaneously the position and momentum of an electron. Nor, for that matter, is writing a work of fiction. In arguing that fiction can both represent reality and reflect on the processes of artistic creation and that reading can encompass an awareness of both, Strehle herself unwittingly suggests as much. (P & Q) is a quantum logical contradiction: the irony in the end is that Strehle and other theorists of postmodernism who have sought to establish a connection between quantum physics and contemporary fiction should reject the 'binary logic' in which (P & Q) is not a contradiction in order to make claims about contemporary fiction that are formally equivalent to (P & Q).

Either Lady or Tramp?

The pattern of Strehle's argument is replicated in a essay on John Fowles's *The French Lieutenant's Woman* by M. Keith Booker. Booker argues that 'by suggesting parallels between the construction of his book and the way in which we construct our everyday reality, Fowles offers a powerful commentary on history and society' and notes that '[s]uch direct "real world" involvement in a text that is so avowedly metafictional would appear to be a paradox' (1991: 195). But paradox, he asserts, 'is precisely the central defining feature of *The French Lieutenant's Woman*' and 'may, in fact, be the most important defining feature of postmodernism in general' (195). Paradox is also generated, he claims, by the 'self-referential nature of Fowles' text and language.' He suggests, for example, that '[w]hen [the] narrator proclaims the fictionality of his text, when he warns us that "I am lying," he is repeating the gesture of Epimenides, a gesture that leads to an infinite regression of back-and-forth cancellation and restatement of meaning' (190). 'This self-referential "liar paradox" effect is,' he asserts

> of critical importance to the dynamics of Fowles' text, undermining as it does the attempt to reduce any aspect of the book to a univocal interpretation or even to peacefully coexisting multiple interpretations along the lines of a New Critical appeal to unity in multiplicity via concepts such as irony or ambiguity.
>
> (190)

There is, first of all, as I have already suggested, nothing paradoxical about the idea of a novel being both about novel writing and about reality (indeed, isn't novel writing a part of reality?). Second, with respect to Booker's claim that the self-referentiality of Fowles's novel generates paradox, it's important to note (a) that the fact that a sentence is self-referential doesn't necessarily mean that it is paradoxical – e.g., 'This sentence is about itself,' though self-referential, is unequivocally true, and (b) that what Fowles's narrator says – 'This story I am telling is all imagination' (1981: 80) – is neither self-referential nor paradoxical. It is not, in particular, the same as liar sentences like 'This sentence is false' or 'What I am now saying is false.' What makes these paradoxical, as I noted earlier, is that it appears that if they are true, they are false, and if they are false, they are true. This is not the case with 'This story I am telling is all imagination,' nor would it be even if what Fowles's narrator had claimed was 'This story I am telling is not true.'

At the same time that Booker proclaims the novel to be paradoxical,[3] he also suggests that it is indeterminate. The problem with this conjunction is that if a sentence is truly paradoxical then its truth value is not indeterminate – rather the sentence is determinately both true and false. Where one is not committed to the idea that a seemingly paradoxical sentence is in fact a true contradiction, one might well call it 'indeterminate,' 'ambiguous,' or 'equivocal.' That is, one might well deem such a sentence 'equivocal' where one suspects that it is an apparent paradox, but where one is unable to determine what's gone wrong, either with the reasoning that leads to it or with the premises. Booker thinks that a novel being both about itself and about reality is paradoxical. He doesn't claim, however, that since (according to him) a novel, by the laws of logic, can't both be about itself and about reality, *The French Lieutenant's Woman*, seeming to be about both, is equivocal; rather, he claims that the novel is determinately, unequivocally, about both itself and reality.

Be this as it may, however, Booker argues that Fowles 'in keeping with his theme of existential freedom . . . proposes no alternative dogma of his own, but merely seeks to subvert the kind of totalizing interpretations upon which all dogmas rely' and that 'this subversion is made particularly effective by the way in which the text constantly employs the ambiguity of sexuality as an analogue for the indeterminacy of the text itself' (195). 'The undecidability embodied in *The French Lieutenant's Woman*,' he states, 'is infinite and can never be brought to rest by appeals to irony and ambiguity as hypostatized categories of textual functioning' (190).

On the one hand, however, it can't be that what renders the meaning of the novel indeterminate is that it is impossible to decide which among the existing interpretations of it are most persuasive. Booker himself asserts that 'the resistance to final interpretation that Fowles demonstrates in relation to sexuality and textuality should not be construed as an attitude of nihilism, as a suggestion that all interpretation is pointless,' nor 'as an endorsement of total interpretative anarchy, as a suggestion that any and all interpretations are just as good as any and all other interpretations' (196).

On the other, the nature of the claims Booker makes on behalf of the novel belies his suggestion that its meaning is undecidable. Not only does he argue that the novel is about both reality and novel writing; he also argues that paradox is the central *defining* feature of *The French Lieutenant's Woman*, as well as perhaps of postmodernism itself, thus reducing not just some aspect of the novel or the period, but the novel and possibly the period as a whole, to what seems to be a 'univocal interpretation.' He further claims that

> Fowles achieves ambiguity not through chaos or meaninglessness, but through paradoxical, undecidable, and nondialectical conflicts between clearly and specifically stated opposing forces, whether they be inside/outside, art/reality, truth/fiction, male/ female, freedom/determination, nineteenth century/twentieth century, or Marxist history/bourgeois progress.
>
> (196)

According to him, for example, the novel 'seems to openly invite a Marxist reading,' but at the same time 'goes even further, calling historical progress so strongly into question that a classical Marxian reading, too, is undercut' (192):

> Marxism itself is seen as merely another opiate of the masses – both the Victorian bourgeois notion of progress and the Marxist notion of dialectical history depend in a fundamental way upon the same Hegelian narrative of history that Fowles' text problematizes.
>
> (192)

'The net effect,' he concludes, 'is that Fowles' novel sets these two opposing views of history one against the other and then proceeds to make it impossible to establish a preference of [*sic*] one over the other' (192). In claiming, however, that these two views are fundamentally alike in their dependence on the same Hegelian narrative of history, Booker in effect denies that they propose opposing accounts of the nature of history, and so it should hardly be surprising that the novel makes it impossible to decide in favor of one or the other. If Fowles's novel 'problematizes' the teleological aspect of this Hegelian narrative, and if both of these views of history rely on it, then the net effect is that the novel rejects both. What's undecidable or ambiguous about that?

Overlooking this, however (and overlooking the fact that what he argues with respect to the art/reality distinction is that the novel affirms both), one might suppose that what Booker is gesturing toward in claiming that 'Fowles achieves ambiguity [through] paradoxical, undecidable, and nondialectical conflicts between clearly and specifically stated opposing forces' is something like the idea that the novel presents the reader with a series of compound statements having the logical form (P ∨ ~P) but makes it impossible for her to affirm either disjunct. The *locus classicus* for this argument is Paul de Man, who in *Allegories of Reading* claims that 'a text such as [Rousseau's] *Profession de Foi* can literally be called "unreadable" in that it leads to a set of assertions that radically exclude each other. Nor are these assertions mere neutral constations; they are exhortative performatives that require the passage from sheer enunciation to action. They compel us to choose while destroying the foundations of any choice' (245). This situation does not arise, however, in the case of the 'opposing forces' Booker identifies because they are not contradictories (with the possible exception of the freedom/determination opposition, though some philosophers espouse compatibilism, which, as the name suggests, is the view that free will and determinism are compatible). One is not logically compelled to affirm, for example, either the nineteenth century or the twentieth century, and so one is not presented with a paradoxical, undecidable, nondialectical conflict in a novel such as *The French Lieutenant's Woman* that, as Booker sees it, fails to establish a categorical preference for either one or the other.[4]

Con men and Cretans

A misunderstanding of the liar's paradox is also apparent in an essay by Richard Kuhns concerning contradiction, repression, and the indeterminacy of the truth of beliefs in Melville's *The Confidence-Man*. Invoking Freud's account of the significance of an analysand's use of negation in the psychoanalytic exchange as one of his starting points, Kuhns claims that 'repression is one the vicissitudes suffered by an instinctual impulse or demand' and that, although such a demand or impulse 'may be pushed out of consciousness or never allowed to enter consciousness' if it 'comes into conflict with others,' the instinct nonetheless 'continues to exist as a force, a psychic reality, however much denied,' revealing itself on occasion through our 'denying that something said or referred to is true' (1992: 188). This, he notes,

> takes the form of a negation: 'I did *not* mean such-and-such'; 'What I said does not refer to such a person, thought, wish, belief, etc.' And as soon as that is said, there is some evidence for

imputing to the utterer just the opposite of what is claimed. So we find ourselves in something like the liar's paradox: What I say is false if true, true if false, but – put more accurately in the psychological context – what I say is *both true and false*. Or, if you will, what I say violates the law of contradiction.

(188)

One's denying, then, that what one meant was such-and-such amounts to a disguised acknowledgment that one did mean such-and-such. However, this fact, if it is one, doesn't render 'I did not mean such-and-such' a violation of the law of noncontradiction – if I claim that I didn't mean such-and-such, but in fact I really did mean that (whether I consciously know that I did or not), then my claim that 'I didn't mean that' is false *simpliciter* (whether I consciously know it or not).[5] On the assumption that when I say 'I didn't mean such-and-such,' the opposite of what I'm asserting is true, then the falsity of my assertion that 'I didn't mean such-and-such' implies the truth of the claim that the analyst (presumably) has made. So we have two statements here, one that is true and one that is false, rather than one statement that is both true and false. (Note that a paradox would arise if, at the time the analysand (A) were saying 'What B is saying is false,' the analyst (B) were saying 'What A is saying is true.')

It may be that Kuhns believes that negations of this sort violate the law of noncontradiction because he is assuming that deception of some kind is crucial to the generation of the liar's paradox. However, an intention to deceive, or, in this case, unwitting self-deception that is considered at the same time to be self-revealing, is irrelevant to the liar's paradox. Suppose I am thought to be a person who habitually lies and I assert that 'Snow is white.' The fact that I habitually lie does not in any way affect the truth-value of 'Snow is white': if snow is white, then what I've said is true. I will have just failed in this case to live up to my reputation (and someone who didn't know whether snow was white or not but knew that I habitually lied might be misled into thinking that snow wasn't white). By the same token, the assertion 'What I am now saying is false' is paradoxical, whether uttered by habitual liar or an unfailing truth-teller.

That Kuhns is assuming that the intention to deceive is relevant to the liar's paradox is suggested by his discussion of *The Confidence-Man*. He argues, for instance, that the mysterious and mute stranger of the opening chapter who writes the words of St. Paul from 1 Corinthians, Chapter 13 – 'Charity thinketh no evil,' 'Charity suffereth long, and is kind,' etc. – on a slate could be, given the way he is described (as being dressed in 'cream colors,' as wearing a 'white fur' with a 'long, fleecy nap') either the Lamb, 'the long departed Christ, returned to preach the Gospel of Paul' or 'a wolf in sheep's clothing' (190). 'If the man in cream colors is a false prophet,' Kuhns claims, 'then what he writes on the slate is true if false, and false if true – and therefore the reader is entangled in the liar's paradox' (191).

However, if it is true that charity thinks no evil, that it suffers long and is kind, then what the man in cream colors writes is true, regardless of whether he is a false prophet or not. Whether it is true may be one question raised by *The Confidence-Man* – a heterodox question, perhaps, but not one that entangles the reader in the liar's paradox. The novel certainly raises the question of whether one should trust the person who asserts as much – a question that may have heterodoxical implications (if, say, asked of St. Paul),[6] a question that, its possible heterodoxical implications aside, raises epistemological concerns.[7] But, again, neither of these is a question to which the liar's paradox is relevant.

Kuhns points to the story of Mocmohoc the Indian chief, recounted in Chapter 26 of the novel, as another example of the way in which the liar's paradox informs *The Confidence-Man*. The colony of Wrights and Weavers, the story goes, after having been repeatedly persecuted by, and after having lost two of their kin in hostilities with, a neighboring Indian tribe, were induced to enter into a treaty with its chief, Mocmohoc, not only on account of 'the harrowings of the enemy, leaving them no peace,' but also because of 'the suddenly changed ways of Mocmohoc, who, although hitherto deemed a savage almost as perfidious as Caesar Borgia, yet now put on a seeming reverse of this, engaging to bury the hatchet, smoke the pipe, and be friends forever' (Melville, 1967: 209). The Wrights and Weavers, amenable to this, but still wary, made a pact that not all of them should ever enter the chief's lodging at the same time when visiting him, so as to ensure that, should he revert to his old ways, some of them would survive; however, on one occasion the chief 'did, with such fine art and pleasing carriage win their confidence, that he brought them all together to a feast of bear's meat, and there, by stratagem, ended them' (210). 'Once again,' Kuhns argues, 'we are confronted by paradox':

All Indians are deceivers: when an Indian says, or acts as if, he is not a deceiver, he is lying. Analogous to the paradox of the Cretan, we are presented with the paradox of the Indian. That paradox is a paradox of action: We cannot know if an action is friendly or perfidious. It is as if we cannot assign a truth value to human behavior, as we cannot to human utterance.

(195)

This 'paradox of the Indian' is not, however, analogous to the paradox of the Cretan – *viz.*, 'All Cretans are liars,' uttered by a Cretan. This statement, made by a Cretan, is paradoxical regardless of whether in point of fact all Cretans are liars or not – that is, no assumptions about the nature of Cretans are required to generate it. By the same token, 'This sentence is true' uttered by whomever, though semantically pathological (it is either true or false, but the assignment of one or the other truth value will be arbitrary), generates no paradox, and so even if one assumes that all Indians are liars, no paradox ensues if an Indian says 'I am telling the truth now.'

It is unclear, moreover, what to make of Kuhns's claim that 'it is as if we cannot assign a truth value to human behavior, as we cannot to human utterance' (human behavior, of course, isn't either true or false – I take it that this is why Kuhns says that it is 'as if' we cannot assign a truth value to human behavior) or of the related assertions that 'representations of truth, whether in assertion or action do not deserve trust, for they are of indeterminate value' (196) and that 'neither truth nor falsity attaches to sentences and actions' (196). For one thing, he seems to assume that it follows from one's not knowing whether a statement is either true or false that it is in fact neither true nor false (or that it follows from not knowing whether an action is friendly or not that is in fact neither friendly nor unfriendly). In so assuming, he not only conflates a question about what we can know with a question about what might in fact be the case, but also renders the question of trust, central to *The Confidence-Man*, a moot one.

With respect to the former, perhaps Kuhns thinks, with Dummett, that a statement is true only if it is capable of being known to be true by us. However, this is something that needs to be argued rather than assumed. With respect to the latter, if Kuhns is claiming that there are statements that are *in principle* unverifiable, and hence neither true nor false,[8] and if he's right, then what could there be to trust or distrust about them? It is statements that we believe are determinately either true or false, but don't know which, that are candidates for trust or distrust – it is with respect to statements like this that what we believe about the person who asserts them may make a difference to whether we believe they're true or false. That is, if I trust the person who asserts something I believe to be effectively decidable, but whose truth-value, for whatever reasons, is unknown to me, I might be inclined to believe that what he or she says is true.

For another thing, though Kuhns argues that actions and utterances in *The Confidence-Man* are of indeterminate value, what he says both about analysands and Indians suggests a different principle, one to the effect that any time one says or does anything, one really means or intends the opposite of what it is one has said or done. Not only is this at odds with his claim that, for example, 'we cannot know if an action is friendly or perfidious' – since on the assumption that a friendly action is always just a front for perfidy, we can know – but it also has ideological ramifications of which he seems to be unaware. The psychoanalytic concept of negation, thought of in relation to an undifferentiated class of analysands, might seem innocuous enough; however, when some specific group is substituted for that undifferentiated class it becomes clear just how hazardous a concept it is: consider, e.g., the idea that when women say 'no,' they really mean 'yes,' or, more to the point here, the appellation 'Indian-giver.'

Kuhns is not incognizant of the fact that *The Confidence-Man* is exposing the blind prejudice of the 'backwoodsman' who assumes, according to Judge James Hall, whose story is recounted in Chapter 26, that 'when a tomahawking red-man advances the notion of the benignity of the red race, it is but part and parcel with that subtle strategy which he finds so useful in war, in hunting, and the general conduct of life' (208). However, Kuhns doesn't object to the principle he thinks underlies the assumption because to him it signals the truth, not just about Indians, but human beings generally – i.e., that they are living, breathing, violations of the law of noncontradiction. The problem, from Kuhns's perspective, is that human beings want to repress this 'truth' rather than just simply acknowledge it, and in the case of the white man's relations with Indians, he argues, this repression takes the form of genocide:

> To trust an Indian is to enter into a contradiction, just as to believe what a Cretan says is to get caught up in a contradiction.

But now we are at the lowest level of the descent into repression: the story of Mocmohoc occurs within the story of Colonel Moredock, which occurs within the story of the stories told by the confidence man, which themselves occur within *The Confidence-Man*. And at that level of repression, the story of Mocmohoc is a substitute formation for lying in speech. The Indian does not talk, he acts. Paradoxes of action are more destructive than simple lying, for they end in death. The only way to overcome them is in a life devoted to eradication of the paradox – that is, kill all Indians.
                                                                                    (195)

In this way, Kuhns is, I think, unwittingly dignifying racial prejudice by attempting to represent it as a sort of logical paradox – what he implies is that the white man is right to believe that when an Indian acts friendly, this is just an act (never mind that Kuhns is mistaken in thinking this to be a logical paradox); however, rather than seeking to 'repress' this 'contradiction' by killing Indians, the white man should have just accepted it.

This ideologically problematic aspect of Kuhn's argument is a function of only one of the ways in which he defines contradiction, i.e., as a denial that is really an affirmation – a definition, which, ideological issues aside, neither accords with the strict sense of the term as he thinks it does, nor yields the radical indeterminacy he believes it does. He also defines contradiction in a way that he seems to think is synonymous with the notion of a denial that is really an affirmation, but isn't, and that also does not accord with the definition of a true contradiction that he originally appeals to (i.e., that violates the law of noncontradiction).

He claims, for example, that all human beings can be, like Colonel John Moredock – the Indian-hater of *The Confidence-Man*, who nonetheless was also a lover, 'contradictory in affection' (196) – both lovers and haters. Not only is this not a contradiction in the strict sense – as James Hall, according to the teller, puts it, 'Moredock was an example of something *apparently* self-contradictory' (218; my emphasis) – but it also conflicts with Kuhns's claim that 'persons,' like texts, 'are indeterminate in their claims to be true, or to be false' (196). For, if like a proposition that fails of a truth-value, or, as in some three-valued logics, has the value 'neuter,' humans beings are neither lovers nor haters, are 'gappy' in lacking the capacity either to love or to hate, or are simply indifferent as such to everything, then how can they be both lovers and haters? And if, as Kuhns suggests, 'telling stories allows the introduction of sentences that are properly speaking both true and false, sentences that do indeed violate the "firmest of all principles"' (188) (*viz.* the law of non-contradiction – Kuhns is quoting Aristotle), and if *The Confidence-Man* is one such story, then how can it be that the sentences of *The Confidence-Man* are neither true nor false?

3

Postmodernism, Logic, and Politics

A case of mistaken identity

Contrary to what many theorists of postmodernism seem to think, the law of noncontradiction is not among the secret protocols of the Elders of Philosophy, intended to prevent what would be, in its absence, certain political insurgence on the part of the oppressed. In stating, as Aristotle formulates it, that '[i]t is impossible for the same thing at the same time to belong and not to belong to the same thing and in the same respect' (1952: iv.3.1005b18–20) the principle excludes only this, and nothing else. Whether it is true or not aside, what it states can hardly be construed in such as a way as to warrant the claim that it 'represses,' 'marginalizes,' or 'excludes' difference.

The insinuation that as a result of some desire on their part to contain difference, western thinkers have consistently 'repressed' the possibility of predicating both terms of a 'binary opposition' of something, and the equation of this repression with an adherence to the law of noncontradiction, is made explicit in Iris Marion Young's account of what she calls, following Adorno, 'the logic of identity':

> The irony of the logic of identity is that by seeking to reduce the differently similar to the same, it turns the merely different into the absolutely other. It inevitably generates dichotomy instead of unity, because the move to bring the particulars into a universal category creates a distinction between inside and outside . . . Because the totalizing movement always leaves a remainder, the project of reducing particulars to a unity must fail. Not satisfied then to admit defeat in the face of difference, the logic of identity shoves difference into dichotomous hierarchical oppositions: essence/accident, good/bad, normal/deviant. Difference as the relatedness of things with more or less similarity in a multiplicity

of possible respects, here congeals as the binary opposition a/ not-a. In every case the unity of the positive category is achieved only at the expense of an expelled, unaccounted for chaotic realm of the accidental. In the history of Western thought this logic of identity has created a vast number of such mutually exclusive oppositions that structure whole philosophies: subject/object, mind/ body, nature/culture. These dichotomies are structured by the dichotomy good/bad, pure/impure. The first side of the dichotomy is elevated over the second because it designates the unified, the self-identical, whereas the second lies outside the unified as the chaotic, unformed, transforming, that always threatens to cross the border and break up the unity of the good.

(1990: 99)

Like Schrift, Young renders the dichotomies she lists as formally equivalent to A/not-A, when in fact they are equivalent to A/B – it is mind/not-mind, for example, that would be equivalent to A/ not-A, not mind/body (not-A signifies the negation of A, and B signifies a property other than A). Having rendered what is equivalent to A/B as A/not-A, Young thus puts herself in a position to conclude that the 'logic of identity' has created a vast number of 'mutually exclusive oppositions that structure whole philosophies.' If something is, or has the property, A, it cannot, according to classical logic, not be or not have the property, A, at the same time. But if something is, or has the property, A, that does not exclude the possibility that it might also be, or have the property, B, at the same time. And so since the 'binary oppositions' Young identifies do not 'congeal' as A/not-A, there is no reason to view them as being necessarily mutually exclusive – having a mind does not exclude the possibility of having a body at the same time; having essential properties does not exclude the possibility of having accidental properties at the same time.

In illicitly substituting A/not-A for A/B, Young also arrives at the odd conclusion that the 'first side of [a] dichotomy is elevated over the second because it designates the unified, the self-identical.' She seems to construe A/not-A as the proposition that if A is not A, A is not self-identical, and to render that, in turn, as the proposition that whatever is other than A is not-self-identical because it is not A. That is, her reasoning seems to proceed as follows: A is A, not-A is not A, hence whatever is not A – whatever is other than A – is not identical with itself. Because what she represents as not-A is B, this is in effect to argue that A is A, B is not A, therefore B is not B.

The 'inference' from A is A and B is not A to B is not B, seems to be what Young is in part ascribing to the western philosophical tradition – she implies that it is an inexorable consequence of the logic that underlies western thought that, if subjects are self-identical, then objects, not being subjects, are not self-identical. This, of course, is nonsense – the chair I am sitting on is no less identical with itself than I am. On the other hand, in supposing that this tradition regards mind/body and essence/accident, for example, as formally equivalent to A/not-A, Young also appears to be suggesting that, as the conjunction (A & ~A) is a contradiction, it follows that the western philosophical tradition has to deny that subjects can have both minds and bodies, or both essential and accidental properties – for to allow that they could would to be allow that they weren't self-identical. But what could it mean to say that because I have the accidental property of brown hair, I am not identical with myself? Such are the absurdities theorists of postmodernism end up attributing to the 'western metaphysical tradition' by assuming that 'binary oppositions' 'congeal' as A/not-A.

Young's concern is with the 'denial of difference' that 'some feminists and postmodern writers have suggested . . . structures Western reason' and with showing how 'such a denial of difference contributes to social group oppression' (10). It is true that throughout western history women have been associated with the body, the irrational, the chaotic, and men with mind, rationality and order, and that women have been deemed inferior to men on the basis of such associations. But these associations are not a function of logic – that is to say, they do not follow by some sort of necessity from the structure of western logic. If western culture has deemed women to be mindless, it's not because allowing that they possessed minds would entail a violation of the law of noncontradiction. Such associations do not even inhere in metaphysical theories that 'privilege' mind over body or in theories that reduce mind to body. For if they did, it would not only be impossible to conceive what is perfectly conceivable, but it would be impossible for theories to exist that do in fact exist – *viz.*, dualistic theories that don't associate mind with masculinity and body with femininity, and materialist theories that don't associate the reduction of mental events to a species of physical events with femininity.[1]

It is worth noting, in addition, that Young's claim that the 'logic of identity' – a logic, which, she says, 'seek[s] to reduce the differently similar to the same' and in so doing 'turns the merely different into the absolutely other'[2] – structures western thought is questionable, in so far as it doesn't structure the thought of one of the most important and influential philosophers in western history, Aristotle:

> One might raise the question of why woman does not differ from man in species, when female and male are contrary and their difference is a contrariety. . . . We should recall the distinction between a thing's definition and its matter. Contrarieties which are in the definition mark a difference as to species; but those which are in the individualized matter do not. Hence white or black does not divide men into species; white men are not a different species from black men . . . For in this case men are being taken as matter, and the matter does not make the difference; since color does not make different kinds of men. The flesh and the bones of which this and that man consist are different, to be sure, and any concrete individual is, indeed, distinct, but not therefore of another species . . . Similarly, male and female . . . do not make an essential difference, but only a difference of matter or body.
>
> (1952: x.9.1058a29–1058b24)

On Aristotle's account here, difference amounts precisely to what Young describes as 'the relatedness of things with more or less similarity in a multiplicity of possible respects.' Difference does not 'congeal' as A/not-A, or human being and not-human being; Aristotle does not equate man with 'white male' and anybody who is not white and male with 'not-man' or 'absolutely other.' Furthermore, the accidental material differences that Aristotle mentions – black skin, white skin, female anatomy, male anatomy – are neither expelled nor unaccounted for. Indeed, he offers a rather detailed account of just these sorts of differences in the *Generation of Animals*. This is not to say that he didn't think women were inferior or that the female form wasn't a deficiency. But since he did, it is to say that Young's proposed replacement for the 'logic of identity' – what one might call the 'logic of difference' – is not the answer to the problem of social group oppression, inasmuch as it is Young's 'logic of difference' that describes Aristotle's logic. But neither is the 'logic of difference' the problem, and that is because the causes of social group oppression are fundamentally extra-logical.

Addressing the opposition

Although it is generally postmodernist theorists with strong post-structuralist credentials who tend to misconstrue the law of noncontradiction, a misunderstanding of it is also apparent in the work of Stephen Yarbrough, who, in the name of a 'postmodern humanism,' takes poststructuralist postmodernism to task for privileging the supposedly devalued halves of various 'metaphysical oppositions' (1992: 33). Drawing on Irving Babbitt's concept of the 'New Humanism,' Yarbrough suggests that poststructuralist postmodernism displays 'the perspective of traditional metaphysics, which necessarily promotes one pole of a categorical opposition and therefore requires the negation of the other' (33):

> By taking up an exclusive perspective, the individual falls into the 'indolence of monism,' Babbitt's term for what Heidegger calls inauthenticity. 'Monism,' as Babbitt says in *The New Laokoon*, 'is merely a fine term that man has invented for his own indolence and one-sidedness and unwillingness to mediate the diverse and conflicting aspects of reality.' Monisms do not establish an original relation toward the world but only 'novel' ones. Becoming novel is easy for the monist because all he has to do is take over the categories of his predecessors and promote the opposite side. Thus, the history of man is a record of movement from one form of critical indolence to another.
>
> (33)

Ironically, Yarbrough ends up implicitly criticizing the disciples of 'the logic of both/and' for bowing before the altar of western logic and failing to transcend the law of noncontradiction. And in the course of his critique he makes the same mistake that they make – he confuses acceptance of the truth of the law of noncontradiction with the 'promotion' of one pole of a dualism:

> [F]or Western man, who because of his history understands his world through metaphysical oppositions, the only access to that which underlies the phenomena of the changeable world is to hold open willfully the possibilities contained by such oppositions. Submission to [Babbitt's notion of] the higher will is fundamentally a cancellation of the law of noncontradiction. It is a holding open of the possibilities that logic would obliterate.
>
> (33)

Yarbrough is not the only critic of postmodernist theory to make such an observation. In 'Nietzsche's Theology of History and the Redemption of Postmodernism,' Bernard Zelechow, for one, also criticizes poststructuralist postmodernists for 'asserting the flip side of . . . traditional definitions and canons' (1993: 120). 'If,' he claims, 'traditional philosophical and religious thinking embraced Presence and Being then the postmodernist project in its most radical form superficially rejects all theological, metaphysical and philosophical meditation. At its furthest extreme, postmodernism spurns the very concept of knowledge' (124). 'Structuralism and deconstruction with all their strategies,' he argues, 'remain mired in the dialectics of the absolute and dualistic dialectic of presence and absence' (124). And he suggests that challenging this postmodernism would involve, among other things, replacing 'the logic of the excluded middle' with 'relationship (covenant) and mutuality' (124–5).

Like Yarbrough, then, Zelechow criticizes postmodernists for failing to 'go beyond' classical logic, but where Yarbrough frames his critique in terms of their failing to transcend the law of noncontradiction, Zelechow frames his in terms of their failing to transcend the law of the excluded middle. They both, however, commit the same sort of error: Yarbrough thinks regarding dualisms in terms of 'both/and' rather than 'either/or' transgresses the law of noncontradiction; Zelechow thinks that rejecting the law of the excluded middle enables one to regard dualisms in terms of 'both/and,' and that doing so (it should come as no surprise) involves embracing paradox. 'To go beyond a mere dissenting critique of postmodernity,' he writes, 'epistemology cannot be defined in terms of classical concepts. Epistemology must overcome the dualism inherent in classical concepts and embrace the paradox uniting "either" and "or" existentially' (126).

Michael Roemer, for another, argues that postmodernist theorists and critics reduce reality to text and, in so doing, reflect a rationalist unwillingness to accept the existence of true contradictions:

Perhaps only the rationalist, convinced that we can attain a perfect or totalized understanding of reality, is threatened by traditional story. Postmodern theory claims to oppose totalization and stresses contradiction and undecidedness, yet is unwilling to entertain the duality of text *and* reality. Though deconstruction is often charged with endorsing irrationality, it is committed to reason and, with respect to the 'real,' obeys the precept of classical logic that:

Either the statement or the negation of the statement must be correct. *'Tertium non datur,'* a third possibility does not exist.

(1995: 90)

'Most of us,' he claims, continue to see story 'from a traditional perspective – as at once reflecting reality *and* separate from it'; 'most of us haven't the intellectual rigor to be consistent rationalists.' Rather, 'we accept the "either" *and* "or" implicit in the contradictions of story' (90). Roemer here makes the mistake (as Zelechow does above) of assuming that the third possibility ruled out by the law of the excluded middle is (P & ~P), but elsewhere in his book he frames the acceptance of 'the "either" *and* "or"' in terms of a negation of the law of noncontradiction:

> In our rationalist context, it is often assumed that contradictions *undermine* a system. Logic persuades us that a thing and its opposite cannot both be true. Thus Marx and Marxists point to the contradictions in capitalism as a symptom of its inevitable demise. Yet the opposites – which imply contradiction even when they don't openly express it – insure the *survival* of the system; they endow it with tensile strength and the capacity for change and renewal.
>
> (120)

It may well be that true contradictions, if they exist, do not undermine a system but rather ensure its survival (notice, however, the vacillation in the above between talk of true contradictions and just contradictions). However, the belief that story at once reflects reality and is separate from it does not openly express or imply a contradiction, and so it can't openly express or imply a true contradiction.

F.F. Centore, too, claims that postmodernism, 'in its effort to overcome the old dichotomies found within the traditional doctrines of science, philosophy, and theology' has 'rolled everything together into one Great Unknown' (1991: 2). He argues that 'what our life-centered experience of reality demands is *both* essence *and* existence, fixed meanings *and* multiple variations, the traditional *and* the modern' and that 'however *avant-garde* it may appear at the moment, any philosophy, interpretation or hermeneutic which affirms one at the expense of the other is doomed to failure' (2). Unlike Yarbrough, however, he doesn't assert that 'hav[ing] both aspects of reality simultaneously' (2) requires a 'cancellation' of the law of noncontradiction, and unlike Zelechow, he doesn't suggest that it involves embracing 'the paradox uniting "either" and "or" existentially.' He claims, rather, to be recapitulating Thomistic philosophy. Which is to say that it is not logic that obliterates the possibility of affirming, say, both mind and body – it's not the law of noncontradiction or the law of the excluded middle that stops Augustine, for example, from promoting both spiritual contemplation and bodily pleasure. Rather, that Aquinas affirms both and that Augustine doesn't is a consequence of, among other things, their different metaphysical commitments: Aquinas represents one (Aristotelian) strain in the western theological tradition, and Augustine another (Platonic) strain.

Like Young, Yarbrough seems to view logic – and the law of noncontradiction in particular – as repressive:

> The law of noncontradiction requires the assumption of a stable, unitary self that thinks within a temporally uniform world – such as the world of geometry – wherein changes in the self's circumstances do not affect the object of the self's thought. Modern scientific discourse, by organizing itself about a self-grounding cogito and adhering to the law of noncontradiction, consequently, has tended toward totalitarianism and cultural solipsism.
>
> (29)

Exactly how the belief that any given proposition cannot both be true and false at the same time and in the same respect, or how the belief that any given entity cannot both have and not have some property at the same time and in the same respect, leads to totalitarianism and cultural solipsism is left unexplained by Yarbrough.[3]

On the one hand, however, it could be that he thinks that it does because he misconstrues the law of noncontradiction – that is, because he thinks that what the law excludes is the possibility of 'affirming' both halves of a 'binary opposition.' A misconstrual of the law of the excluded middle leads another theorist, Robert Nadeau, to a similar conclusion:

> There is, as I see it, the prospect that the law of the excluded middle, which is very much in force in the recent epistemological debates among quantum physicists, will eventually be understood to be incommensurate with the life of nature. Since that principle is a basic feature of all controlling symbolics, and since

the defense of the absolute ontological authority of such symbolics in the sphere of political reality threatens to destroy us daily, some fundamental reorganization of the manner in which we use our minds could well be our only hope of survival. If either-or categorical thinking could be perceived as an arbitrarily, culturally derived mechanism in the construction of our symbolic universe which is not ontologically grounded in the life of nature, then perhaps we can once again similarly consider, and plan for, the future we hope our children and grandchildren will enjoy.

(1981: 63)

What Nadeau identifies as 'the mechanism[ ] of control' (155) in western thought – 'either-or categorical thinking' – is not, however, the law of the excluded middle. Nadeau is operating on the mistaken assumption that false dichotomies are generated by an acceptance of the law, as the following excerpt from his discussion of Barth's *Giles Goat-Boy* suggests:

We are asked in *Giles Goat-Boy*, to realize that the tendency of Western man to make either-or judgments, or to frame our experience in terms of irreconcilable categorical abstractions, is a principal source of division and conflict in human society.... Barth suggests that we abandon [this habit of mind] in favor of a new mode of understanding in which we recognize distinctions between particulars while affirming at the same time that those distinctions are not absolute. The intended result is that we become as much aware of *sameness* as we are of *differences*, which will not only make for a more realistic assessment of a given situation or problem, but also greatly facilitate meaningful compromise.

(93–4)

If it is the tendency of western man to make the sorts of either-or judgments Nadeau ascribes to him, it is because he commits a logical fallacy, not because he is committed to logic. That is, if there is something that 'threatens to destroy us daily,' it is not the defense of the absolute ontological authority of the law of the excluded middle, but the fallacy of bifurcation – that is, the presumption, as S. Morris Engel puts it, 'that a distinction or classification is exclusive and exhaustive, when other alternatives exist' (1986: 135).[4] (One of Engel's examples of this fallacy speaks to the threat Nadeau alludes to: 'There can only be one capital, Washington or Moscow.

There can be one flag, the Stars and Stripes or the godless hammer and sickle' (135–6).)[5]

On the other hand, it is possible that Yarbrough's belief that, in adhering to the law of noncontradiction, modern scientific discourse tends toward totalitarianism and cultural solipsism, is the product of another of his misconceptions about the law of noncontradiction. Discussing the differences between Aristotle's *Politics* and *Ethics*, on the one hand, and his *Metaphysics*, on the other, he comments that

> The starting point of ethics and politics . . . differs from that of metaphysics. The *Metaphysics* is concerned about 'that which is *knowable* in the highest degree.' Knowing is not subject to choice, whereas deliberation can occur only in an indeterminate situation. Adherence to the first principle of metaphysics, the law of noncontradiction, can distinguish true from false statements only when the being or nonbeing of the subjects is clear.
>
> (9)

By the law of noncontradiction, any compound statement of the form $\sim(P \& \sim P)$ is necessarily true, and so any compound statement of the form $(P \& \sim P)$ is necessarily false. But this is of no help in determining which conjunct is true and which false. That is, the law of noncontradiction cannot distinguish true synthetic statements from false synthetic statements. Yarbrough apparently believes that it can, and so perhaps he thinks that armed solely with it, scientists are able willy-nilly to declare certain theories true and others false. No appeal to the law of noncontradiction, however, can settle the question of which among a number of internally consistent, but conflicting, theories may be true.

Yarbrough, like many theorists of postmodernism, also seems to confuse the law of noncontradiction with the law of the excluded middle. Quoting Aristotle, he writes ' "Thought" in the *Metaphysics* "either affirms or denies every object of thought or intelligible object." ' 'Deliberation,' he adds, 'begins precisely when this affirmation or denial is impossible' (10). This remark, which Yarbrough makes in the context of claiming that the law of noncontradiction 'can distinguish true from false statements only when the being or nonbeing of the subjects is clear,' suggests he thinks that to claim that the truth value of some proposition is indeterminate entails the 'cancellation of the law of noncontradiction.' One explanation as to why he thinks this could be that, like Schrift, Zelechow, and Roemer, he is taking the negation of (P ∨ ~P) to be (P & ~P) and so assumes that to reject the former is to commit oneself to the latter, or at least, to the possibility of the latter. But since the negation of (P ∨ ~P) is ~(P ∨ ~P), the 'middle' excluded by the law of the excluded middle is not the possibility of both P and ~P being true, but the possibility of neither P nor ~P being true. Yet although Yarbrough explicitly invokes the law of noncontradiction, he makes no mention of the law of the excluded middle. He quotes from Aristotle's account of the law of the excluded middle in Book Gamma of the *Metaphysics*. But he does not point out that this is what Aristotle is discussing, and the substance of his analysis of Aristotle's claim that 'every concept and thought is expressed either as an affirmation or a negation' (iv.7.1012a1–2) suggests that he thinks Aristotle is outlining the law of noncontradiction.

Whether Yarbrough's attack on the law of noncontradiction is really an unknowing attack on the law of the excluded middle or whether he thinks that in attacking the one he is attacking the other, his discussion of Chapter 7 of Book Gamma suggests that, ultimately, his most basic misconception with respect to logic is his thinking that the law of noncontradiction and, implicitly, the law of the excluded middle, can tell one whether a synthetic statement is true or false. He seems, for example, to interpret Aristotle's claim that every proposition is either true or false as meaning that to believe that a proposition is either true or false is to know whether it is true or false, when in fact what Aristotle is saying is that every proposition has a determinate truth-value, independently of whether it is known. A compound statement of the form (P ∨ ~P) is, by the terms of classical logic, necessarily true, but to accept that this is so does not help one to decide which disjunct is true – that is, the law cannot settle the issue as to whether P or its negation is true and thereby render deliberation superfluous.

If one believes that the law of the excluded middle is true, one believes that a proposition whose truth value is unknown nevertheless is either true or false. But to believe this does not make it any less likely that one will deliberate than if one didn't (though if one rejects the law of the excluded middle, on, for example, intuitionist grounds, there will be fewer propositions one will consider worthy of deliberation than there would be if one accepted it). What Yarbrough is suggesting in claiming that 'deliberation can occur only in an indeterminate situation' is that deliberation can occur only when one doesn't know whether a given statement is true or

false. He confuses this, however, with the idea that 'deliberation
begins . . . when affirmation or denial [of a statement] is impossible.' For, if with respect to a given statement, neither affirmation
nor denial is possible, then the situation is not only determinate,
but determinate in a way that, in contrast to the situation in which
one assumes that a statement whose truth-value one does not know
is nonetheless determinately either true or false, would render deliberation unnecessary. That is, if the parties to a debate about – to
take Dummett's example – whether Jones was brave or not all agreed
that affirmation or denial of 'Jones was brave' was in principle
impossible, there would be nothing for them to deliberate about.

Insubstantial charges

There are a number of explanations one might offer as to what
lies behind the grudge against the law of noncontradiction apparent in theories of postmodernism, one of which has emerged above
– namely, that it, along with the law of the excluded middle, are
viewed as the source of political oppression, as principles that mar-
ginalize women and other groups, and that legitimate totalitarian
impulses. A related but more general antipathy to exclusion as
such, however, as well as a concern with the exclusion, marginaliza-
tion, and devaluation of 'anything that is not substantial,' emerges
in Yarbrough's explanation of the source of the antagonism, which
he claims is 'Aristotle and his metaphysics.' In the *Metaphysics*,
Yarbrough argues, Aristotle

> is concerned about the determination of beings, and his prelimin-
> ary discussion about experience is limited to the experience of
> things, as such. It reflects a craftsman's mentality – someone who
> wants to be able to 'work things out' in his head or on paper and
> have it work out the same in actuality.
>
> (6–7)

In essence, the *Metaphysics* is, according to Yarbrough, 'an elaborate
denigration of experiences that cannot conform to Aristotle's primary principle of contradiction.' And, he continues,

> [q]uite a few people have been concerned about this attitude . . .
> since it necessarily devalues anything that is not substantial, that
> has its being bound up in the circumstances of its appearance,

that is not infinitely repeatable as the same, or that violates the logic of contradiction. Even today invocations of the names of Nietzsche, Heidegger, Derrida, James, Deleuze, Foucault, and many others are ultimately aimed at Aristotle and his metaphysics, particularly the law of noncontradiction. There have been attempts to reset the logic on new ground, to reverse the hierarchy of values implicit in it, to retrieve the primal, authentic experience preceding the determination of beings, to deconstruct the logic and our faith in it, to posit a multiplicity of grounds and thus affirm a plurality of possible meanings, and so on.

(7)

The concern which Yarbrough describes here, however, is unwarranted. First of all, it is not clear that Aristotle believes there are experiences that don't conform to the law of noncontradiction. That is, the charge that Aristotle must necessarily devalue 'anything that is not substantial, that has its being bound up in the circumstances of its appearance' rests on the assumption that he regards them as violations of 'the logic of contradiction.' But it is precisely the assertion that such phenomena do violate the law that Aristotle contests in Chapter 6 of Book Gamma:

[O]ne and the same thing may appear to sight to be honey and to taste not to be; moreover, since we have two eyes, it may not appear to be the same thing to each eye, if the eyes differ. So that when [someone] say[s] . . . that things are as they appear and that therefore all things are alike false and true, since things do not appear the same to all or always the same to the same man, and even appear contrary at the same time (as when we cross our fingers, we feel two things but see only one), we may reply: 'Yes, but things are not both so and not so to the same sense, in the same respect, in the same way, and at the same time; to be truly, they must satisfy all these conditions.'

(4.vi.1011a25–1011b)

Secondly, it's not clear what 'reset[ting] the logic on new ground' and 'revers[ing] the hierarchy of values implicit in it' would accomplish. On the one hand, no cancellation of the law of noncontradiction is required in order to 'affirm a plurality of possible meanings,' since it does not exclude affirming that a word or sentence, say, may have a plurality of possible meanings in the first place. On the other, if the law is not a fundamental presupposition of all meaningful discourse, it is at least the case that a cancellation as such of it would render language trivial. If *all* sentences were both true and false, then, as Aristotle points out, 'all men alike [would be] both right and wrong' and 'no one [could] say anything meaningful' (iv.4.1008b8–9).

Yarbrough not only implies that the law of noncontradiction excludes affirming a plurality of possible meanings, but also seems to be suggesting that it impinges on our ability to experience the world in all its diversity. But again, on the one hand, it does not oblige us to look at the world in only one way. On the other, it is arguable that a cancellation as such of it would result in us experiencing the world in just the monistic, one-sided way that Yarbrough is criticizing. As Aristotle notes, 'if all contradictories were true at the same time and of the same thing, it is clear that all things would be one' (iv.4.1007b18–19, and 'if contradictories apply to anything, one thing will not differ from another' (iv.4.1008a27–29).[6] That is, in retrieving, were it possible, the primal, authentic experience preceding the determination of beings, it seems that what we would be retrieving would not be multiplicity and difference but something like what Hegel described as the dark night in which all cows are black.

Yarbrough sheds further light on what motivates the attack on the law of noncontradiction when he notes that 'rhetoric (as well as poetics, politics, ethics and other "inexact sciences")' tends to despise metaphysics and science 'since the latter can view tropes only as violations of the law of noncontradiction, while tropes are the very matter of rhetoric' (7). This, coupled with Yarbrough's claim that modern science tends toward cultural solipsism and totalitarianism because of its adherence to the law of noncontradiction, makes the attack on the law begin to look something like an assertion of the right, or even obligation, to be inconsistent in defiance of a caricature of science and metaphysics. These eminently logical fields, so the caricature goes, are populated by creatures who have no tolerance for the trivialities of literature, and who would deny that its instruments – e.g., metaphor, simile, metonymy, synecdoche – could serve as a medium for the expression of truth.

As stereotypical as this picture is, it is true, nevertheless, that literary theorists and critics – in the United States, in particular – have been plagued for some time now with the problem of justifying their profession in the eyes of a society that is rather uncritical in its reverence of science. One solution to this problem has been to abandon the defensive tactic of arguing that the inexact sciences are engaged in work different from, but nonetheless as important as, that of the exact sciences, in favor of an offensive strategy which challenges the validity of what many postmodernists think of as the unquestioned assumptions of both the hard sciences and analytic philosophy (another has been to suggest that the hard sciences – in particular, physics – have themselves rejected the fundamental principles of classical logic). It becomes essential to the success of this offensive strategy to insist that tropes, for example, are not words or phrases 'turned from their usual meaning to an unusual one' (Frye, 1985: 472) – this definition clearly being one that denies tropes the power they would require to live up to the task of disorganizing and resisting 'binary logic' – but rather honest-to-God violations of the law of noncontradiction.

This strategy, however, is not likely to shake the conviction of those scientists and philosophers who consider the law to be true. As insensitive to the subtleties of literary language as they are assumed to be, their belief that there are no true contradictions is not likely to be confounded by

> Suffering the evils of both day and night,
> (While no night is more dark than is my day,
> Nor no day hath less quiet than my night),
> With such bad mixture of my night and day
> That, living thus in the blackest winter night,
> I feel the flames of hottest summer day.
>
> > (Sidney, 1986: 496)

Nor even by the arguably non-tropological opening of Robbe-Grillet's *In the Labyrinth*, where we are told:

> outside it is raining, outside you walk through the rain with your head down, shielding your eyes with one hand while you stare ahead nevertheless, a few yards ahead, at a few yards of wet asphalt. . . . Outside the sun is shining, there is no tree, no bush to cast a shadow, and you walk under the sun shielding your eyes with one hand while you stare ahead, only a few yards in front of you, at a few yards of dusty asphalt . . .
>
> > (1965: 141)

Neither of these violates the law of noncontradiction. Sydney's sonnet presents the reader with an apparent contradiction. The opening of *In the Labyrinth*, excluding for the sake of argument the possibility of interpreting it as describing two different episodes in time (i.e., excluding the possibility of interpreting it as an apparent contradiction), presents the reader with a contradiction. Apparent contradictions and contradictions, however, are not the same as true contradictions.

4

Apparent Contradictions, True Contradictions, and Meaning

Heirs of the apparent

In the same spirit as Yarbrough, Brian Caraher, noting that '[i]n Aristotelian and later analytic and symbolic logics, contradiction poses a problem for systematic thought,' argues that it is 'very difficult for either finely trained intellects or the ordinarily opinionated to get much beyond the view that logical, verbal, and argumentative contradictions seriously disable discourse of any kind' (1992: 1–2). Caraher suggests, for example, citing propositions 4.462 and 4.464 of the *Tractatus* ('Tautologies and contradictions are not pictures of reality. They do not represent any possible situations. For the former admit of *all* possible situations, and the latter *none*. A tautology's truth is certain, a proposition's possible, a contradiction's impossible'), that the 'visual, spatialized, and pictorial qualities of Wittgenstein's representational or correspondence theory of logical language and truth . . . promote an intellectually austere regard for the kind of propositions that can speak the truth of things' (2). Wittgenstein, he notes, asserts that '[i]t is impossible to represent in language anything that "contradicts logic" as it is in geometry to represent by its co-ordinates a figure that contradicts the laws of space, or to give the co-ordinates of a point that does not exist' (2). According to Caraher, however, M.C. Escher's *Ascending and Descending* and *Waterfall*

represent visual loops that defy the logic of 'the laws of space' or depict 'co-ordinates of a point that does not exist.' Escher's art models a visual manner of representation that allows contradiction of logical and analytic forms of rendering the truth of things. Moreover, Escher's work permits intimate conflict among word-pictures, world-models, and our ways of rendering things visible, representable, indeed *possible*. Escher invents a visual language that lets us see the laws of visual logic, spatial relationships, and analytic geometry speaking against themselves in figurations that generate rather than vacate possibility. The austerity of the early Wittgenstein's propositions regarding the impossible truth-claims of contradictions would strive to delimit and circumscribe the instructive possibilities of contradiction for discourse.

(2–4)

But whatever instructive possibilities there might be in Escher's lithographs, they don't in fact defy the law of noncontradiction. As Wendell V. Harris points out in his review of the collection of essays on contradiction of which Caraher is editor, what Escher's lithographs 'offer us are *apparent* contradictions, visual equivalents of the kind of verbal play found in Heraclitus' assertion that one cannot step into the same river twice' (1993: 335). Which is to say that neither Wittgenstein nor any other philosopher who believed that 'a contradiction's [truth is] impossible' would argue that the examples of contradiction Caraher provides – all of them apparent – 'cancel, undermine, or paralyze cognition or discourse' (1) or that such apparent contradictions cannot be 'discursively generative' (4).

Nor would they argue that 'the strife or contradiction' that arises from competing truth-claims cannot be 'itself vital and empowering,' as Caraher seems to imply in outlining the argument of Henry Johnstone's contribution to the volume, 'Strife and Contradiction in Hesiod.' Caraher reads Johnstone as arguing that Hesiod, in 'construct[ing] a passage [in the *Theogony*] about strife breaking out among the immortals [that] yields evidence of a problem without clear resolution,' poses a situation where 'the principle of noncontradiction cannot afford the rule for choice or the law of exclusion' because 'it offers neither the force nor principle for selection in a contest of conflicting claims' (20). In claiming this, Caraher implies that philosophers committed to the truth of the law of noncontradiction believe it does offer force and principle for deciding which claim is true in a contest between two contradictory assertions. He, like Yarbrough, appears to think that the law of noncontradiction is considered by those who accept it to be something that can distinguish true synthetic statements from false ones, and so he seems to be construing it as something that would eliminate in advance of any deliberation the 'contradiction or strife' that could be 'vital and empowering' – i.e., that could generate a productive argument even if no resolution of the conflict were achieved (the corollary of his thinking this seems to be that, since the law of noncontradiction doesn't have the force or principle for selection in a contest of competing claims, it can't be true). But since the law of noncontradiction cannot, and has never been thought to be able to, resolve disputes between parties making conflicting claims, the belief of the parties to a dispute that the law is true will not stop them from having a possibly productive debate (indeed, if the parties believed that the law wasn't true, there might well be nothing for them to argue about). As Harris notes,

> Johnstone's primary point is simply that Hesiod seems to have been the earliest to treat 'strife of a certain kind as evidence that a lie has been told.' Johnstone is not making the obvious point that the principle of noncontradiction does not in itself help one to resolve a contradiction – I don't know of anyone who has ever thought it does – but simply that when we encounter two contradictory statements each purporting to report the facts, the contradiction causes us to seek to find the truth. Such a contradiction is 'vital and empowering' only in that it causes us to resolve it. (Since such a contradiction lies in conflicting assertions about contingent facts, it is theoretically resolvable.)
>
> (339)

Both Caraher and Yarbrough give voice to a sentiment that informs a number of postmodernist attacks on the law of noncontradiction in implying that Aristotle's and Wittgenstein's belief that the law is true is motivated by some sort of puritanical dislike of, or aversion to, true contradictions – witness, for example, Yarbrough's assertion that Aristotle seeks to denigrate experiences that do not conform to 'his' principle of noncontradiction, and Caraher's suggestion that Wittgenstein chooses to believe that all contradictions are false because he wishes to delimit and circumscribe the instructive possibilities of contradiction. Caraher, it will be recalled, does point out that 'in Aristotelian and later analytic and symbolic logics, contradiction poses a problem for systematic thought' (1). But because the contradictions he adduces to support his thesis that 'contradiction yields creative or generative activity' (14) are apparent ones and so do not pose any problems, I think he has trouble seeing that there could be any reason for rejecting the suggestion that there are true contradictions other than a preference for austere 'models of representation.'

An apparent paradox like Eliot's 'In my end is my beginning,' for example, which Caraher cites, poses no logical difficulties. Yet if one believes that a logician committed to the truth of the law of noncontradiction would think it did, it's going to be hard to understand why he or she would. And so one might come to the conclusion that such a hypothetical logician's rejection of the possibility that 'In my end is my beginning' could 'speak the truth of things' stems simply from a dislike of such formulations. Philosophers who deny that there are true contradictions may be wrong (at least there are some logicians who think they are), but their reasons for doing so are not, I suggest, that they wish to delimit the instructive possibilities of contradiction.

As R.M. Sainsbury notes, 'historically, one thing that has deterred many people from seriously entertaining the thought that a contradiction could be true is the classically valid inference rule: From a contradiction, anything follows' (1988: 141). If the classical inference rule is valid, then, as Sainsbury points out, 'it would be crazy to believe a contradiction, for this would commit one to believing everything' (141). It is perhaps *ex contradictione quodlibet* ('from a contradiction, anything whatever')[1] that Caraher is alluding to when he remarks that Aristotelian and later analytic and symbolic logics regard contradiction as something that 'cancel[s], undermine[s], or paralyze[s] cognition and discourse.' But he doesn't address the objection directly, nor does he attempt to answer it (again, I think he doesn't because the contradictions he discusses are apparent, and so do not raise the problems that have traditionally troubled logicians in considering the possibility of the existence of true contradictions).

A number of logicians have argued that there are problems with this objection. R.M. Dancy, for example, points out that 'there are formalizations of elementary logic in which [the argument (P & ~P) → Q] fails' (1975: 12–13).[2] 'Although,' he goes on, 'these formalizations are very difficult to work with, they are not impossible to work with,' and so, he concludes, what 'the claim "a contradiction entails anything" . . . at most supports' is that it is 'easier to accept the law of noncontradiction than to reject it' (12–13). And Sainsbury notes that '[r]ecently it has been shown that one can have a great deal of what one wants from classical logic without accepting this rule. The result is that there can be no knockdown argument against the view that a rational system of belief may contain a contradiction' (141). But however weak the objection that 'a contradiction entails anything' may be, Dancy's suggestion that what it at most supports is that it is easier to accept the law of noncontradiction than to reject it, speaks, I think, to another thing, more important than *ex contradictione quodlibet*, that has seriously deterred philosophers from accepting the idea that there are true contradictions: the sheer difficulty, if not impossibility, of conceiving how something could both have and not have the same property at the same time and in the same respect (for if it has that property, how could it not have it?).

It is worth considering in this context what a logician who does believe that there are true contradictions thinks follows, or rather, doesn't follow, from such position. Graham Priest, for example, who has argued for dialetheism at length, points out that 'if the dialetheias in our concepts were to spread everywhere, this would be dysfunctional,' since 'a trivial theory/language would be useless, and would frustrate any point it was supposed to have' (1987: 251). However, he, like Dancy,[3] argues that '*ex contradictione quodlibet* fails'[4] and so 'there is no automatic move from inconsistency to triviality; quite the reverse, since triviality is a special case' (251). (There does appear to be some disagreement on this point, however. Jean Norman and Richard Sylvan, for example – who likewise note that '[i]n inconsistent theories, it is important to ascertain that sufficient *control* has been gained over contradictions,' since 'otherwise an inconsistent theory could be so counterintuitive or so near to triviality as to be fairly useless' – write that 'satisfactory criteria even for what constitutes damaging contradictions, and for the spread of inconsistency appear some way off' (1989: 417).)

Priest also points out that though an objector to dialetheism might conclude that accepting dialetheism doesn't prevent one from distinguishing between theories that are rationally acceptable and those that are not (that is, might concede that given the invalidity of *ex contradictione quodlibet*, the 'mere assumption of dialetheism, or of some particular contradiction, does not help one iota . . . in producing good reasons for the hypothesis that I have three hands, that London has just disappeared off the face of the planet, or for classical logic' (127)), she or he might argue that dialetheism disrupts 'another crucial aspect of rationality' – namely, the obligation to give up a belief under the appropriate circumstances. If dialetheism were true, the argument goes, then 'no one could be rationally obliged to give up something they believe' (127–8):

For suppose someone believes a theory, T. Any impetus for giving up T will come from an argument or experiment in which it
makes it reasonable to believe something inconsistent with T, α.
But now, the argument continues, if dialetheism is correct, there
is nothing to stop the person from simply adding α to their belief
set and believing the whole inconsistent totality. The very notions
of rational criticisability and change of belief therefore disappear.

(128)

In response, Priest asserts that the fact that

a person may sometimes be able to accept a contradiction rationally, and that there is nothing in the domain of formal semantics
ever to stop a person accepting a contradiction, I do not dispute.
That a person can always accept a contradiction rationally, is a
blatant *non sequitur*, which I reject. It does not follow from the
fact that some contradictions are rationally acceptable that all are,
nor from the fact that there is nothing in formal semantics against
it, that it can be done rationally.

(128)

That, he writes elsewhere, 'it may be possible to accept a contradiction *logically* (i.e., without trivialising one's position) does not mean
that it is possible to accept it rationally'

obviously raises the question of when it is rationally possible to
accept a contradiction. No algorithmic answer to this question is
to be expected. However, the acceptance of a contradiction in an
area where a theory leads one precisely to expect that there should
be contradictions is obviously not a rational black mark for the
theory. By contrast, the acceptance of contradiction when there is
no such presupposition may be little more than an *ad hoc* evasion,
with little to recommend it rationally.

(1984: 161)

Finally, 'very few contradictions,' Priest points out, 'are dialetheias,' and hence, 'most contradictions one normally comes across
are not dialetheic' (1987: 144). He explains that a general argument
for 'the low frequency of dialetheias in ordinary discourse' can
be made by appealing to the fact that people commonly use what
he refers to as 'quasi-valid' inferences – the disjunctive syllogism,

(P ∨ Q), ~Q, therefore P, for example, is only 'quasi-valid' on Priest's account, because it will fail in inconsistent situations – and to the fact that 'such reasoning is, by and large, successful' (144):

> I know that you are either at home or in the supermarket. I ascertain that you are not in the supermarket. I go to your house and lo! you are there. Now if dialetheias were common, we would expect quasi-valid inferences to go wrong quite frequently. But they do not. Hence they are not common. The normal success of quasi-valid reasoning therefore provides the basis of a transcendental argument for the infrequency of dialetheias.
>
> (144–5)

These issues are not addressed by theorists of postmodernism who attack the law of noncontradiction, and I suggest that this is so in part because many such theorists are inclined to regard the notion that there are constraints on what is rationally acceptable as the expression of a veiled desire to delimit and circumscribe the possibilities of discourse. The assertion, for example, that in inconsistent theories, it is important to ascertain that sufficient control has been gained over contradictions is one that I think a number of postmodernists would be suspicious of. Yet, as Norman and Sylvan (1989) point out, gaining such control is critical to ensuring the nontriviality of inconsistent theories.

Making sense

The consequences of the failure to confront and address such issues are apparent in Elizabeth Ermarth's analysis of Robbe-Grillet's *Jealousy* in her recent *Sequel to History: Postmodernism and the Crisis of Representational Time*. Ermarth claims that the novel 'continually forces the reader to violate that long-standing Western article of faith, the principle of noncontradiction' (76). A sequence like that in which one of novel's personae, A . . . , 'discovers on p. 64 "a centipede!" that was already crushed on p. 62,' she argues, affects us in such a way that 'we find ourselves forgetting about "meanings" and "messages"' (76). Details of this sort, she notes, 'have no meaning in themselves or any referential frame,' but instead have 'value as *markers* with which to anticipate variation in their arrangement' (77). Needless to say, however, if we were *continually* forced to violate the law of noncontradiction, we could not discern any arrangement at all, much less 'become absorbed in noticing minute variations and making complex discriminations of [it]' (76).[5] Nor would we be in a position to appreciate even the idea that the novel has no meaning 'in the conventional sense having to do with the actions of individuals and the causes of events' (76).

Despite the fact that Ermarth initially seems to assume the objective existence of an arrangement in Robbe-Grillet's novel that all readers must naturally perceive (a theoretical no-no in postmodernist circles), she nonetheless proceeds to cite the following passage

> The table is set for two. A . . . 's place will have to be added. On the bare wall, the traces of the squashed centipede are still perfectly visible. Nothing has been done to clean off the stain, for fear of spoiling the handsome, dull finish, probably not washable. The table is set for three, according to the usual arrangement . . .

and to ask, 'well? Is the table set for two, or for three? Are these descriptions of two different occasions? Is some mad individual narrating the story?' (76) Her conclusion is that 'such questions are not answerable in this novel' because 'they are questions that insist on the world of "same and different," "after and before," "normal" and "individual," and in *Jealousy* there is no sequence except the reader's sequence, no identities or events except those involved in reading the writing' (77).

Yet no reader could impose even her own subjective and idiosyncratic arrangement or sequence on the novel if she didn't possess the concepts of 'same and different,' and 'after and before.' Lacking these concepts, she would not be able, for example, either to grasp the appearance of the centipede on p. 64 as possibly being an encore performance by the *same* centipede – miraculously reborn – that was encountered on p. 62, or to interpret each centipede episode as involving two *different* centipedes. Or, to put this another way, if the examples of inconsistency in the novel that Ermarth cites – A . . . and Franck have ' "finished the book" about Africa' but 'a few pages later they still "are reading it" '; 'at one time Franck's car "is always having engine trouble," ' but 'later it "never gives its owner any trouble" '; 'A . . . is both in bed and in town' (77) – are contradictions at all, much less violations of the law of noncontradiction, then the Franck whose car is always giving him trouble and never giving him trouble, for example, has to be the *same* Franck and the car the *same* car.

Given that Ermarth claims that Robbe-Grillet's novel 'forces' the reader to violate the law of noncontradiction, that there are no sequences in it but the reader's, that it defies the world that insists on concepts like 'same and different,' 'after and before,' 'normal,' and 'individual,' it is rather surprising to find her arguing in the theoretical discussion that precedes her analysis of *Jealousy* that

> postmodernism acknowledges not a single but multiple constraints. Unlike the discourse of modernism with its common denominators for extension to infinity, postmodern time and space are warped and made finite . . . This awareness of finitude, of limit, is the basis of an entirely new aesthetic and provides the main restraint on construction that postmodernism respects.
> (65–6)

Her own awareness of finitude and limit apparently abandons her when it comes to explicating Robbe-Grillet's novel. It would be one thing, say, to suggest that some of the more blatant inconsistencies in the novel point in a hyperbolic way to the fact of human fallibility – that is, to suggest that the fact that human beings are capable of inconsistency points to their finiteness; it's another thing to argue that the novel continually forces the reader the violate the law of noncontradiction, which, since this seems to amount to the claim all contradictions are rationally acceptable (Ermarth doesn't suggest that there are some contradictions in or out of the novel that are not rationally possible to accept), would mean that all human beings were infallible and that there were no constraints on construction.[6]

Ermarth's assertion that the novel continually forces the reader to violate the law of noncontradiction is odd, not just because the novel is ambiguous enough to admit an interpretation that renders its logical inconsistencies apparent, but also because Ermarth argues that there are no sequences in the novel but the reader's. If the reader chooses to view

> [t]he bedroom windows are closed. At this hour A . . . is not up yet. She left early this morning in order to have enough time to do her shopping . . .
> (77)

as indicating that at 6 a.m. A . . . was not yet up, but that at 7 a.m. she was already on her way to town, or as indicating two different possible worlds in which the reader might imagine A . . . , then what is there to stop the reader from so doing? What could possibly 'force' her to accept that A . . . is simultaneously in bed and not in bed? If the sequence is her own sequence, what ground is there for claiming, as Ermarth does, that these 'contradictions are irreducible and render completely inaccessible the time of historical mediation' (77) (i.e., the world of 'same and different' and 'before and after,' 'normal,' and 'individual')? 'If what a reader really wants is a rationalization of the world,' Ermarth claims, 'then he or she should stay away from Robbe-Grillet' (83). However, she goes on, 'if a reader wants to practice paying attention to the mechanisms of a discourse, and to exercise from the root his or her power to imagine and change the tools of thought, then he or she must attend to the making of patterns' (83). But a 'rationalization of the world' just is one way of making patterns. And if, as she argues, quoting the following passage from Robbe-Grillet's *Future for a New Novel* –

> The author today proclaims his absolute need of the reader's cooperation, an active, conscious, *creative assistance*. What he asks of him is no longer to receive ready-made a world completed, full, closed upon itself, but on the contrary to participate in a creation, to invent in his turn the work – and the world – and thus to invent his own life . . .
>
> (115)

– then why can't the reader invent the work by making whatever patterns he or she likes? If the point is to 'forc[e] readers to read and write creatively' (116) – and Ermarth insists again and again in her book that this is the point of postmodernist fiction (yet, ironically, one finds her taking issue with Lyotard's 'militaristic metaphors' (114)) – why should she care how they go about reading and writing creatively?

Given that she claims both that there are no sequences but the reader's and that the contradictions of *Jealousy* render completely inaccessible the time of historical mediation, it is also puzzling to find her arguing the following:

> [T]he postmodern narrative sequence is a continuous process of changing the logic context. The project is already familiar in the images of surrealism – Magritte's locomotive coming out of a fireplace – which simultaneously impose two contradictory 'realities'

so as to emphasize the arbitrariness, the *semiotic surplus* of each. In daily life this is not an unfamiliar experience, as Cortázar is fond of pointing out; the 'warp' is any moment when you perceive something weird – a spider in your shoe – or when your philosophical discussion ends because you run out of beer.

(77–8)

If there are no sequences but the reader's, how does Ermarth know that the postmodern narrative sequence is a continuous process of changing the logic context? And how can she describe anything as weird if the art she discusses creates worlds where, as she argues, there is no such thing as 'normal'? Again, Ermarth seems to overlook the fact that by rejecting those concepts she associates with the 'time of historical mediation,' she deprives herself of any ground upon which to claim that, for example, a spider in a shoe or a philosophical discussion ending because the beer has run out, constitute the simultaneous imposition of two 'contradictory realities.'

Ermarth, like other theorists of postmodernism, is concerned with the exclusions she thinks the law of noncontradiction effects.[7] She fails to see, however, that to argue that readers of *Jealousy* are *forced* to violate the law of noncontradiction is to deny them the possibility of choosing not to – that is, she excludes the possibility of readers choosing to believe that P or that ~P, but not both. If the reader were continually forced to violate the law of noncontradiction, then, whether the reader liked it or not, to believe, for example, that A . . . was in bed would be to believe that she was not in bed. If one abandons the idea that the point of such passages is to force the reader to violate the law of noncontradiction, a number of interpretive choices become possible. For example, one could regard the events of the novel as possibilities, rather than actualities, in which case there is no inconsistency between, for example, Franck's car never giving him trouble and it always giving him trouble. There is textual evidence to support such a reading. A . . . and Franck 'sometimes deplore the coincidences of the plot [of the novel about Africa they are reading], saying that "things don't happen that way," and then they construct a different probable outcome starting from a new supposition, "if it weren't for that"' (1965: 75):

Other possibilities are offered, during the course of the book, which lead to different endings. The variations are extremely numerous; the variations of these, still more so. They seem to enjoy multiplying all these choices, exchanging smiles, carried away by their enthusiasm, probably a little intoxicated by this proliferation . . .

'But that's it, he was just unlucky enough to have come home earlier that day, and no one could have guessed he would.'

Thus Franck sweeps away in a single gesture all the suppositions they had constructed together. It's no use making up contrary possibilities, since things are the way they are: reality stays the same.

(75)

Insisting that the point of the apparent inconsistencies in *Jealousy* is to force the reader to violate the law of noncontradiction, Ermarth is led, ironically enough ('[i]n the postmodern frame,' she writes in her prologue, 'choice is not a question of either/or but a question of emphasis' (15)) to issue the following either/or ultimatum:

This new kind of textual event involves new practices – especially holding simultaneously in awareness what is putatively 'contradictory' but nevertheless *there* as an event of consciousness. A reader can either close the book and give up or forget consistency along with its exclusions and begin to situate his or her awareness where the novel directs it.

(77)

Where before there were no sequences but the reader's, now the reader can either close the book – clearly not the 'correct' choice – or somehow force herself to believe that it is possible for someone to be in bed and not be in bed at the same time (though one would have thought, what with forgetting consistency and its exclusions, that the reader could simultaneously close the book and continue to read it).

It is worth mentioning, however, that, as the bizarre suggestion that a spider in a shoe and a philosophical discussion ending because the beer has run out constitute the simultaneous imposition of two contradictory realities implies, Ermarth does not understand what the law of noncontradiction states. Thus, in claiming that the new kind of textual event that *Jealousy* represents involves 'holding simultaneously in awareness what is putatively "contradictory,"' she might not be suggesting the reader is forced to accept that A . . . could both be in bed and not in bed at the same time. It's not clear what she might be suggesting instead, but it is clear that she misunderstands the law of noncontradiction.

That this is so is underscored by her assertion that 'the art of collage . . . promotes the imaginary and neutralizes the principle of noncontradiction by disconnecting material objects from their "normal" (read, habitual) connections and conditions' (8).[8] No 'neutralization' of the law of noncontradiction, however, is required for the reader of *Jealousy* to regard the centipede on p. 64, for example, as being the same centipede that was squashed on p. 62 – a dead centipede coming back to life may be fantastic, but it is not logically impossible. What would be logically contradictory is if a centipede could be both dead and not dead at the same time, in the same place, and in the same respect (i.e., not just half-dead or half-alive, but dead and not dead).

If Ermarth did not insist on linking the disconnection of material objects from their normal connections and conditions with the neutralization of the law of noncontradiction, one might just assume that what she meant by a phrase like 'the simultaneous imposition of two contradictory realities' was 'the simultaneous imposition of two different, seemingly unrelated realities'; one might just assume that she was using the word 'contradictory' in a very loose sense to mean 'dissimilar.' That she does persist in associating 'disconnected' and 'weird' with the neutralization of the law of noncontradiction, however, strongly suggests that she thinks 'disconnected' and 'contradictory,' in its strict sense, are equivalent in meaning.

It is possible that she believes that the disconnection of material objects from their normal connections and conditions in collage violates the law of noncontradiction because she thinks that what the law concerns is physical impossibility or improbability, when in fact what it concerns is logical impossibility. Her thinking this might explain why she supposes that the promotion of the imaginary neutralizes the law of noncontradiction, since human beings are capable of imagining and representing all sorts of things that are physically impossible (though her thinking this would not explain why she thinks that a spider in a shoe and a philosophical discussion ending because the beer has run out are contradictory, since these are neither logically nor physically impossible). It apparently doesn't occur to Ermarth to wonder why the law of noncontradiction should indeed be, as she puts it, 'that long-standing Western article of faith' if violating it were a simple matter of, for example, representing a locomotive emerging from a fireplace.

In my end is my beginning

None of this is to deny, of course, that the disconnection of material objects from their normal connections and conditions in a work of art may not have both interest and value, or more to the point, to deny the possible interest and value of apparent contradictions in works of art. The 'equivocation. . . . [the] play[ ] on words,' as Harris notes, that 'is present in Eliot's "In my end is my beginning" . . . can open intriguing, sometimes very profitable, trains of thought':

> [I]t may be worth considering whether such equivocations are not in fact the most fruitful form of contradiction: they stimulate thought by juxtaposing different perspectives through the use of the same word with different senses or different referents. Whether or not such an equivocation proves intellectually profitable will depend on the interplay between the two perspectives thus brought into relationship[.]
>
> (336)

Moreover, as situationists Jon Barwise and John Etchemendy point out in their study of the liar's paradox, 'paradoxes in any domain are important' because 'they force us to make explicit assumptions usually left implicit, and to test those assumptions in limiting cases' (1987: 169). 'A common thread,' they argue, 'runs through the solution of many of the well-known paradoxes, namely, the uncovering of some hidden parameter, a parameter whose value shifts during the reasoning that leads to the paradox' (171). Citing Russell's barber paradox – 'there is a barber who shaves all and only the men who don't shave themselves' – they ask:

> Can [this sentence] be used to express a true proposition? Certainly not if the barber himself falls in the range of the quantifier phrase 'all the men,' for then the barber would have to shave himself if and only if he doesn't. But this sentence could express a truth if the context implicitly restricts the quantifier, say, to all the men who live in Oxford. What then follows is only that the barber himself cannot live in Oxford. Here the implicit parameter provides us with some limited collection, Oxford men, and the barber simply 'diagonalizes out' of that collection. No man from Oxford could shave every man from Oxford who doesn't shave himself. But a woman could, or a man from Kidlington.
>
> (172)

The barber's paradox is not, as Sainsbury notes, 'a very deep paradox' (2) – that is, unlike the liar's paradox, it is not difficult to dismiss – and one could just regard it as false rather than as an apparent contradiction that is true; that is, one could allow that the barber does fall in the range of the quantifier phrase 'all the men,' in which case one's conclusion will be that there is no such barber. However, Barwise's and Etchemendy's point is important – the barber's paradox may not be a deep paradox in the sense of being an apparently true contradiction, and it may not even be a very deep apparent paradox, but one should not underrate the extent to which apparent paradoxes can be fruitful in forcing one to make explicit assumptions that are implicit, assumptions that may simply be taken for granted but in fact are false.[9]

Because *pharmakon*, for example, has two opposed meanings, and because in the context of the *Phaedo* a good case can be made for its having both these meanings, its deployment there can be regarded as generating an apparent paradox, an apparent paradox that expresses a thought similar to Eliot's 'In my end is my beginning.' The choice of the word *pharmakon* to denote the hemlock allows the Socrates of the *Phaedo*, then, to juxtapose different perspectives on death through the use of the same word with different senses, and this appropriation of the resources of the Greek language adds force to the challenge he makes to his audience's assumption that his death, and death generally, is wholly an evil.

One can acknowledge, then, that something is lost in the translation from *pharmakon* to, say, 'poison.' Schrift, however, sees its translation as 'poison' as not simply a problem of translation, but as part and parcel of some sort of conspiracy on the part of the western philosophical tradition to repress the fact that the *pharmakon* from Socrates' perspective also functions as a remedy: '[W]hen,' he argues, 'Socrates drinks the *pharmakon* at the conclusion of the *Phaedo*, the metaphysical tradition is quick to translate the *pharmakon* as "poison," and in so doing, [it] must repress Socrates' final speech in the *Apology* [in which Socrates claims that we have reason to hope that death is a good which a virtuous man need not fear], while it forces us to interpret as *ironic* his last words concerning the debt his death will incur with Asclepius' (1990: 104). Is Schrift suggesting that all those in 'the metaphysical tradition' who have glossed the *Phaedo* have craftily avoided mentioning Socrates' extended discussion of the immortality of the soul? Or that the translation of *pharmakon* as 'poison' somehow obliterates the reader's awareness of Socrates' discussion of death as a good in both the *Phaedo* and the *Apology*?

Schrift's claim that translations of the dialogue that render *pharmakon* as 'poison' force us to interpret Socrates' request that a cock be sacrificed to Asclepius after his death as ironic is false, moreover, since G.M.A. Grube, to take a case in point, renders *pharmakon* as 'poison' in his translation but doesn't view Socrates' request as ironic. He explains the reference to Asclepius by noting that Socrates regards death as a remedy that cures the ills of life, and points out in his preface that 'we [are] repeatedly told in the dialogue how and why the philosopher should face death without fear and apprehension – indeed, welcome it with a beautiful hope – and [at the end of the dialogue] we see Socrates do precisely that' (1981: 9 n.24). If Grube can translate *pharmakon* as 'poison' but not thereby be forced to interpret Socrates' request as ironic, there's no reason to necessarily suppose anybody else in or out of 'the metaphysical tradition' should be so forced.

As it is with Schrift's *pharmakon*, so it is with most of the examples theorists of postmodernism offer as evidence of the violation of the law of noncontradiction. That is, as Harris concludes,

> most of the paradoxes of which contemporary literary theory is fond are produced by fallacies like that of equivocation, and most of the contradictions in literary texts espied by eager poststructuralists reflect the impossibility of simplistic reduction which such texts can – may in fact be intended to – help us see.
>
> (342)

It is because many postmodernists have uncritically accepted a hopelessly simplistic and reductive picture of classical western logic that they think that they are posing a radical challenge to it, and it is the fact that what they are attacking, in essence, is not classical western logic, but what is regarded by it to be one of the most common of the fallacies of presumption – *viz.* black-and-white thinking (also known as the either/or fallacy) – that ultimately renders their attack on it superfluous.

Part II
'Modernity,' 'Postmodernity,' and All That: The 'Grand Narratives' of Postmodernism

5

Metaphysically Underdetermined Beliefs

'The death of intelligent writing'

In *The Circus of the Mind in Motion: Postmodernism and the Comic Vision*, Lance Olsen attacks what he calls 'neorealism' – which for him includes fiction published over the last decade or so by such writers as Bobbie Ann Mason, Raymond Carver, and Jayne Anne Phillips – labeling it, following Richard Kostelanetz, 'the death of intelligent writing.' He argues, further, that the 'narrative strategy' of realist fiction is 'conservative' (he attributes its revitalization in the 1980s to the long reigns of Thatcher, Reagan, and Kohl) and that 'such a conservative narrative strategy indicates a conservative metaphysical strategy' (1990: 28):

> It believes in a world out there, an empirical world that the reader can smell, see and touch. It believes in logic, chronology and plot. It believes in a stable identity, in a sense of self, in depth psychology. It believes in a universe of communal reality and common sense, where content is privileged over form, language is transparent, style is secondary, and, it is assumed, the word mirrors the world.
>
> (28)

Despite the postmodernist rage against 'totalization,' the idea that realist fiction is politically and 'metaphysically' conservative is uncritically propagated by many a theorist of postmodernism, and is typically complemented by an equally reductive (but more tolerant) characterization of the contemporary fiction such theorists label 'postmodernist.'[1] This reductivism appears to derive in part from the idea that metaphysical, epistemological, moral, and political views somehow inhere in the conventions of realist and so-called postmodernist fiction. Olsen's assumption of a 'metaphysical strategy' specific to realist fiction, for instance, seems to be predicated on the idea that things like plot, setting, and character not only always have metaphysical implications, but also always have the same metaphysical implications from one realist novel to the next. The idea that, in virtue of its conventions, a literary mode necessarily reflects a certain metaphysics, epistemology, ethics, and politics is, on the face of it, if not palpably absurd, then at least highly implausible. It is, however, so often assumed to be trivially true by theorists of postmodernism as to warrant an investigation of what accounts for its elevation to the status of self-evident truth. Accordingly, what I will explore here are the ideas from which the reductivism that characterizes many recent accounts of realist and postmodernist fiction seems to derive.

'Out there'

To start, I want to address the notion – often lurking in contemporary critiques of literary realism and explicitly voiced by Olsen in the above – that a belief in a world 'out there,' in logic, chronology, and plot, in a sense of self, in a communal reality, and in the idea that the word mirrors the world, are just so many strands of an all-embracing realist philosophy. It is the subscription to such a notion that constitutes the first step, as it were, in the process of the conceptualization of literary realism by theorists of postmodernism that results in the reductive account of it many of them provide; the second step is the assumption that literary realism is perforce grounded in this realist philosophy. Therefore I'll begin by attempting to explain how the beliefs Olsen identifies as comprising literary realism's 'conservative metaphysical strategy' do not describe some one philosophy, much less a distinctively realist one.

Consider, first of all, Olsen's claim that literary realism's 'conservative metaphysical strategy' is informed by 'a belief in a world out there, an empirical world that the reader can smell, see and touch.' Since Olsen takes this belief to be a distinctive component of a metaphysics specific to literary realism, it may be that he thinks it is tantamount to a belief in metaphysical realism – the thesis, simply put, that reality is mind-independent. But a belief in a world out there is not equivalent to an acceptance of metaphysical realism, nor does a commitment to the former entail a commitment to the latter. That someone professes belief in the existence of a world out there does not, in itself, indicate what her or his commitments might be as to the nature of that world. A belief in a world out there, in short, is compatible with both metaphysical realism and metaphysical anti-realism.[2] As Galen Strawson notes, ' "[m]ind-independent" and "external" [the "world out there"] are to be distinguished in so far as "external" suggests simply that there is some reality external to one's own mind or perceptions . . . while "mind-independent" suggests further that there is some non-mental reality. "Mind-independent" entails "external," but the converse is not true' (1989: 62 f.50).[3]

A belief in a world out there not only cannnot be construed as 'metaphysically conservative,' but it also cannot be construed as politically conservative or as entailing political conservatism. Nor even can the belief that there is some non-mental reality. There's nothing about the idea that there are rocks and trees, or about the idea that rocks and trees are mind-independent, that could create any obstacle to being, for example, a pro-choice supporter or a socialist or an anti-colonialist. Conversely, the belief that reality is mind-dependent does not entail progressive political views. The same holds of epistemological theories – as Oscar Kenshur points out, 'the claim that views about knowledge have some intrinsic connection with political views does not rest – to use a metaphor popular among early-modern philosophers – on very solid foundations' (quoted in Morton, 1993: 260). 'Those who,' he notes, 'on the basis of perceived homologies, claim that a given theory or belief logically entails a given [ideologically] legitimating function' err in treating 'historical questions as if they were theoretical ones'; that is, they make the mistake of treating 'a historically contingent relationship as if it were a relationship of logical implication' (quoted in Morton, 1993: 261). '[N]o epistemological position can be *intrinsically* reactionary or *intrinsically* progressive' for the reason that, as Michael Morton suggests in his discussion of Kenshur's argument, 'there is no epistemological position that cannot be (and historically has not been) used in the service of "political views" not only different from, but wholly incompatible with, one another' (1993: 260).

Like a belief in 'a world out there,' the other beliefs Olsen lists are not indicative of a specific 'metaphysical strategy.' A belief in logic, for example, is compatible with any of the following views about the nature of logical laws: that they are constructs of the human mind, that they are inductive generalizations, that they are necessary truths, or that they are linguistic conventions. Moreover, an acceptance of classical logic does not go hand in hand with an acceptance of metaphysical realism, nor does an acceptance of metaphysical anti-realism entail a rejection of classical logic. One could, for example, espouse dialetheism – the view that 'the actual world itself is (irremediably) inconsistent' (Norman and Sylvan, 1989: 417). This would amount to a realist view if one believed that the world, independently of our minds, languages, or schemes, was inconsistent,[4] but it also would be a view that challenged classical logic, which is no doubt the logic Olsen means to single out when he claims that the metaphysics of literary realism includes a belief in 'logic, chronology and plot.'

Similarly, a belief 'in a stable identity, a sense of self' is not confined to metaphysical, epistemological, or moral realists; rather, it is a belief shared by philosophers of all stripes. To be sure, many theorists of postmodernism, influenced by poststructuralism, proclaim the demise of something they call 'the unified and coherent subject.' 'That the self can no longer be considered a unified and stable entity,' writes Edmund Smyth in his introduction to *Postmodernism and Contemporary Fiction*, 'has become *axiomatic* in the light of poststructuralism' (1991: 10; my emphasis). But what this by now veritable cliché in the literature on postmodernism is supposed to mean is not clear. On the one hand, if what it means to say that it has become axiomatic in the light of poststructuralism that the self can no longer be considered a unified and stable entity is that it is now widely believed that human beings change, that they can be inconsistent, that they can have contradictory beliefs and desires, then it has to be said that no one has ever thought human beings to be otherwise. If, on the other hand, what it's supposed to suggest is that human beings no longer experience, say, continuity and connectedness in their mental lives, then it hardly can be axiomatic, since I, for one, do experience such continuity and connectedness in my mental life. And since scores of philosophers continue to attempt to account for this phenomenon, I assume they do too.

The rejection of the notion of a continuous and stable self can perhaps in part be explained by the fact that theorists of postmodernism often appear to assume that if the self were stable and continuous, then that would preclude the possibility of persons having, for example, conflicting beliefs and desires, or of being inconsistent in their beliefs. But this is not so – indeed, the claim that the subject is divided, fragmented, conflicted, and inconsistent requires the assumption of a stable and continuous self. Linda Hutcheon, for one, argues in *A Poetics of Postmodernism* that 'the fragmented, iterative structure' of Doctorow's *Ragtime* 'challenges the traditional realist narrative conventions of the inscription of the subject as coherent and continuous' (1988: 84):

> What Doctorow once called the 'novel as private I' is what he cannot write: that I is social and political, as well as fragmented and discontinuous.
>
> (84)

However, insofar as this 'I' is the *same* 'I' it is coherent and continuous. That is, for this 'I' to be fragmented it has to be the same 'I' – it wouldn't be fragmented if it were two or more different 'I's. Similarly, if I state that I believe both P and ~P, then unless I am the same person, unless there is coherence and continuity between the person who claims to believe P and the person who claims to believe ~P, I cannot be regarded as holding contradictory beliefs. If there were no continuity and coherence between the person who claimed to believe P and the person who claimed to believe ~P, then there wouldn't be one person who was claiming to believe P and ~P simultaneously, but two persons, one of whom was claiming to believe P and another who was claiming to believe ~P.

The rejection of the notion of a 'unified and coherent subject' can perhaps also be explained by the fact that it seems to be regarded by many contemporary theorists as entailed by the supposition that the self is a linguistic construct. Michel Haar, for example, claims that 'the subject, the self, the individual, are just so many false concepts, since they transform into substances fictitious unities having at the start only a linguistic reality' (quoted in Butler, 1990: 21). Granting for the sake of argument that the self is a linguistic construct, how does that make the concept of self 'false' or make the self a 'fictitious unity'? The implication is, as Judith Butler – who cites Haar's argument in her *Gender Trouble: Feminism and the Subversion of Identity* – seems to suggest, that in the absence of a 'metaphysical substance,' there could be no 'stable identity.' Butler writes that the notion of a 'metaphysical substance,' according to Haar, constitutes 'the artificial philosophical means by which simplicity, order, and identity are effectively instituted' (1990: 20) – the insinuation being that if there is no such metaphysical substance, then there can be no such thing as 'the "coherence" and "continuity" of "the person"' (17).[5]

But the belief that there is such a thing as the coherence and continuity of persons is compatible with any number of theories about the nature and source of personal identity. It is not, as many theorists of postmodernism seem to assume, synonymous with a belief in the existence of an immaterial substance – rather, the existence of such a substance is just one possible explanation among others – including, for example, memory and bodily identity – of the continuity of a person over time. Locke, for example, argued that 'nothing but consciousness can unite remote existences into the same person; the identity of substance will not do it, for whatever substance there is, however framed, without consciousness there is no person'; 'the same numerical *substance* is not considered as making the same self,' but rather 'the same continued *consciousness*' (1964: 218–19).[6] If Butler is denying the existence of the coherence and continuity of persons (and it's not clear that she really is), it may well be that other theorists of postmodernism, in repudiating the concept of the 'unified and coherent subject,' are not, but rather are denying that the source of personal identity is an immaterial, self-same substance – in which case, they are belatedly joining the ranks of philosophers who have been denying as much for centuries.

A belief in 'a stable identity, a sense of self,' then, is not a uniquely or quintessentially realist one. Moreover, just as a belief in the existence of a mind-independent reality does not oblige one to accept classical logic, and just as a commitment to classical logic does not necessarily imply a commitment to metaphysical realism, so neither does one's belief in 'a stable identity, a sense of self,' nor, say, one's belief that the source of personal identity is memory, entail a commitment to the idea that reality is mind-independent.

A belief in the existence of 'a universe of communal reality and common sense' is likewise compatible with both metaphysical realism and anti-realism. The anti-realist denies that reality exists independently of beliefs about it – denying this does not rule out arguing that there is a communal reality constituted by shared beliefs about it. A belief in a communal reality is also consistent with moral anti-realism. One could deny the existence of moral facts – that is, reject the idea that moral judgments are cognitive, capable of being true or false – and yet maintain, as Hume did, that 'the notion of morals implies some sentiment common to all mankind, which recommends the same object to general approbation, and makes every man, or most men, agree in the same opinion or decision concerning it' (1988: 272). This Hume called 'the sentiment of humanity,' which he loosely characterized as compassion, love, and benevolence towards others, and to which he appealed to explain apparent moral

differences across cultures and time. 'Had you asked a parent at
Athens, why he bereaved his child of that life, which he had so
lately given it. It is because I love it, he would reply; and regard
the poverty which it must inherit from me, as a greater evil than
death.' (334). 'What a wide difference . . . in the sentiments of morals,'
Palamedes, in Hume's 'A Dialogue,' claims 'must be found between
civilized nations and Barbarians, or between nations whose characters have little in common. How shall we pretend to fix a standard
for judgments of this nature?' 'By tracing matters,' his interlocutor
replies, 'a little higher, and examining the first principles, which
each nation establishes of blame and censure' (335):

> the principles upon which men reason in morals are always the
> same; though the conclusions which they draw are often very
> different. That they all reason aright with regard to this subject,
> more than with regard to any other, it is not incumbent upon any
> moralist to show. It is sufficient, that the original principles of
> censure and blame are uniform, and that erroneous conclusions
> can be corrected by sounder reasoning and larger experience.
> Though many ages have elapsed since the fall of Greece and
> Rome, though many changes have arrived in religion, language,
> laws, and customs; none of these revolutions has ever produced
> any considerable innovation in the primary sentiments of morals.
>
> (335–6)

It is worth noting, in addition, that if one holds the fact/value
distinction to be a valid one, one might be drawn to metaphysical
realism on the one hand, and moral anti-realism on the other. Hume
himself argued that

> . . . the distinct boundaries and offices of reason and taste are
> easily ascertained. The former conveys the knowledge of truth
> and falsehood: the latter gives the sentiment of beauty and de-
> formity, vice and virtue. The one discovers objects as they really
> stand in nature, without addition or diminution: the other has a
> productive faculty, and gilding or staining all natural objects with
> the colours, borrowed from internal sentiment, raises in a man-
> ner a new creation.
>
> (294)

Drawing a distinction between primary and secondary qualities
(which elsewhere he questions), he uses the idea that secondary

qualities like color are not 'in' objects as a metaphor for the process by which human beings morally and aesthetically gild objects as they exist independently of mind, i.e., as things with size, shape, extension, solidity. Likewise, one could deny that either primary or secondary qualities exist independently of mind, and yet maintain that moral judgments have truth values, as Berkeley arguably did.

Neither metaphysical anti-realism nor moral anti-realism, then, necessarily precludes a belief in a shared reality, nor does moral realism necessarily follow from metaphysical realism, or moral anti-realism from metaphysical anti-realism. Moreover, just as there's no necessary connection between a belief in the existence of a mind-independent reality and reactionary politics, or between metaphysical anti-realism and radical politics, there's no necessary connection between political conservatism and moral realism, or between political radicalism and moral anti-realism. Many theorists of postmodernism appear to believe, for example, that moral relativism is politically progressive. Moral relativism, however, is a species of moral realism, not moral anti-realism. Moral relativists, in contrast to moral anti-realists, argue that moral judgments have a truth value – i.e., that they are relatively true or false. So even if it were the case that there was a historically contingent relationship between moral relativism and radical politics, the existence of such a relationship would challenge the general association theorists of postmodernism tend to draw between realism and conservatism.

Finally, the belief that language refers to reality (what Olsen tendentiously terms the belief that 'the word mirrors the world') is also not a distinctively realist one. Olsen, however, perhaps thinks that such a belief is tantamount to an acceptance of the correspondence theory of truth (although it is not), and may be assuming that the correspondence theory of truth goes hand-in-hand with metaphysical realism. Often enough, realists do entertain the correspondence theory of truth, and anti-realists the coherence theory of truth. Yet, as Michael Devitt argues,

> correspondence truth is in no way constitutive of realism as I have defined it, nor of any other doctrine along similarly metaphysical lines. On the one hand, such doctrines do not entail the correspondence nor any other theory of truth. One can be a realist and yet be eliminativist about the semantic prperties of thoughts and language. This has been nicely demonstrated by Stephen Leeds (1978) drawing on the views of Quine. Indeed,

many philosophers interested in cognitive science, and not in any way tainted by antirealism, are dubious of the need for a correspondence notion of truth. On the other hand, the correspondence theory does not entail realism. It is the theory that truth consists in some way in correspondence to reality that is usually taken to be the objective. Beyond that, the correspondence theory says nothing about the nature of that reality. The theory leaves open what entities make representations true.

(1988: 159–60)

On this view, whether the correspondence theory of truth is true is irrelevant to the question of whether metaphysical realism is true. What Devitt is insisting on is the importance of keeping the metaphysical issue distinct from the semantical one. Devitt himself argues that a naturalistic account of meaning and reference and a correspondence account of truth might well be the best explanation of language and truth in a realist world, though, as he indicates, there are a number of philosophers who espouse realism but who are not committed to correspondence truth. The point is that, having established the truth of realism, one might well want to opt for correspondence truth – correspondence truth is not, however, entailed by realism.[7]

That correspondence truth, on the other hand, does not entail realism seems obviously right. What the correspondence theory posits is that truth is a function of a relation between statements and reality; as such, it is, as Devitt notes, 'compatible with *absolutely* any metaphysics' (1991: 47; his emphasis). One might hold that reality is mind-dependent and also argue that what makes sentences true is their correspondence to mind-dependent situations. The correspondence theory makes no claims about the nature of the reality to which sentences correspond. The addition of the criterion of reality's objective independent existence to the correspondence theory does, as Devitt points out, 'bring us closer to Realism [the doctrine that tokens of most common-sense, and scientific, physical types exist independently of the mental]' (47). This addition, however, he says, 'seems like a gratuitous intrusion of metaphysics into semantics' (47).

It may be the belief that this addition is a necessary aspect of the correspondence theory that partly explains why anti-realists have typically rejected it, and, in many cases, opted instead for a coherence account of truth. Or, perhaps, as Devitt suggests, anti-realists have been led to anti-realism by adopting certain views of reference, meaning, and truth – he argues, for instance, that Dummett, in adopting a verificationist account of meaning and truth, is led to reject realism. Devitt thinks that trying to derive a metaphysics from a theory of language is to put the cart before the horse.

It should be also noted, as Devitt points out, that 'the crude notion of resemblance (or mirroring) has no place in contemporary correspondence theories' (1988: 161). This unfortunate metaphor is traceable, he claims, to both Descartes and the British empiricists, who assumed that 'what we immediately perceive are ideas in the mind' and 'that objects outside the mind cause and resemble these ideas' (161).[8] He suggests that once this notion is dropped, however, there still remain a number of viable ways of explaining truth in terms of correspondence. He, for instance, thinks that

> sentence meaning is to be explained largely in terms of truth conditions; those conditions are to be explained in terms of syntactic structure and the reference of words; reference must then be explained part causally, part descriptively. The notion of truth in this theory has a sufficient number of the properties of the traditional correspondence notion – without the obscure mirroring metaphor – to be called a correspondence notion.
>
> (167)

One can see how the idea that impressions or ideas in the mind are caused by and resemble objects in the world could give rise to the notion of mirroring. But many contemporary theorists seem to have something else in mind than (a popular conception of) eighteenth-century British empiricist epistemology when they criticize the idea of the word 'mirroring' the world. What they very often seem to be attacking, rather, is a position that they represent as having been universally accepted before the twentieth century, but which in fact has been long-contested in western philosophy, *viz.* the notion that language is isomorphic with reality, or that words are isomorphic with their concepts (e.g., that the word 'cat' bears some natural relation to the idea of 'catness'). One, for instance, finds J. Hillis Miller in his 1986 MLA Presidential address referring to 'a *now* exploded Cratylism, the stubborn belief that the phenomenality of words somehow naturally corresponds to the essence of things' (1987: 282; my emphasis). Similarly, one finds Peter Currie remarking that 'there can be no emergent postmodernism without its residual Modernist component, nor without the shadow of an ill-defined realism, the rough magic of which – the Cratylist tradition with its belief in the intrinsic connection of word and object, "the Voodoo at the heart of mimetic theory" in Ronald Sukenick's phrase – both Modernist and postmodernist alike abjure' (1987: 54–5). But the idea of 'a now exploded Cratylism' is an ill-informed one, as is the notion that 'the Cratylist tradition' informs literary realism. Both Hillis Miller's and Currie's claims appear to be predicated on the assumption that cratylism went unchallenged until the twentieth century; Currie's claim, I would further suggest, is grounded in two other suppositions – namely, that philosophical realisms are committed to cratylism and that literary realism is based in them, and therefore itself cratylist. The idea that literary realism can be defined in terms of a relation to philosophical realisms is one I turn to below; for now, it simply needs to be noted that a commitment to, say, metaphysical realism does not entail a commitment to the belief that there is an intrinsic connection between word and object, so that even if literary realism could be seen as bound up with metaphysical realism, it wouldn't follow that realist fiction reflected cratylism. As Andrzej Gasiorek notes:

> One need not subscribe to a belief in the isomorphism of sign and referent to be a realist. In fact, metaphysical realism repudiates most of the views attributed to it by its critics. It acknowledges that there can be no theory-neutral description of the world in either the social or natural sciences and embraces fallibilism; it rejects the metaphor of the mirror and the 'copy' theories to which it gives rise; and it dissociates itself from *a priori* principles, defending a causal account of truth.
>
> (1995: 187)

That many theorists of postmodernism do indeed suppose that the idea that signs are unmotivated constitutes a new theory of the relationship between words and objects is suggested by the frequent appeals they make to Saussure's account of the arbitrary nature of the sign in describing twentieth-century theories of language. Alison Lee, for instance, argues that the notion 'that words have a "magic" relationship to the objects they represent' is one that 'twentieth-century structuralist linguistic theories have called into question' (1990: 20):

Particularly important here are the theories of Ferdinand de Saussure. . . . Saussure's most influential premise is that the relationship between the word in its graphic or spoken form (signifier), and the thing it represents (signified), is a purely arbitrary one. In the English language, for example, the four black marks T-R-E-E, or their sound equivalent, signify 'tree,' but there is no eternal, magical correspondence between the two. Historically and culturally, English speakers agree that these marks indicate some sort of vegetation with a trunk and leaves. However, to assume that the correspondence between word and thing is natural is to forget that in other languages the same concept is signified by an entirely different signifier.

(20)

Terry Eagleton similarly claims that structuralism 'made it impossible any longer to see reality simply as something "out there," a fixed order of things which language merely reflected' (1983: 107–8):

On that assumption, there was a natural bond between word and thing, a given set of correspondences between the realms . . . This rationalist or empiricist view of language suffered severely at the hands of structuralism: for, if, as Saussure had argued, the relation between sign and referent was an arbitrary one, how could any 'correspondence theory' of knowledge stand?

(108)

And, in their *Postmodern Theory*, Stephen Best and Douglas Kellner likewise aver that

Saussure emphasized two properties of language that are of critical importance for understanding contemporary theoretical developments. First, he saw that the linguistic sign was arbitrary, that there is no natural link between the signifier and signified, only a contingent cultural designation. Secondly, he emphasized that the sign is differential, part of a system of meanings where words acquire significance only by reference to what they are not: 'In language, there are only differences *without positive terms*.'

(1991: 19–20)

That Lee should think that what Saussure regarded as a truism – '[n]o one,' he claims, 'disputes the principle of the arbitrary nature of the sign' (1966: 68) – is his 'most influential premise' is indicative of a serious lack of familiarity with the history of ideas, and that Best and Kellner consider it to be of critical importance to understanding contemporary theoretical developments suggests how unrevolutionary such developments are.[9] For the idea that signs bear a magic relationship to their referents (or signifiers to signifieds – Lee conflates word/object and signifier/signified) was 'called into question' by Locke, empiricist *par excellence* (and rationalism and empiricism are not, as Eagleton seems to imply, the same thing), among others (e.g., Hermegones in Plato's *Cratylus*), a couple of hundred years before Saussure noted that no one disputes the principle of the arbitrary nature of the sign.[10] Words, Locke claimed, 'come to be made use of by men as the signs of their ideas . . . not by any natural connexion that there is between particular articulate sounds and certain ideas,' for if that were the case 'then there would be but one language among all men'; words, rather, come to be made use of 'by a voluntary imposition, whereby such a word is made arbitrarily the mark of such an idea' (1964: 259). In pointing out that the notion that linguistic signs are motivated was questioned long before Saussure observed that no one disputes the principle of the arbitrary nature of the sign, I am not claiming that there was unanimous agreement on this matter before Saussure, or indeed that there is now. (That I should suggest that there is no unanimous agreement even now might seem surprising – I would note, however, that the debate over whether signs are motivated or not appears to be more complicated than theorists of postmodernism imagine, as Linda Waugh, for one, suggests in her 'Against Arbitrariness: Imitation and Motivation Revived,' and as Cary Plotkin, for another, points out in a discussion of Gérard Genette's *Mimologiques* by noting that the history of the debate of the question cannot be understood in terms of the 'oversimplified antithesis' of 'cratylism versus hermogenism' (1989: 139).) Rather, I am contesting the tidy account of the history of ideas promoted by theorists of postmodernism in which they imply that the belief that signs are motivated is characteristic of seventeenth- eighteenth- and nineteenth-century thought (or, indeed, of western thought 'since at least Plato') and that the 'revolutionary' belief that signs are unmotivated is characteristic of twentieth-century thought.

In addition to mistakenly assuming the principle of the arbitrariness of the sign to be a revolutionary development in twentieth-century thought, many theorists of postmodernism also draw questionable conclusions as to what follows from it, such as, for example, that it rules out of court the possibility of signs referring to objects – hence Eagleton's suggestion that the idea that language refers to reality requires the assumption of a 'natural bond' between word and thing (and the concomitant suggestion that unless the knowledge, for example, that the earth is round doesn't somehow look like the earth's roundness, that a correspondence theory of knowledge cannot stand). Alternatively, one finds Elizabeth Ermarth arguing that '[t]he crisis that puts an end to classically defined subjects and objects also produces a crisis of the referential sign' and that '[t]his means first and most simply that a sign cannot be conceived as a traveling pointer because there are no longer any simply located things to point *at*' (1992: 139; her emphasis). There is no evidence of a 'crisis' of the referential sign – people today continue successfully to use linguistic signs to refer to objects – but if there were such a crisis, it wouldn't follow that there was because there 'no longer' were any 'simply located' things to point at. That is, it wouldn't follow that if stones, chairs, trees, cats existed only in virtue of their relation to other entities (which is what Ermarth seems to mean by the claim that there are 'no longer' any 'simply located' things to point at – the 'everything is connected' idea, though the 'no longer' is baffling – that the signs 'stone,' 'chair,' 'tree,' 'cat' could not refer to those things.[11] It is worth noting, moreover, that Ermarth's claim that 'there are no longer any simply located things to point at' is predicated on the idea that signs are 'differential' ('[t]he linguistic model so often invoked in postmodern writing,' she states, 'reconstitutes subjectivity as difference, or rather as a differential process' (113)), so that her argument that signs cannot be conceived of as traveling pointers because there are no longer any simply located things to point at, is, for one thing, circular (further, even if the meaning of signs were purely relational, it would by no means follow from this that objects existed only in virtue of their relation to other objects). For another, since *how* signs mean is not identical with *what* they mean,[12] the fact that how they mean is through their differences from other signs does not entail that, as Raymond Tallis notes, 'the differences . . . are what is meant' (1988a: 82) or that they cannot refer to objects. 'Even if,' Tallis argues,

> we were to accept Saussure's view that the status of the signifiers as values makes them pure forms whose contents are immaterial, this would not oblige us to believe the same thing of the sign

considered as a totality. If this distinction had been kept in mind by many structuralists, then it would not have been possible for them to confuse that by virtue of which a sign signifies (its values ... plus its textual and non-linguistic context) with that which it signifies (its meaning or reference).

(82)

The source of the assumption that the arbitrariness of the linguistic sign rules out of court the possibility of words referring to objects seems to be the idea that a word could secure reference to a thing only if it somehow 'mirrored' the thing. The reasoning that leads to such a conclusion, Devitt and Kim Sterenly observe, would appear to go something like this: 'If signs were "pictures" of things then ... they would not be arbitrary: they would be constrained by what things were like. Yet signs are arbitrary. So, they are not pictures. So, reference must be rejected' (1987: 217). Tallis makes a similar point. Commenting on Terence Hawkes's claim that the 'behavior' of the word 'dog' 'derives from its inherent structural status as a noun rather than its referent's actual status as an animal,' he quips:

Would we expect a word to behave like its referents? Clearly not. Does anyone claim that the word 'dog' barks, pees on the floor or gets under my feet? ... [T]he difference between the word's behaviour and that of its referents – the type 'dog' is instantiated, while actual dogs bark; 'dog' tokens associate with other tokens while dogs prefer the company of dogs – hardly counts as a case against the referential nature of language. Even pre-linguistic modes of signification do not operate by mimicry. In pointing, neither the pointer nor the act of pointing behaves or looks like the pointee but no one would conclude that pointing was a closed system, sealed off from its 'referents.'

(77)

He too concludes that '[b]ehind the many fallacies of post-Saussurean literary theory may be the assumption that if there is no simple (e.g., numerical) correlation between terms and pre-linguistic entities, then there can be no reference to, or veridical account of, extralinguistic reality' (114). Insofar, then, as Olsen's summary dismissal of the notion that words 'mirror the world' rests on either on the idea that almost everyone except theorists of postmodernism take the mirroring metaphor literally or on the idea that the arbitrary nature of signs makes their reference to objects impossible, it is unwarranted.

So, how does the foregoing bear on the issue of literary realism? Well, in short, since a belief in 'a world out there,' in 'logic, chronology, and plot,' in 'a stable identity, a sense of self,' in 'a universe of communal reality and common sense' and in the idea that 'the word mirrors the world' are, as it were, underdetermined, compatible with all kinds of theories about the nature of reality, thought, time, history, identity, knowledge, morality, and truth, and since, further, being a metaphysical realist, for example, doesn't entail being an epistemological realist, a moral realist, a political realist, or any other kind of realist, it follows that no all-embracing realist 'metaphysical strategy' can be imputed to literary realism on the grounds that such beliefs inform its narrative strategy.

6
Myths about Literary Realism

The real thing

One of the myths about literary realism commonly subscribed to by theorists of postmodernism is that it is naive and uncritical. Michael Boyd, for example, maintains that

> [a] contradiction implied by the aesthetics of realism is its failure to be concerned about the nature of reality. Although their characters may be uncertain about what is really real, realist novelists never are: reality is simply the given. . . . This attitude must create problems for modern antirealists when they read a realistic novel. Do they find themselves taking sides against the novelist with certain fictional madmen who dare to wonder if the world is real? Or dare to wonder what 'real' means?. . . . If the realist pretends that fiction is life, the antirealist *knows* that life is a fiction. (Antirealists are themselves involved in a contradiction here. How can they disavow all claim to reality and at the same time claim knowledge of that reality? Their one defense – which is at the same time their *raison d'être* – is that they know that they cannot know.) For the antirealist, reality is protean, a mental construct bereft of the certitude given by the belief in any universal laws of the mind. Everyone is a novelist.
>
> (1983: 18)

In claiming that the aesthetics of realism implies a contradiction[1] in its failure to be concerned about the nature of reality, Boyd assumes, first of all, that realism does as a matter of course fail to evince such concern. (Nor is he not alone in assuming as much. Lyotard, for example, in 'Answering the Question: What is Postmodernism?' claims that the only definition of realism is 'that it intends to avoid the question of reality implicated in that art' – unlike Boyd, however, Lyotard makes no attempt to argue the point

(1984: 75). The evidence Boyd marshals in support of this proposition is slim, and essentially negative – that is, he proceeds as if the truth of the claims he makes about realism follows from his (likewise unsubstantiated) claims about anti-realism. He asserts, for example, that '[a]ll writers reacting against realism are essentially concerned with the question of the nature of reality' (19), a contention that implies no realist writers are, but which, in the absence of any evidence demonstrating this, simply begs the question.

His account, moreover, of the ways in which anti-realists demonstrate a concern with the question of the nature of reality suggests that his assertion that realists fail to address it is predicated on a rather arbitrary definition of what it means to question the nature of reality – i.e., he conveniently restricts what counts as questioning the nature of reality to the promulgation of the views he ascribes to anti-realists (that those views, as will become apparent, are incompatible need not concern one here).

On the one hand, Boyd claims that insofar as 'symbolic fiction' (fiction that 'points to the ideal rather than to the objects of the senses') 'wishes to make a statement, albeit oblique, about the nature of reality, [it] is compatible with the epistemological naiveté of literary realism' (21), which, coupled with his assertion that anti-realists 'know that they cannot know,' implies that his view is that realists display a lack of concern about the nature of reality in assuming that it is possible to know what its nature is. But even if it were the case that realist writers in general assumed it was possible to know the truth about the nature of reality and that anti-realist writers in general assumed it wasn't, the difference between them would not be that anti-realists evinced a concern with the question and realists did not; rather the difference would be that the latter manifested an interest in the subject by expressing the view that it is possible to know the truth about the nature of reality, while the former indicated an interest in it by expressing the view that it is not.

On the other hand, Boyd argues that for the anti-realist, reality is a mental construct, which suggests that what he means by asserting that realism fails to be concerned about the nature of reality is that realist writers assume the truth of metaphysical realism. But to posit that reality exists independently of the mental is to demonstrate as much of an interest in the question of the nature of reality as is to posit that it is a mental construct – so, again, even if realists did assume the truth of metaphysical realism and anti-realists the truth of metaphysical anti-realism, the difference between them would be that they each proferred different accounts of the nature of reality, not that the latter demonstrated a concern with the subject while the former did not.

The idea that what counts as an expression of concern with questions such as that of the nature of reality, knowledge, truth, etc., is the expression of a commitment to metaphysical anti-realism, or global skepticism, or relativism, is widely voiced by theorists of postmodernism, even by those who object to the view of literary realism as naive and retrograde promulgated by many of them. Patricia Waugh, for example, takes issue with the tendency of theorists of postmodernism to represent postmodernism 'as an authentic exposure of the illusions of preceding systems of knowledge and representation' (1992: 60), arguing that 'in claiming a radical break . . . postmodernists nearly always undo their own argument because they are forced to "totalise" what has come before in order to see it as bygone history' (58). In particular, Waugh claims, theorists of postmodernism are often 'guilty of reductive totalisation for polemical purposes' in their 'theorisation of Realism' (58):

> Just as Eagleton ignores the specific strategies of postmodern artefacts in order to proclaim a generalised condemnation of Postmodernism as the logic of commodification, so too its defenders often set Postmodernism against some other generalisation in order to show its greater authenticity. In my view this is where theory can learn from literature, for just as many postmodern artefacts can be shown to bear little resemblance to Eagleton's generalised categorisation of them, most realist novels involve modes of irony and linguistic playfulness which are ignored in many of the theoretical formulations of Realism.
>
> (58)

Waugh, however, despite her objecting to the practice of setting postmodernism against some other generalization in order to show its greater authenticity, effects her own 'reductive totalization' in claiming that 'postmodern fictions, like its theories, do play with fictionality in ways which challenge ontological and epistemological certainty,' while '[a] realist text such as Jane Austen's *Emma*, for example, clearly does not' (60). Waugh notes that throughout the novel, Austen is 'preoccupied with issues about the difficulty of critical interpretation and judgement,' 'the nature of the connection between social manners and ethical foundations,' and 'the social determinants of class, gender, urban and rural values' (60), and yet she arbitrarily decides that this preoccupation does not constitute a challenge to ontological or epistemological certainty: '*Emma* is clearly not postmodern: there *is* a correct way of seeing' (60; her emphasis). In so asserting, Waugh seems to assume, like Boyd, that there is only one 'correct' way of challenging ontological and epistemological certainty, namely, by embracing what she apparently regards as being a categorically 'postmodern' idea (but that, since it is an idea that has been promulgated throughout the history of western thought – i.e., that there is no one correct way of seeing – does not warrant being called 'postmodern').

I say that she 'seems to assume' and that she 'apparently regards' because Waugh is not consistent in this matter – she also argues (on the preceding page) that 'it is most fruitful to see Postmodernism in its literary modes not dissolving but rescuing the possibility of coherent subjectivity, historical significance and ethical stability by re-examining rather than refuting their foundations in modern thought and representation' (59), which suggests that she might not necessarily be committed to the idea that to posit that there is no correct way of seeing is the only way to challenge epistemological and ontological authority. Yet even if she weren't committed to that idea, there would still be no grounds for her to claim that postmodernist fiction plays with fictionality in ways that challenge epistemological and ontological authority, but that realist fiction does not, since her description of what Austen is preoccupied with in *Emma* accords with her description of postmodernism in its literary modes as engaged in the project of reexamining the foundations of, e.g., subjectivity and ethics in modern thought.

Either way, then, Waugh ends up wedging a distinction between realist fiction and the fiction she labels 'postmodernist' on the grounds that the former is less philosophically savvy than the latter, even though in so doing, she not only militates against her better intuitions, but also against what she explicitly asserts about *Emma*. (Why it is that any number of theorists of postmodernism who claim to be critical of certain tendencies in theories of postmodernism are unable to avoid duplicating the problems they identify in them is a matter I address in the last chapter.)

The difficulty with attempting to force a distinction between literary realism and anti-realism (anti-realism being what many theorists of postmodernism regard as the salient feature of literary postmodernism) in terms of philosophical sophistication is further borne out by the only positive evidence Boyd offers to support his initial claim that realism fails to be concerned about the nature of reality, which is J.P. Stern's remark that 'realism doesn't ask whether the world is real, but . . . occasionally asks what happens to persons who think it isn't' (18) and Stern's description of realism as 'philosophically incurious and epistemologically naive' (18). Boyd offers no account of what he thinks these remarks mean – he merely cites them – but on the face of it, the latter claim seems manifestly false (as well as inconsistent with what Stern maintains elsewhere in his *On Realism*, the book Boyd cites, *viz.* that 'any simple statement of the kind 'realism = x + y' is likely to be unsatisfactory' (1973: 57). The context in which Stern makes this assertion, however, does qualify the scope Boyd gives the claim by omitting mention of it:

> Realism (unlike a discussion of what it is) is philosophically incurious and epistemologically naive: the idealists' claim that we can have no reliable proof of external reality strikes the realist as egregious, just as G.E. Moore's famous refutation of that claim ('Here is one hand, and here is another') would strike him as supererogatory.
>
> (54)

But since epistemological questions are distinct from metaphysical ones, realism's purported epistemological naiveté is not indicative of a failure to be concerned about the nature of reality. To think that the claim that we can have no reliable proof of external reality is egregious, and that it is unnecessary to try to refute it, neither resolves the question of the nature of reality, nor precludes speculation as to whether external reality is mind-independent or not.

Stern's argument here thus fails to lend support to Boyd's; it is, moreover, itself an unwarranted generalization for which Stern offers no evidence. The only way one could substantiate such a claim would be if one could identify some convention of realist prose in which this epistemological naiveté made itself apparent. Stern perhaps thinks that it is manifested in the fact that the world of the realist novel is one in which characters typically behave as if there were an external reality capable of being described. But since this sort of behavior is compatible with the view that we can have no reliable proof of external reality, with the view that we can and do have such proof, and with the view that the debate over whether

we can have proof or not is a silly one (and none of these is necessarily naive), one cannot just assume that such behavior in a realist
novel indicates epistemological naiveté. Indeed, questions concerning, *inter alia*, the origins of knowledge, the kinds of knowledge that
there are, and the limits of human knowledge have always been,
and continue to be, critically reflected upon in realist novels. (Would
Stern or Boyd really be prepared to maintain that *What Maisie Knew*,
for example, is epistemologically naive?)

Stern, of course, is sympathetic to literary realism. However, he
unnecessarily limits its scope. The aim of his endeavor, he claims,
is to 'show, occasionally in a philosophical way, the irrelevance to
realism of philosophical enquiries into the nature of reality' (31).
'More than most other literary critics,' he writes, 'the writer on realism is apt to be told that his undertaking is impossible':

> 'How can you say anything sensible about realism unless you
> have first defined what reality is – and to do that, surely, is the
> business of a philosopher, not a literary critic!' It is an irrelevant
> objection. What we require for our present undertaking is not a
> 'definition of reality' at all but a certain kind of description of the
> world. Such a description, moreover, is not antecedent to or a
> condition of realism, it is the thing itself. That is what realism is.
> (31–2)

The writer on literary realism, I agree, does not require a 'definition
of reality' to define it – indeed, literary realism cannot be defined
in terms of a commitment to a theory about the nature of reality.
But it hardly follows from this that realist fiction doesn't conduct
philosophical enquiries into the nature of reality. That is, the question of the nature of reality is not irrelevant to realist fiction; it is
irrelevant to the definition of literary realism.

Stern's assertion that realism doesn't ask whether the world is
real likewise lends no support to Boyd's contention that it fails to
be concerned about the nature of reality, since, again, to assume
that the world is real does not preclude questioning its nature, or
even preclude arguing that the question of its nature is a meaningless
one – again, the latter amounting to as much of a show of concern
with the question as does positing that its nature cannot be known
or that it does not exist independently of perceptions about it.
Consider, for example, the logical positivist position as A.J. Ayer
describes it:

Let us suppose that a picture is discovered and the suggestion made that it was painted by Goya. There is a definite procedure for dealing with such a question. The experts examine it to see in what way it resembles the accredited works of Goya, and to see if it bears any marks which are characteristic of a forgery; they look up contemporary records for evidence of the existence of such a picture, and so on. In the end, they may still disagree, but each one knows what empirical evidence would go to confirm or discredit his opinion. Let us now suppose that these men have studied philosophy, and some of them proceed to maintain that this picture is a set of ideas in the perceiver's mind, or in God's mind, others that it is objectively real. What possible experience could any of them have which would be relevant to the solution of this dispute one way or the other? In the ordinary sense of the term 'real,' in which it is opposed to 'illusory,' the reality of the picture is not in doubt. The disputants have satisfied themselves that the picture is real, in this sense, by obtaining a correlated series of sensations of sight and sensations of touch. Is there any similar process by which they could discover whether the picture was real, in the sense in which the term 'real' is opposed to 'ideal'? Clearly there is none. . . . The question at issue between idealists and realists becomes fictitious when, as is often the case, it is given a metaphysical interpretation.

(1952: 40)

Neither does assuming that the world is real preclude, as Boyd implies it does, having doubts about 'what is really real'[2] – one could believe the world was real without being certain as to whether psychokinesis or telepathy was real; one could believe the world was real without being sure whether events one heard about or saw were real, as was the case for many who heard the famous broadcast of H.G. Wells's radio play and as is the case for Nicolas Urfe in John Fowles's *The Magus*.

Finally, the distinction Boyd draws between realist novels and realist novelists in claiming that '[a]lthough their characters may be uncertain about what is really real, realistic novelists never are' is fraught. On the one hand, the assertion that realist novelists are never uncertain about what is really real is utterly lacking in justification. Boyd apparently thinks there is some fundamental connection between being a realist writer and being certain about what is real, but just as such certainty doesn't follow from the fact that one is an American, or a woman, or a doctor, so it doesn't follow from the fact that one is a realist writer. Moreover, if one assumes, as Boyd admits he does, that writers are capable of conveying something of what they themselves believe through their fiction, and if there is nothing to stop either realist or anti-realist writers from using their characters as mouthpieces for their own views, how can Boyd be so sure that a character in a realist novel who is uncertain about what is real doesn't reflect the author's uncertainty?

On the other, whether realist writers are never uncertain about what is really real is beside the point if there are indeed characters in realist fiction who are. For if there are, then at least some realist fiction concerns itself with the question of what is really real. Boyd conflates the issue of what is real with the issue of the nature of what is real, but even if he had argued that while their characters may concern themselves with the question of the nature of reality, realist novelists never do, the same objection could be made: if there are characters in realist fiction who do, then, *ipso facto*, it is false that no realist fiction concerns itself with the question of the nature of reality.

Since Boyd does not show that realism fails to be concerned about the nature of reality, his claim that it contradicts itself because of this purported failure is questionable. But even if it were true that realism failed to be concerned about the nature of reality, what could it mean to assert that this involved it in a contradiction? Boyd seems to presuppose, oddly enough, that 'realist' means 'to demonstrate a concern with the question of the nature of reality.' This definition is not a conventional one, but even if it were, and even if realist fiction did in fact fail to display such a concern, it still wouldn't follow that it contradicted itself. For it is untenable to predicate, *a priori*, f of x, and then claim, *a posteriori*, that because f cannot in fact be predicated of x, x contradicts itself – that would be like classifying whales as fish, and then claiming, after having discovered that in fact no whales are fish, that because no whales are fish they contradict themselves. If, for the sake of argument, one were to allow that the fiction generally labeled 'realist' did not address the question of the nature of reality, then, by the definition in question, it would not in fact be realist and so no 'contradiction' would ensue from its failure to be concerned with the question of the nature of reality – rather, it would simply have been mislabeled. Indeed, Boyd, in claiming that 'all writers reacting against realism are essentially concerned with the nature of reality' and that '[t]herefore, there is some justice in their claim to the title of neo-realists' (19), suggests that that's his view on the matter.

The untenability of the assertion that realism contradicts itself and the fact that 'a concern with the nature of reality' is not a conventional definition of realism aside, it would seem that what Boyd is at least in part assuming when he claims that realism contradicts itself is that certain specialized, nonliterary senses of the word 'realism' bear on the definition of literary realism. The reductivism of a number of recent accounts of literary realism seems in part to be precisely the result of assuming that there is, or ought to be, a connection between philosophical meanings of the word 'realism' and the definition of literary realism – hence, the commonly articulated notion in theories of postmodernism that metaphysical and epistemological realism underwrite literary realism. But there is no such one-to-one correspondence. The idea that there is dies hard, however, even among literary critics who are at pains to contend it. Andrzej Gąsiorek, for example, argues that:

[a] major problem bedevilling all debates about the nature and validity of realism is that critics tend to conflate epistemology and aesthetics. Terry Lovell has pointed out that realism in epistemology and realism in art are distinct and should be kept separate, since they do not necessarily entail one another.

(1995: 183)

And yet, having seemingly given his tacit support to the idea that neither necessarily entails the other, Gąsiorek goes on to qualify that support:

Lovell's argument that epistemological realism does not *ipso facto* entail aesthetic realism seems obviously right. There is no necessary reason why an epistemological realist should produce realist art. On the other hand, to be a realist in art is implicitly to be some sort of realist in epistemology, since the belief that art can represent reality rests on a prior conviction that the world can be known.

(184)

Gąsiorek's argument here is puzzling. For the fact that an artist could be a believer in epistemological realism and yet produce anti-realist art – which, *pace* Gąsiorek implies that a believer in epistemological anti-realism could produce realist art – is irrelevant to the question of whether epistemological and aesthetic realism entail each other (though an artist's belief that they entail each other might well prove important to understanding her or his work). And indeed, Gąsiorek himself intimates as much – that is, in pointing out that there is no necessary reason why an epistemological realist should produce realist art, he implies that art is realist or not irrespective of the artist's epistemological beliefs. What makes realist art realist, he suggests, is its representing reality – which representation, he claims, is grounded in epistemological realism since it implies that the world can be known. The upshot of his thinking that he has countered the conflation of epistemological and aesthetic realism by observing that there is no necessary reason why an epistemological realist should produce realist art is that he fails to question the assumption that gives rise to this conflation in the first place – namely, that the belief that the world can be known is synonymous with epistemological realism. However, epistemological realism (of which there are several varieties, as Gąsiorek points out), is one theory – and not the only theory – *about* how we acquire knowledge of the external world; it is not the theory *that* we can acquire knowledge of the external world. So realist art, insofar as it implies that the world can be known, need not be grounded in epistemological realism.

That said, I would note that I am largely sympathetic to Gąsiorek's aims. Pointing out that his book is 'in certain respects a modest exercise in retrieval,' he observes that 'postmodernism is so often invoked as a cultural dominant that a diverse range of literary forms come to be seen in a homogenous fashion as part of a general "crisis of representation"' (vi). He continues:

> This is in my view deeply misleading. To read authors who engage in quite different ways with the epistemological and aesthetic difficulties entailed by representation as though they are all participating in the same pursuit is to 'flatten out' the post-war period in a way that can only contribute to the very dehistoricization that critics of postmodernism lament. One of my most basic assumptions in writing this book has been that careful attention to the specific political and aesthetic contexts in which writers work militates against the subsumption of their quite diverse novels to the current preoccupation with postmodernism.
>
> (vi)

His position is thus similar to my own; not only do theorists of postmodernism homogenize the contemporary fiction they label 'postmodernist,' but, as he notes, they also pit it against realist fiction, which they tend to regard as lacking 'the epistemological sophistication of contemporary critics' (13). 'This view,' he rightly ascertains,

> rests on a theory of belatedness symptomatic of much postmodernist thought; it is 'we' who are doubting, ironic, self-reflexive and detached, whereas 'they' are innocent, gullible, benighted and unable to stand back from the beliefs of the day. We pit 'our' self-reflexive scepticism against their 'naive' realism in an act of gross historical condescension. Equally, however, the current concern with reflexivity may result in realism being valued because it too can be shown to be theoretically up-to-date, rather than because of its cognitive power and its ability to challenge various contemporary assumptions about the nature of reality.
>
> (13)

However, there are problems with his argument other than the one I have already addressed. First, although he claims that realism has the ability to challenge various assumptions about the nature of reality, he also asserts that 'realist writers . . . share a general orientation to the world: they believe it has an existence independent from the perceptions of the cognizing self' (191). Not only is the suggestion that realist fiction in general manifests a commitment to metaphysical realism impossible to substantiate (and by reformulating his claim here, I am again suggesting that Gąsoriek, despite his implying in the above that what in part makes art 'realist' is that the artist who produces it believes that reality exists independently of perceptions of it, in fact believes that an artist's metaphysical beliefs do not determine what kind of art she or he might produce, and hence that what makes art 'realist' art is not a function of an artist's metaphysical beliefs), but, were it true, it would also rather limit the ability of realist fiction to challenge various assumptions about the nature of reality. Second, I think that Gąsiorek fails to heed sufficiently his own warning that realist fiction might come to be valued because it can be shown to be theoretically up-to-date. He argues, for example, that

> [t]he work of those writers who do not reject realism outright (Lamming, Naipul, Berger, Lessing, Fowles, Wilson, Maitland,

Rushdie) seeks in distinctive ways to retain realism's strengths, particularly its attention to the social and intersubjective nature of human life, while at the same time confronting the problem of representation. Although the works of this group of novelists are heterogeneous, they all extend realism by disclosing the constitutive function of language and narrative in human beings' production of meaning. This emphasis on the construction of meaning is predominantly the counterpart of a textuality rooted in a particularized and historicized social domain. Thus these novels avow realism's referential impulse but reject any simple reflectionist aesthetic and any straightforward truth-as-correspondence epistemology.

(181–2)

Yet Gąsiorek opens his book by challenging those contemporary critiques of realism in which nineteenth-century realist fiction is represented in terms of a simple reflectionist aesthetic and a straightforward truth-as-correspondence epistemology. Using George Eliot's novels and Colin McCabe's and Catherine Belsey's critiques of the 'classic realist text' as references points, he argues that Eliot's 'conception of realism is certainly inseparable from empiricism and from a correspondence theory,' but that that 'does not commit her to the naive representationalism associated with classic realism' (10). Eliot, he claims, citing a review by her of Ruskin, 'acknowledges that art depends on selection and thus cannot reproduce reality entire'; her emphasis, he continues, 'on the artist's interpretative and synthesizing function goes hand in hand with a complex view of language, which is far from a "mirror" theory' (10). The standard account of the 'classic realist text'

offers a misleading account of realism's epistemology: It is not just Eliot who eschews the naive reflectionism attributed to classic realism; her emphasis on the synthetic role of the imagination in processing experience is shared by Balzac, de Maupassant, and James.

(11–12)

So given that naive reflectionism never was a feature of realism as such to begin with – 'it may be,' Gąsoriek notes, 'that some nineteenth-century writers thought that realism 'mirrors' reality, but this can hardly be claimed of realists *tout court*' (12) – it can't be that the twentieth-century realist novels he discusses have, as he suggests, 'taken realism in new directions' by 'reject[ing] reflectionism and embrac[ing] reflexivity' (182). Gąsiorek falls into the trap – despite his own warning – of thinking that defending realism against recent attacks on it requires demonstrating that post-war realist writing is 'theoretically up-to-date.' In so doing – again, despite himself – he concedes unnecessary ground; that is, he allows that the discrediting of naive reflectionism is indeed owed to poststructuralist and postmodernist theory.

To be fair, Gąsiorek does not blatantly contradict himself. Having defended nineteenth-century realism against the charge of naive reflectionism, he goes on to argue that we can nonetheless see why

> the kind of writing favoured by someone like Eliot has been superseded and why the poststructuralist account of realism, despite its weaknesses, has highlighted the decisive break with nineteenth-century narrative modes ushered in by modernism and postmodernism.
>
> (15)

Many of the post-war novels he considers, he claims, 'both look outward to an external world that they attempt to depict in all its complexity and inward to the very processes by which such depiction is brought into being.' But Eliot, he continues,

> remains caught in a subject–object dualism that, however subtle her conception of language, conceives it as designative rather than constitutive. Poststructuralism's break with this conception draws attention to the way that language shapes, constrains, and to some extent determines, the terms in which reference can be thought at all. It is on these simultaneously creative and confining aspects of language that so many contemporary writers dwell.
>
> (15)

Gąsiorek's claim, however, that Eliot conceives of language as designative rather than constitutive, and that, by extension, nineteenth-century realist fiction in general represents language as designative rather than constitutive, lacks force because it poses a false opposition that he himself challenges. A wholly designative conception of language would stand opposed to a wholly constitutive view of it, but Gąsiorek has already argued that Eliot's conception of language is far from a simple mirror theory, and since what a simple mirror theory would offer, if there were such a theory, would be a wholly designative account of language, it follows that, within the terms of his own argument, Eliot's conception of language is not wholly designative – indeed, the oft-cited excursus from Chapter 17 of *Adam Bede*, which Gąsiorek discusses (and to which I will return below), looks 'inward to the very processes by which [the depiction of an external world] is brought into being,' embracing the reflexivity that Gąsiorek suggests is one of the new directions in which post-war realist fiction has taken realism. Furthermore, Gąsiorek does not assert, as his claim that Eliot's conception of language is designative rather than constitutive might suggest he would, that the post-war realist novels he discusses represent language as wholly constitutive of reality. Rather, he argues that they

> emphasize that the discourses people necessarily use constitute their experience of reality, but . . . shy away from a textualism that conceives reality to be so fundamentally constructed out of language that it seems to possess no extra-discursive features, which might constrain or shape the way that language configures it.
>
> (183)

Within the terms of his own argument, then, the distinction Gąsiorek proposes between realism before, and realism after, modernism and postmodernism collapses. It collapses, in part, because he is attempting to defend realism by situating it with respect to theories of postmodernism – the assumptions of which he does not question – and since these theories define postmodernism in substantive positive terms, define it in terms of, for example, the idea that language constitutes reality, he is forced to posit a distinction between realism and postmodernism, and a distinction between realism 'before' and realism 'after' postmodernism, in substantive positive terms as well. Hence his suggestion both that realist writers as such – whether of the nineteenth or twentieth century – share a general orientation toward the world in believing that objects exist independently of perception (which he appeals to to distinguish them from so-called postmodernist writers who, he implies, believe they don't) and that post-war realist writers believe that language is not wholly designative (which he appeals to to distinguish them from their nineteenth-century forbears).

But literary realism eludes substantive positive definition. Indeed,

as Raymond Tallis notes, trying to define literary realism in positive terms 'gets one into all sorts of messes' (1988b: 190). However,
following Robert Scholes, he suggests that

> [r]ealism presents . . . a world recognizably *bound* by the same
> laws as that of the author. Realism is bounded by external, non-
> literary constraints. We may not be able to say what lies at the
> heart of realism, but we can say what, in general, determines its
> edges.
>
> (190; his emphasis)

The definition of realism as a literary mode that is bounded by
external, non-literary constraints seems to me to be a workable one.[3]
It is not, strictly speaking, a negative definition, but it comes close
– it posits that realism cannot characterized in terms of, for example, specific metaphysical, epistemological, moral, or political
content. So in creating worlds bounded by external, non-literary
constraints, realism doesn't necessary reflect a commitment to, say,
metaphysical realism. Nor for that matter does literary anti-realism,
in flouting such constraints, necessarily reflect a commitment to
metaphysical anti-realism, contrary to what Diane Elam, for one, suggests in her *Romancing the Postmodern*. 'A significant implication of
[romance's] self-excess, which (re)marks a generic departure from
purely realistic representation,' is, Elam argues, that

> romance troubles the simple reference of novels to a political and
> historical 'reality.' That is to say, romance's ability to go beyond
> itself is also a capacity to go beyond realism. . . . If literary real-
> ism considers reality as its ontological ground, romance threatens
> to expose 'reality' as a constructed referent rather than as a 'nat-
> ural' state of existence to which we all naturally, textually, refer.
>
> (1992: 8)

In claiming that romance 'troubles the simple reference of novels
to a political and historical 'reality,' Elam assumes, first of all, that
realist fiction does 'simply' refer to reality. That that assumption
is questionable[4] need not, however, concern one here, since Elam,
following Henry James, also describes romance as 'the genre that
liberates the representation of experience from known conditions
and measurable states' (6–7), which suggests that what she means
by saying that romance 'troubles the simple reference of novels to

a political and historical reality' is that realist fiction is constrained by known conditions and measurable states.[5]

Yet it hardly follows from the fact that romance creates worlds dissimilar to the actual one in many respects that it therefore exposes 'reality as a constructed referent,' or even that it is committed to the idea that reality is a constructed referent. Spenser's Error and the Gawain-poet's Green Knight are language-dependent constructions that 'liberate the representation of experience from known conditions and measurable states,' but that doesn't prove either that reality is a linguistic construct or that such a notion informs *The Fairie Queene* and *Sir Gawain and the Green Knight*.[6] By the same token, that realist fiction creates worlds similar to the actual one in many respects does not entail either that realism is committed to metaphysical realism or that metaphysical realism is true; that the Dublin of Joyce's *Ulysses* is a language-dependent construction constrained by known conditions and measurable states is neither evidence that reality exists independently of language nor that *Ulysses* gives expression to the idea that it does.

Because one cannot define realism (or any literary mode, as far as I am concerned) in substantive positive terms, the only reason that I can see for attempting a definition of it at all (and so of any literary mode) would be to do justice to the intuition that there *are* different modes of fiction. And I think the definition of it as a mode that is bounded by external, non-literary constraints not only does justice to that intuition, but also, importantly, provides all that is needed to do justice to it. The problems with many accounts of realism and anti-realism seem to me to arise from the need or desire to construct a 'grand narrative' that would explain the existence of different modes of fiction. That is, most theorists and critics are not satisfied merely to define anti-realism, say, as a mode that 'liberates the representation of experience from known conditions and measurable states' and leave it at that (thus allowing that the implications of such a representation of experience from one anti-realist novel to the next novel to the next could, for a multitude of reasons, vary widely), but also want to read some general underlying philosophical sensibility into such a representational mode. Many also want, furthermore, to characterize the underlying philosophical sensibility they attribute to narrative modes as the reflection of *Zeitgeister* like 'victorianism,' 'modernism' and 'postmoderism.' ('Realism' and 'anti-realism,' are, I believe, serviceable terms; 'victorianism,' 'modernism,' and 'postmodernism,' on the other hand, as period concepts, strike me as being very nearly useless, for reasons that if not already apparent will become so – periodization is not, I would argue, the 'necessary fiction' it is often claimed to be. That it is a fiction cannot be doubted; that it is necessary is far from evident.) To be sure, the definition of realism (and by extension, of anti-realism) I've offered is not without its problems, but, if one is to posit one at all, it seems to me to be the most promising, and so I will, for now, adopt it as a working one.

It is important to note what does *not* follow from such a definition of literary realism. For one thing, it is no consequence of being bounded by external, non-literary constraints that literary realism privileges content over form, or renders style secondary, as Olsen puts it. This popular misconception about literary realism is well put paid to by Valentine Cunningham in his brilliant *In the Reading Gaol: Postmodernity, Texts, and History*. Dickens's *Hard Times*, he claims, for example, 'is a famous test for assumptions about reading texts, in this case novels – novels in general and nineteenth-century novels in particular' (1994: 129):

> On the one hand, it has long been a *locus classicus* of Victorian realism. You could hardly invent a sharper instance of the so-called classic realist novel than this one. And it has indeed been an appropriately happy hunting-ground for moralists and historians and Marxists, for any ideologue, in fact, who believes that fiction, and above all nineteenth-century fiction, connects with the real world, mirrors it clearly, instantiates it by numerous particularities and by thickness of Jamesian detail in the pages of the book . . . Such readings reinforce the view that the Victorian novel – and possibly all good novels, certainly the ones not wrongly contaminated by false modernist preferences – is, like this one, worldly, metonymic, imitative of social realities . . . The Condition of England Novel, on these assumptions, represents the right condition of the novel . . . It's the kind of writing clearly demarcated from the fiction that preceded it – that is, playful, gaming, self-referential eighteenth-century texts, fictional modes climaxing in *Tristram Shandy* – or that succeeded it – anti-realist, modernist, and postmodernist writing that takes its cue from the likes of *Tristram Shandy*, textualized texts, increasingly gamey, highly metaphoric, [texts that] artfully retreat[ ] from any suspicion of merely transcribing the real.
>
> (129)

On the other hand, he notes that

> in keeping with the fashion for post-Derridean notions that all
> the old referential assumptions about literature are misplaced,
> *Hard Times* has been subjected, along with many of the canonical
> classics, the standard items of the literary syllabus, to re-readings
> aimed at proving rather that it is essentially of the order of *Tristram
> Shandy* or *Finnegans Wake*, is really about the condition of text
> and textuality rather than the Condition of England.
>
> (130)

Theorists of postmodernism, eager to demarcate postmodernism
from both modernism and realism, have in recent years tended to
align realism with contentism, modernism with formalism, and postmodernism with both; an early articulation of this position is found
in John Barth's 'The Literature of Replenishment' (originally published in *The Atlantic* in 1980):

> If the modernists, carrying the torch of romanticism, taught us that
> linearity, rationality, consciousness, cause and effect, naïve illu-
> sionism, transparent language, innocent anecdote, and middle-
> class moral conventions are not the whole story, then from the
> perspective of these closing decades of our century we may appre-
> ciate that the contraries of those things are not the whole story
> either. Disjunction, simultaneity, irrationalism, anti-illusionism,
> self-reflexiveness, medium-as-message, political olympianism, and
> a moral pluralism approaching moral entropy – these are not the
> whole story either.
>   A worthy program for postmodernist fiction, I believe, is
> the synthesis or transension of these antitheses, which may be
> summed as premodernist and modernist modes of writing.
>
> (1984: 203)

'The ideal postmodernist novel,' Barth concludes, 'will somehow rise
above the quarrel between realism and irrealism, formalism and
"contentism," pure and committed literature, coterie and junk fiction.' (203).

In similar terms, Linda Hutcheon explains in her preface to *A
Poetics of Postmodernism* that her focus

> is on those points of significant overlap of theory with aesthetic
> practice which might guide us to articulate what I want to call a
> 'poetics of postmodernism,' a flexible conceptual structure which

could at once constitute and contain postmodern culture and our discourses both about it and adjacent to it. The points of overlap that seem most evident to me are those of the paradoxes set up when modernist aesthetic autonomy and self-reflexivity come up against a counterforce in the form of a grounding in the historical, social, and political world.

(1988: ix)

T.V. Reed, for another, argues that *Let Us Now Praise Famous Men* is representative of 'postmodernist realism': its 'aesthetic sophistication stands in critique of simple realism, while its political concerns (as embodied in the tenants) critique the now normative self-referentiality of (post)modernism' (1992: 24). Postmodernist realism 'features self-reflexive, realism-disrupting techniques, but places those techniques in tension with "real" cognitive claims and with "realistic," radically pragmatic political needs' (18). For Hutcheon, postmodernist fiction in general is defined by its confrontation with 'the problem of the relation of the aesthetic to the world of significance external to itself . . . in other words, to the political and the historical,' is marked 'by both history and an internalized, self-reflexive investigation of the nature, the limits, and the possibilities of the discourse of art' (22); for Reed, it is rather only 'postmodernist realism' that is. But the problem with both arguments is the same: driven by a teleological impulse to represent, in Hutcheon's case, postmodernist fiction in general as marking an 'advance' over both realist and modernist fiction, and, in Reed's case, 'postmodernist realism' as transcending realism, modernism, and what he calls 'normative' postmodernism, they are forced to posit strawmen. Thus, Reed, in order to claim that 'postmodernist realism' is superior to nineteenth-century realism has to figure the latter as a 'simple realism,' lacking 'aesthetic sophistication.'

Needless to say, the idea that a concern for both world and word is unique to postmodernism, or even 'postmodernist realism,' is just not on. As Cunningham remarks:

What *Hard Times* does dramatically is to challenge the either-or ism of the critical postures that cluster about it. It very firmly undoes, it disallows, the absolute polarities that critics have erected between Victorian and Modernist, realist and rhetorical, Condition-of-England and Condition-of-Text, old-fashioned reading and progressive reading, reference and self-reference, metonymic and metaphoric, that have sadly infected readings of this novel ever since Leavis' *The Great Tradition*. In particular, the difficulties this novel experiences in handling the apparent opposition it sets up between Fact and Fancy focuses with extraordinary (and, of course, I think exemplary) clarity the real impossibility of separating world issues from word ones, realism from irrealism, metonymic from metaphoric.

(130–1)

That 'we not only need not choose' (60) between 'inside and outside, historicism and formalism, rhetoric and reference, form and content' (56) but that 'rigorous analysis will not allow us to choose' (60) is what Cunningham seeks to demonstrate by looking, as he says, at 'some classic fictions' – e.g., *Tristram Shandy, Emma, Jane Eyre, Middlemarch, Hard Times, Bleak House, Heart of Darkness* (and 'occasionally not so classic fictions' – e.g., Golding's *Rites of Passage*) (61). It is of no matter that Cunningham seems to be unaware of the popularity currently enjoyed by the argument that what distinguishes postmodernist fiction from realist and modernist fiction is its commitment to both form and content, world and word, since his ingenious, and often incisive, analysis of these classic novels exposes for the strawman that it is the schema to which theorists of postmodernism have had to appeal to make this argument.

It doesn't follow from what Cunningham deems to be the impossibility of separating world issues from word ones that it is impossible to distinguish realism from anti-realism. (And so one might want to quibble with his infelicitous yoking of realism with world issues and irrealism with word ones, which, given his claim that world issues are inseparable from word ones, could give license to the idea that all novels are both realist and anti-realist, and hence to the idea that realism and anti-realism are indistinguishable.) Realism 'presents . . . a world recognizably *bound* by the same laws as that of the author'; anti-realism doesn't. 'Realism is bounded by external, non-literary constraints'; anti-realism isn't. This is what, in light of the working definition of literary realism that I offered above, I think the fundamental difference between realism and anti-realism can be understood as consisting in (and by using the word 'fundamental,' I mean to suggest that there is a spectrum here – a novel such as Christine Brook-Rose's *Textermination*, for example – in which characters from various classic novels convene to pray for their continued existence – is an anti-realist novel that would stand, on my proffered distinction between realism and anti-realism, at the far anti-realist end of the realist-anti-realist spectrum, whereas, say, Alisdair Gray's *Lanark* would stand in the middle of it). It's not that realism concerns itself with world issues and that anti-realism doesn't: anti-realist fiction, in varying degrees, flouts external, non-literary constraints, but it is, so far as I can tell, as concerned with world issues as is realist fiction.

Nor does the difference between anti-realism and realism, as I see it, hinge on the presence or absence of foregrounding of fiction-ality, *pace* Robert Holub, for one, who argues that 'when a given text makes no claim to mirror or reflect reality, but instead insists upon its nonrelationship to the world, it forfeits its potential for pro-ducing an effect of the real,' and that 'realist texts, therefore, must stop short of foregrounding fictionality if they are to have a realist effect' (1991: 16). Realist texts, he claims 'in most instances . . . conceal any traces of their nature as fantasy and invention: the fiction they perpetuate is that they are not fiction at all' (16). What Holub's claim that to foreground fictionality is to forfeit the potential for producing an effect of the real seems to be predicated on is the rather odd assumption that to produce an effect of the real requires creating the illusion that what are merely words on a page are instead bits of reality.

Such an assumption might owe something to Roland Barthes's 'effet du réel.' As Christopher Prendergast notes:

The implication of 'nous sommes le réel' is that the words of the text try to perform a kind of disappearing act upon themselves; the text plays a trick whereby the reader undergoes the 'illusion' of being confronted not with language but with reality itself; the sign effaces itself before its 'referent' in order to create an 'effect': the illusion of the presence of the object itself. The reader believes he is faced not with words, but with things, as if the referent were actually *there*, in the statement. What in fact he is faced with is, of course, not things, but a rhetorical category (la catégorie du réel). But Barthes's hypothetical reader *does not know this*; he is bewitched by the stratagems of realist writing into confusing category with thing (otherwise there could be no sense in positing him as the victim of an 'illusion'). To maintain such a position vis-à-vis the text, such a reader would have to be in state approach-ing hallucination . . . [I]t is difficult to believe that Barthes is asking us to believe that this is actually what happens to ('naive') readers of *Un Coeur simple* or *Histoire de France*. Assuming that Barthes cannot in fact be asking us to believe that, the point, then, is that the rhetorical device supplants rather than serves argument. It promotes the idea of a relationship between language and reality that is rightly described as an 'illusion,' but leaves us in a state of uncertainty as to who could ever fall victim to such an illusion in the first place.

(1986: 70–1)

'Barthes,' Prendergast concludes, 'mobilises his combined semiological artillery and rhetorical infantry to fight what appears to be an imaginary enemy in a phoney war' (72).

Whatever its source, the idea that the production of the effect of the real depends on tricking readers into believing that what they are confronted with is not language but reality itself is common among theorists of postmodernism. Fredric Jameson, for example, claims that ' "[r]ealism" is ... a peculiarly unstable concept owing to its simultaneous, yet incompatible, aesthetic and epistemological claims, as the two terms of the slogan, "representation of reality," suggest':

> [T]he emphasis on this or that type of truth content will clearly be undermined by any intensified awareness of the technical means or representational artifice of the work itself. Meanwhile, the attempt to shore up the epistemological vocation of the work generally involves the suppression of the formal properties of the realistic 'text' and promotes an increasingly naive and unmediated or reflective conception of aesthetic construction and reception. Thus, where the epistemological claim succeeds, it fails; and if realism validates its claim to being a correct or true representation of the world, it thereby ceases to be an *aesthetic* mode of representation and falls out of art altogether. If, on the other hand, the artistic devices and technological equipment whereby it captures the truth of the world are explored and stressed and foregrounded, 'realism' will stand unmasked as mere reality- or realism-*effect*, the reality it purported to deconceal falling at once into the sheerest representation and illusion.

(1992: 157)[7]

The realism of a realist novel, however, has nothing to do either with its trying to pass itself off as a piece of unmediated reality or with its trying to pretend that it is not fiction. Rather, as I've been suggesting, the realism of a realist novel consists in its creation of a fictional world that is bounded by external, non-literary constraints, and so the realism achieved by the creation of such a world is not necessarily undermined if 'the artistic devices and technological equipment whereby it captures the truth of the world are explored and stressed and foregrounded' (consider, for example, Iris Murdoch's *The Black Prince* – I can't imagine anyone denying that it is a realist novel (even if one regarded the definition of realism I've chosen to work with as problematic) and yet it actively explores, stresses, and foregrounds the artistic devices and technical equipment whereby it represents the truth of the world).

That the narrator of *Adam Bede*, for example, pauses to address concerns she imagines the reader might have – ' "This Rector of Broxton is little better than a pagan!" I hear one of my lady readers exclaim. "How much more edifying it would have been if you had made him give Arthur some truly spiritual advice. You might have put into his mouth the most beautiful things – quite as good as reading a sermon" ' – and answer those concerns – 'Certainly I could, my fair critic, if I were a clever novelist, not obliged to creep servilely after nature and fact, but able to represent things as they never have been and never will be. Then, of course, my characters would be entirely of my own choosing, and I could select the most unexceptionable type of clergyman and put my own admirable opinions into his mouth on all occasions' (1985: 221) – certainly foregrounds the fictionality of the novel, but it does nothing to mar its realism.

Nor does the fact that *Adam Bede* expresses an 'intensified awareness of the technical means or representational artifice of the work itself' undermine whatever truth content it may lay claim to.[8] What leads Jameson to believe that an intensified awareness of the representational artifice does undermine 'the emphasis on this or that type of truth content' is suggested by the way he parses the slogan 'representation of reality.' He attaches 'aesthetic claims' to the term 'representation' and 'epistemological claims' to the term 'reality.' But reality itself (whatever *it* 'really' is) just is: it doesn't make truth-claims. Rather, human beings make truth-claims through language, through verbal representations. The question of how exactly fiction can make truth-claims is the subject of a good deal of controversy, but assuming that it does, however it does, Jameson's 'aesthetic claims' and 'epistemological claims' would both belong on the left side of the 'representation of reality' equation.

What Jameson seems oddly to presuppose is that representations can't be true because what's true is reality itself. Realism, on this account, tries to hide the fact that it is a representation, tries to pretend it is reality itself; by contrast, those novels that explicitly foreground their fictionality make clear that they are representations, make clear that they are not reality itself, and so forfeit the claim to being true. But, again, physical reality itself, whether understood as comprising independently existing, discrete objects or as being 'always already' linguistically constructed, is neither true nor false. That is, even if, as many theorists of postmodernism, à la Lacan, claim, it is the world of words that constructs the world of things, the world of things is not identical with the words that construct it: a table, for example, neither looks nor feels anything like the word 'table.' So, a table, even if it were a linguistic construct, would be neither true nor false. Rather, it is statements about the linguistically constructed table that would be true or false.

There are, of course, novels in which the foregrounding of fictionality has a decidedly anti-realist effect (which is why I claimed above that the realism achieved by a novel is not *necessarily* undermined if the artistic devices or equipment by which it captures the truth of the world are stressed). A case in point here would be Muriel Spark's *The Comforters*, where the protagonist Caroline, hearing the tippity-tap of a typewriter and voices repeating her thoughts verbatim, realizes that she is a character in a novel (and yet, as with realist fiction that foregrounds its fictionality, this intensified awareness of the representational artifice of the work itself does not necessarily undermine whatever truth it may lay claim to). But not all anti-realist fiction foregrounds its fictionality in this way, just as not all realist fiction foregrounds its fictionality in the way that *Adam Bede* does. The point is that the presence or absence of explicit foregrounding of fictionality in a novel just isn't a reliable indicator of its generic status.

Reality check

Realism (and anti-realism, too) has a long history – it is, as Stern notes, 'a perennial mode of representing the world and coming to terms with it' (32). But what it is most commonly associated with is a movement of the nineteenth century, a movement that – as the critical writings of nineteenth-century authors from the continent, from England, and from the Americas, as well as of literary reviewers, suggest – was more or less unified in its opposition to 'romanticism,' narrowly conceived of as an artistic mode committed to the depiction of the fabulous and mired in sentimentalism. It was, however, unified in little else, in contrast to what Alison Lee, for example, supposes in her *Realism and Power: Postmodern British Fiction*. Lee's thesis is that many postmodern novels 'challenge Realist conventions . . . from within precisely those same conventions,' and by so doing 'call into question the basic suppositions made popular by nineteenth-century Realism' (1990: 3).

The literary conventions 'developed in nineteenth-century France and England as a formula for the literal transcription of "reality" into art' ('the dictates of objectivity, impersonality, and documentation' (13)) have, she asserts, 'ideological implications' (ix) – and by 'ideology,' she explains, what she means is 'a general system of beliefs held by a given group which are powerful because unexamined' (142, n.1). These 'basic suppositions,' these 'ideological implications,' Lee discerns in the 'Realist theories . . . often espoused by authors in their critical writings' – rather than in their novels, which, she asserts, 'attest to an opposing practice' (9). 'It would seem,' she adds, 'that many modern literary critics ignore this point. Robert Alter, among others, sees the tradition of the self-conscious novel as one which is in eclipse in the nineteenth century' (9). It is easy, then, she claims, 'to sympathize with Chris Baldick, who, in a review article in the *Times Literary Supplement*, writes:

> Among today's theoreticians of post-modern writing, some remarkable legends about the Dark Ages of nineteenth-century realist fiction have been allowed to gain currency. It can now almost go without saying that the objective of realist fiction was to inhibit any questioning of the world, to induce complacency and stupefying ideological amnesia.
>
> (9–10)

'It could certainly be argued,' Lee states, 'that this is the case with nineteenth- (and twentieth-) century Realist theories, but even the most cursory glance at a nineteenth-century novel will reveal that, for fiction, this is not the case' (10). This is a damaging concession. For, even allowing the wild generalization that the objective of nineteenth-century authors in their critical writings was to inhibit any questioning of the world and to induce stupefying ideological amnesia, if it was not their aim in their fiction, then how could it be that there was a 'general system of beliefs' held by nineteenth-century authors 'which [was] powerful because unexamined'?

Be that as it may, Lee maintains that in nineteenth- and twentieth-century realist theories, 'several now untenable assumptions are clear' (12):

> The first of these is that 'empirical reality' is objectively observable through pure perception. The second is that there can exist a direct transcription from 'reality' to novel. Implicit in this is the idea that language is transparent, that 'reality' creates language and not the reverse. Zola voiced a common hypothesis in 'The Experimental Novel,' that language is 'nothing but logic, a natural and scientific construction.' Finally, there is the notion that there is a common, shared sense of both 'reality' and 'truth.' Fernand Desnoyers has a doctrinaire tone when he writes: 'Since the word truth puts everybody in agreement and since everybody approves of the word, even liars, one must admit that, without being an apologist for ugliness and evil, realism has the right to represent whatever exists and whatever we see.' Similarly, Henry James, in *The Art of the Novel*, explicitly describes reality as 'the things we cannot *not* know sooner or later, in one way or another; it being but one of the accidents of our hampered state, and one of the instances of their quality and number that particular instances have not yet come our way.' This, of course, assumes an objective, eternal essence which, in time, will become readily apparent to all.
>
> (12)

What Lee is ascribing to realists in stating that they assume that empirical reality is objectively observable through pure perception can be inferred from what she asserts twentieth-century linguistic theories have questioned – *viz.* 'our ability to perceive the world as unmediated by language' (34). No such assumption, however, is apparent in the writings of the nineteenth-century authors and critics she mentions; there is nothing to suggest that they would deny the truism that our experience of the world is mediated by language.[9] Nor is there anything to suggest that they believed, as Lee claims, 'that we can apprehend history as a synthetic structure of pure, non-linguistic fact' (34). The idea that prior to the development of postmodernist and poststructuralist theory, writers, critics and philosophers in the west universally believed we could have unmediated access to the past is widely shared by theorists of post-modernism. In terms similar to that of Lee, Nancy J. Peterson, for example, argues that Louise Erdrich's difficulty in completing her 1988 novel, *Tracks*, 'is symptomatic of a crisis: the impossibility of writing traditional history in a postmodern, postrepresentational era' (1994: 983). She claims:

> It seems epistemologically naive today to believe in the existence of a past to which a historian or novelist has unmediated access. Radicalized in the poststructuralist movement, language and linguistics have not only led to skepticism concerning access to the past but also instigated a debate about whether historical narratives can be objective representations or are (merely) subjective constructions of a researcher's and a culture's ideologies. Following Lacan, Saussure, and Althusser, prominent poststructuralists have without regret or nostalgia asserted the textuality of history – that there is no direct access to the past, only recourse to texts about the past.
>
> (982–3)

But who – except perhaps those who believed in the existence of time travel – ever thought we could have direct access to the past? (Indeed, in light of the speculations of some contemporary astrophysicists, people today might be inclined to give more credibility to the possibility of direct access to the past than the people of any other period would have been.) Given that we have only ever had access to the past through texts about the past (and through memories), Peterson's suggestion that 'a historical position in postmodern culture necessitates the recognition that history is a text composed of competing and conflicting representations and meanings,' a recognition that 'precludes any return to a naive belief in transparent historical representation or even in realism' (984), is superfluous – there is nothing to preclude a return to, since historical works, whether in the form of the realist novel or otherwise, have never pretended to be anything other than 'texts about the past.' (And since writers continue to produce texts about the past, continue to produce 'competing and conflicting representations' of it, how can it be that we live, as Peterson claims, in a 'postrepresentational era'?) That is, like Linda Hutcheon, T.V. Reed, and other theorists of postmodernism, Peterson, in arguing that '[t]he new historicity that *Tracks* inscribes is neither a simple return to historical realism nor a passive acceptance of postmodern historical fictionality' (991), is forced to posit a mythical 'naive' realism in order to be able to claim that 'truly' postmodern novels – i.e., those that also respond to 'the excesses of poststructuralism and postmodernism, which attempt to reject the referential function of language and narrative' (991) – have moved beyond it. (This, after she has claimed that 'Erdrich's writing lays tracks . . . for a revisionist history and a new historicity' by defamiliarizing 'the popular narrative of American history as progress' (985).)

That our experience of reality and our access to the past is mediated through language does not necessarily mean, however, that there is no difference between true and false statements, as Lee suggests in asking how fiction and history could 'really be antithetical, if both are related in language' (34), and as Peterson implies in noting that E.L. Doctorow argues in 'False Documents' that 'there is no difference between history and fiction, that both are narratives constructing the only world that can be known' (988).[10] 'Even the facts of history,' Peterson writes, 'are constructed in language' (983). Of course they are, but so what? The implication is that because facts are constructed in language they can't be true. Yet that 'The moon is round' and 'The moon is made of green cheese' are both 'related in language' (indeed, *all* truth-claims are 'related in language') doesn't make the former a fiction, any more than it makes the latter a fact. As Tallis points out:

> the constructed or artefactual nature of facts – their being '*facta*,' 'mades' – does not impugn their truth . . . Facts are selected and constructed but they are not invented; they are made but they are not made up. Between the reality that determines the truth value of the statement and the statement itself there intervenes an enormously complex process of selection, abstraction, generalization, analysis, synthesis, etc. But this will not preclude the latter from being true or false. Just because physical reality – material objects, sensory experiences, perceptions of presence – is not a nexus of 'natural facts,' we are not entitled to conclude that there are no true or realistic facts or that factual truth is an illusion.
>
> (1988b: 25)

That our language and theories are not 'neutral' – that there is no 'view from nowhere' – likewise does not mean that our statements and theories cannot be objectively true, *pace* Peterson, who, in arguing that the narratives of Nanapush and Pauline in *Tracks* 'suggest that history is not objective and impartial, as traditional documentary historians assert,' but 'is always constructed in the interests of a particular party or ideology' (991) sets up a false opposition between objectivity and interest (having, say, an interest in writing a history of the achievements of women because, among other things, I believe that writing such a history will aid in the fight to attain equal rights for women, doesn't necessarily make it any less objectively true that the women I write about did the things that they did).[11] As David Wiggins notes in a discussion of Tarski's T-schema:

> A condition that definitely need not be placed upon replacements for 'p' [in the schema 's is true in L if and only if p'] – and need not be placed upon it even by a card-carrying realist still in possession of his faculties – is that the replacement be a neutral, eternal, placeless-and-timeless, nonperspectival or standpoint-less sentence. Why should *anyone* require this? There is a long standing tendency in controversy about these matters to burden the scientific realist, who thinks that science can aspire to see the world as it is, not only with the correspondence theory of truth, but with this strange unnecessary supposition too.
>
> (1991: 335 n.19)

Wiggins notes that Nicholas Jardine, for example, 'in sidestepping the idea of the "identification of truth in science with representation of the world as it is"' in his *The Fortunes of Inquiry*, 'feels he must gloss the realist's use of the latter phrase with the words (themselves standing in an ambiguous construction) "undistorted by the standpoint of any observer."' Jardine, Wiggins argues, 'thereby implicates the aspiration "to see the world as it is" with the aspiration to see it from no particular standpoint – as if standpoint *itself* were a distortion' (335 n.19). But perspective, Wiggins remarks, 'is not a form of illusion, distortion, or delusion' (108).

As for the related idea that, as Lee puts its, 'there can exist a direct transcription from "reality" to novel' ('[h]istory was seen,' Lee claims, 'as accessible as pure fact, independent of individual perception, ideology, or the process of selection necessitated simply by creating a written narrative' (29)),[12] even Zola, the most outspoken defender of the 'experimental method in the novel,' regarded it as a 'stupid reproach made against us naturalist writers' that 'we wish to be merely photographers' (1963: 168):

In vain we have asserted that we accept temperament and personal expression; people go right on answering us with imbecile
arguments about the impossibility of the strictly true, about the
necessity of arrangement of facts to make any work of art what-
soever. Well, with the application of the experimental method to
the novel all argument comes to an end. The idea of experiment
carries with it the idea of modification.

(168)

The idea that fiction should aim to be a literal transcription or
exact copy of reality is not a realist one. It is, rather, a strawman
of anti-realist polemics, a means of dismissing realism by way of a
sophistical knock-down argument, and, in some cases at least, of
generating a smokescreen for the dubious notion that fiction that
respects external, non-literary constraints cannot be art (as with
Jameson's position that I discussed above). Such a notion appears
to be lurking, for example, in Baudelaire's review of the 1859 Salon,
where he claims that '[i]f photography is allowed to supplement art
in some of its functions, it will soon have supplanted or corrupted
it altogether, thanks to the stupidity of the multitude which is its
natural ally' (1956: 232). He couches his attack on naturalism in
familiar anti-realist terms – 'In matters of painting and sculpture,
the present-day *Credo* of the sophisticated . . . is "I believe that Art
is, and cannot be other than, the exact reproduction of Nature"'
(230) – yet what he is really objecting to is not the naturalist's alleged
desire to transcribe reality literally, but to art that, as he tendentiously puts it, 'bow[s] down before external reality' (233). For, in
so doing, it, in his estimation, degrades itself, 'diminishes its self-
respect' (233).

What Baudelaire thinks accounts for this degradation of art, its
reduction to industry, is a disdain of the 'most honourable and
the most useful of the moral faculties' (236) namely, imagination,
and his encomium to that 'Queen of the Faculties' in his review of
the 1859 Salon is repeated in the critical writings of a number of
twentieth-century writers hostile to literary realism. 'Reality,' writes
Beckett, 'whether approached imaginatively or empirically, remains
a surface, hermetic. Imagination . . . is exercised in vacuo and cannot
tolerate the limits of the real'; 'The reality of imagination,' Federman
asserts, 'is more real than reality without imagination, and besides,
reality as such has never really interested anyone'; 'Our imagination,' Robbe-Grillet states, 'is the organising force of our life, of *our*

world' (quoted in Nash, 1987: 110). Postmodern literary theorists would not, by and large, I think, be comfortable with these appeals to 'imagination,' but the belief that realism threatens the autonomy and distinctiveness of literature, and hence of the autonomy and distinctiveness of the profession of literary criticism, perhaps accounts in part, as Bruce Robbins argues, for 'the strange near-consensus in literary studies today that realism is naive and self-contradictory.' 'I have asked myself,' Robbins writes,

> why it is that the construction of an argument in our discipline so often relies on using 'naive realism' as a negative or scapegoat term that a given author, text, period, or genre can be shown to rise sophisticatedly and self-consciously above. The repetitiveness of this rhetorical structure ought to suggest what in any case [George Levine] has long argued: that 'naive realism' in this sense is not realistically accurate but rather a fiction enlisted for its usefulness in generating arguments. There must be other, less simplistic, ways of generating arguments than this blatant strawmanism. Why then do we persist in it? The answer, I think, is that such arguments are ritualistic reiterations of what the discipline of literary criticism takes to be its founding postulates, reenactments of its creation myth. Realism is not any old subject for criticism; it's what we have told ourselves we exist by not being. . . . Every time a text is triumphantly shown to transcend realism, therefore, the demonstration is only partly about the text; it is also a pious exercise in disciplinary self-corroboration, a demonstration that the discipline of literary criticism is justified in its distinctiveness and autonomy.
>
> (1993: 216–17)

Given that the idea that art that respects external constraints is not art does not bear scrutiny, one ought perhaps to regard Baudelaire – and others who attempt to justify a rejection of realism on like grounds – as simply expressing a preference for anti-realist art (though one should not ignore the extent to which the 'blatant strawmanism' that Robbins refers to has been useful to theorists of postmodernism in generating the kind of grand arguments they are fond of making – there are not other, less simplistic ways of generating such arguments). As Tallis points out in noting his own preference for realist fiction, there is, of course, no God-given reason why fiction, or, indeed, any other form of art, should attempt to be realistic. But this can be acknowledged only after it has been made clear that there is equally no sound reason for rejecting realism – in favour of the various forms of anti-realism. Anti-realism does not have the arguments on its side.

(1988b: 189)

Lee does not have the arguments on her side even if one allows that what she means in claiming that realism assumes 'there can exist a direct transcription from "reality" to art' is that realism assumes that there can be such a thing as art that is constrained by reality, since the assumption that there can be such art is hardly untenable (even if one assumes reality to be a linguistic construct, since there is nothing untenable about the idea of there being art that is constrained by a linguistically constructed reality).

Implicit – or, rather, explicit – in the assumption that there can be fiction that is constrained by reality is certainly the belief that language is intelligible – if that's what Lee means by 'transparent' – but, again, the idea that language is intelligible is far from untenable – indeed, it is a belief shared by anti-realist writers, as well as by postmodernist theorists and critics, including Lee. Language can, of course, be equivocal, vague, ambiguous (though the capacity to recognize equivocality, vagueness, and ambiguity presupposes the 'transparency' of language); it can, moreover, be employed in such a way as to deliberately underscore this fact about it. Zola, for one, however, associates such a use of language with the excesses of romanticism, and, accordingly, inveighs against it: 'Today,' he states, 'we are rotten with lyricism, we wrongly believe that a great style is made of a sublime disorder, always ready to tumble over into madness.' On the contrary, he asserts, a great style 'is made of logic and clarity' (192).

Despite his remarking, then, that once the experimental method is fixed, '[we can] accept all the rhetorics which may be produced' – 'let us,' he writes, 'regard them as the expression of the literary temperaments of the writers' (191–2) – Zola is nonetheless advocating here a certain style for naturalism – a clear, dry, analytical one that was by no means everyone's cup of tea. Which is to say that he does not voice a common hypothesis in claiming that language is 'nothing but logic, a natural and scientific construction.' Flaubert criticized Zola for what he saw as Zola's lack of concern for 'poetry and style, which are the two eternal elements [of literature]' (quoted in Grant, 1970: 29).[13] James, for another, in a review of *Nana*, takes Zola to task not for choice of subject, which, James states, has not 'shocked us,' but for 'the melancholy dryness of his execution, which gives us all the bad taste of a disagreeable dish and none of the nourishment' (1963: 243.) 'The real has not a single shade more affinity with an unclean vessel than with a clean one,' James claims, 'and M. Zola's system, carried to its utmost expression, can dispense as little with taste and tact as the floweriest mannerism of a less analytic age' (240).

Lee's suggestion that implicit in Zola's description of language is 'the idea that "reality" creates language and not the reverse' is likewise questionable. On the one hand, as Zola indicates, language is a *construction*: inanimate physical reality doesn't create language; rather, human beings (among other sentient organisms) create language. On the other, in claiming that postmodernist novels affirm that 'reality is a purely linguistic construct' (25), that 'language creates "reality"' (39), Lee is, of course, implying that implicit in realist theories is the idea that language does not create reality. In suggesting that it does she seems to mean not that our experience of reality is mediated by language – something, in any event, as I have indicated, no one would deny – but that reality does not exist independently of our language, conceptual schemes, or theories. However, like the assumption that there can be fiction that is constrained by reality and like the assumption that language is intelligible, the assumption that reality exists independently of our languages, conceptual schemes, or theories is hardly untenable (it might be false, but it is not untenable).

As plausible as it is, though, Zola does not assume its truth in his exposition of the experimental method; rather, like many positivists, he claims to reject metaphysics altogether. The task of the experimental novelist, Zola states, citing Charles Bernard's *Introduction to the Study of Experimental Medicine*, is to observe and analyze phenomena, and not to engage in futile questioning regarding their ontological status; '[t]he experimental physiologist,' Bernard writes, 'should have neither spiritualism nor materialism. . . . We shall never know either mind or matter, and if this were the occasion, I could easily show that on the one hand as on the other, you quickly reach scientific negations, whence it results that all considerations of this nature are idle and useless' (190).

Whether the positivism Bernard espouses and Zola claims to adopt is in fact anti-metaphysical is another issue. It has often been argued that positivism is implicitly anti-realist. Devitt and Sterelny, for example, note that, according to the (in this case, logical) positivists, 'whether there [is] a reality external to the mind, as the realists claim, or whether all reality is made up of "ideas," "sense data" or "appearances," as idealists claim, is a "meaningless pseudo-question" (Schlick),' that since 'both parties to the dispute agree on the "empirical evidence" (Ayer), the "given" (Schlick),' there is 'nothing substantive [left] to disagree on' (1987: 189). But, they point out,

> at the same time that the positivists are rejecting the metaphysical dispute about the nature of reality, they are making a strong metaphysical assumption about reality: it consists only of the given. What exactly *is* the given? The positivists find it very hard to say. However, a certain view of it always comes through in their writings: it is *the indubitable content of experience*. In other words, the given is indistinguishable from the ideas and sense data of traditional idealists. The positivists are closet anti-realists. Despite their disavowal, they are committed to a powerful and, we claim, thoroughly false metaphysics.
>
> (190)

Galen Strawson, for another, argues that the positivist insistence that 'there is definitely no reason in the nature of things why regularity rather than chaos . . . occurs from moment to moment' is 'a typical dogmatically anti-realist overshoot: a strict empiricist claim about what we can observe flowers into a vast and spectacular metaphysical claim about the nature of things': 'positivist methodology turns into *positivist metaphysics* – a contradiction in terms' (1989: 21–2; his emphasis).

Zola, rather tediously following Bernard in outlining the experimental method for the naturalist writer, talks a lot about data and phenomena. But whether Bernard's claim about the limitations on what we can know (Bernard, Zola remarks, 'made great discoveries' but 'he died admitting that he knew nothing, or nearly nothing' (172)) is more than just that, whether there is enough here to convict him, and by extension, the Zola of 'The Experimental Novel,' of closet anti-realism, I cannot say.

Likewise, James' description of reality as 'the things we cannot *not* know sooner or later,' is, at best, an epistemological, not metaphysical, assertion. There is nothing about it that suggests James assumed the existence of 'an objective, external, essence which, in time, will become readily apparent to all.' Indeed, as Renford Bambrough notes, James, after having read his brother's *Pragmatism*, wrote in acknowledgment that '[a]ll my life I have (like M. Jourdain) unconsciously pragmatized' (quoted in Bambrough, 1986: 169) – though, Bambrough adds, 'it is debatable whether [James] can reasonably enrol himself in his brother's philosophical school, or in any other' (1986: 169). 'What is unquestionable,' he claims, 'is that [James] consciously and unconsciously constantly philosophized. And that is what he thought the novelist must do' (169).[14]

Finally, Desnoyers may well have a doctrinaire tone when he writes that 'realism has the right to represent whatever exists and whatever we see' – after all, he is writing a manifesto. And, to be sure, the notion that there is a common, shared sense of both reality and truth informs his assertions – but no more so than such a notion informs Lee's own claims about postmodernist fiction.[15] Indeed less so, since Desnoyers, in the course of his anti-romanticist tirade, has nothing to say about the nature of truth or reality:

> It is through this underbrush, this battle of the Cimbri, this Pandemonium of Greek temples, lyres, and jews' harps, of alhambras and sickly oaks, of boleros, of silly sonnets, of golden odes, of rusty daggers, rapiers, and weekly columns, of hamadryads in the moonlight and the tenderness of Venus, of marriages in the manner of M. Scribe, of witty caricatures and unretouched photographs, of canes and false collars, of toothless discussions and criticisms, of tottery traditions, of ill-fitting customs and couplets addressed to the public, that Realism has made a breach.
>
> (1963: 87)

To appreciate this rhetoric (and fine rhetoric at that) requires no more in the way of a common, shared sense of reality and truth than is required to appreciate Shakespeare's 'My mistress's eyes are nothing like the sun' – whatever the nature of reality and truth, it is widely believed that women are not goddesses, and that Venus, 'diaphanous nymphs,' and 'gods with silver bows' (81) do not exist. To suggest that in the late twentieth century there is no common, shared sense of reality and truth is not only disingenuous, but also pragmatically self-refuting – it is an instance of what David Stove wittily calls the 'Ishmael effect,' which theorists of postmodernism are plagued by. Ishmael, by the end of *Moby-Dick*, is the only survivor, and on being found he quotes from the Book of Job: 'I only am escaped alone to tell thee.' But suppose, Stove suggests, that:

> a man told us that he had been one of those on board a certain ship, and that, in an encounter with a whale, *everyone* on board the ship had perished. Then his statement would suffer from a severe defect, of a peculiar kind, which I call (by a slight licence) the Ishmael effect: for if his statement were true, he could not have made it.
>
> (1991: 61)

If the statement that there is no common, shared sense of reality and truth were true, Lee could not have made it.[16] Or, as Tallis puts it, citing Bernard Bergonzi's pronouncements that 'we have no common sense of reality,' that '[w]e are saddled with all kinds of relativistic structures,' and that '[w]e do not believe in there being "one reality" out there as Tolstoy undoubtedly did':

> We should note how the scope and confidence of Bergonzi's assertions is at odds with what they say about the 'we' who have no common sense of reality. The total lack of confidence that should follow from the collapse of such a reality is signally absent. Who, moreover, is this 'we'? Does it include me? Does Bergonzi mean to include the whole world? Or only the students in his seminars? If his 'we' encompasses more than the few people he knows, does this not imply that the common sense of reality that he deems to have come to an end is in fact very much alive?.... Bergonzi's merely typical claims about contemporary reality and the modern novel illustrate the way in which many critics' assertions presuppose a much more understandable and unified reality than common sense would normally allow while at the same time they postulate a lesser degree of either of those things than anyone in his senses would accept.
>
> (1988b: 17–18)

Lee's assertion, moreover, that the 'attacks on Realism' provided by 'recent linguistic and critical theories' pose a 'threat because [they] question[ ] the very nature of "reality" and "truth,"' that in claiming that 'these are merely linguistic constructs with no absolute value,' such theories 'radically undermine[ ] a whole system of social and pedagogical control which depends for its power on there being a "good" or a "truth" which is transcendental' (27), betrays an ignorance of the fact that, for example, both defenders and detractors of Zola's naturalism discerned in it a repudiation of a ' "good" or "truth" which is transcendental.' One W.S. Lilly, a detractor, writes in an 1885 essay entitled 'The New Naturalism' that

> the writings of M. Zola and his school ... are the most popular literary outcome of the doctrine which denies the personality, liberty, and spirituality of man and the objective foundation on which these rest, which empties him of the moral sense, the feeling of the infinite, the aspiration towards the Absolute, which makes of him nothing more than a sequence of action and reaction, and the first and last word of which is sentism.
>
> (1963: 288)

And, Roger Sherman Loomis argues in a 'A Defense of Naturalism' that it 'discards as obsolete ... absolute morality':

> Naturalistic morality differs ... from conventional morality in its relativity. The notion of an eternal code, confided by Infallible Wisdom to the visions of seers and the conscience of every individual does not appeal to the Naturalistic thinker. ... The Naturalist has come to believe that conscience, an emotional assurance of the rightness of one's actions, varies so uniformly with the social conventions about it that it can no more be relied on than a compass in the neighborhood of masses of iron.
>
> (1963: 538–9)

Lee's assertions about the 'untenable assumptions' of realism, the 'ideological implications' of its conventions, then, are, specious. The most prominent and recurring theme of the nineteenth-century realist criticism and theory that George Becker has usefully collected is, as he himself notes, the expression of 'a general aspiration toward a literature which would have to do directly with contemporary life and would break away from hackneyed subjects and stereotyped formulas, particularly those of romanticism' (1963: v). 'At the point where modern realism began,' he writes, 'romanticism was the enemy, something against which young writers could unite, however much they ultimately differed as to the course literature should follow'; the 'complaints against romanticism' in realist critical writing 'add up to a very simple observation: the prevailing mode was thin and lifeless because it had lost touch with ordinary, everyday life' (5).

No consensus about the nature of reality, truth, knowledge, self, or morality emerges from this attack on what was regarded as conventional, hackneyed, and stereotypical in romantic writing. And no such consensus emerges from twentieth-century anti-realist attacks on what came to be seen as conventional, hackneyed, and stereotypical in realist writing either (or from twentieth-century neorealist attacks on what has come to be seen as conventional, hackneyed and stereotypical in anti-realist writing) – which is to say that Lee's imposition of postmodernist dogma on the fiction she discusses, her reduction of it to an expression of linguistic idealism (a metaphysics that many theorists of postmodernism unquestioningly suppose[17] is not only the truth about the nature of reality, but about everything else as well) is as troubling as her account of realist theory and criticism.[18]

7

Literature, Science, and Postmodernist Theory

The invention of the episteme engine

In 'Why Realism Matters: Literary Knowledge and the Philosophy of Science,' Paisley Livingston discusses what he terms 'sociological holism' and the problems with it as an approach to literary study. 'A central problem,' he claims,

> has been the failure of critical theorists to grasp the most basic lessons of methodological individualism. Critics ask how a particular work 'reflects' or 'contests' some social totality or dominant discourse, but they fail to reflect sufficiently on the ontological status of the latter, endowing it with dubious causal powers. Moreover, such critics typically fail to confront the difficult epistemological problems that are raised by this kind of sociological holism, which typically begins and ends with some set of untested theses about the nature of global structures, moments, systems, and sets of institutions. The heroic critic takes on the monumental task of mediating back and forth between claims about the social totality and the particular work, but the results of these dialectical efforts are easily challenged by historians who are closer to the facts. Another typical shortcoming of holist sociologists, and of the literary criticisms inscribed within them, is that they typically fail to attend sufficiently to the processes at work in the individual agent's assimilation of, and resistance to, the influences, discourses, etc., of the putative social totality. Holist critics fail to ask in what concrete ways the many faces of the totality make themselves known to the individual agent. We are simply supposed to take it for granted that social orders are 'habitus forming.'

> (1993: 147)

The story of literary history from realism to postmodernism that many theorists of postmodernism tell is marked by just the kind

153

of problematic holist assumptions that Livingston identifies here. Holism takes a number of forms in theories of postmodernism. Fredric Jameson, for example, sees realism, modernism, and postmodernism as the manifestation of market capitalism, monopoly capitalism, and multinational capitalism, respectively. It is one consequence of multinational capitalism, according to Jameson, that

> [f]or better or for worse, art does not seem in our society to offer any direct access to reality, any possibility of unmediated representation or of what used to be called realism. For us today, it is generally the case that what looks like realism turns out at best to offer unmediated access only to what we think about reality, to our images and ideological stereotypes about it.
>
> (1991: 150)

The problem with this argument is that it is founded on the assumption that 'what used to be called realism' did offer direct, unmediated access to reality. But as I've been arguing, realism never did do that, and so Jameson's suggestion that the condition of possibility of realism doing what it didn't in fact do was the emergence of market capitalism can't be right. By the same token, it can't be that the fact that art today doesn't offer direct, unmediated access to reality is a peculiar consequence of the emergence of multinational capitalism. Most attempts by theorists of postmodernism to define realism, modernism, and postmodernism in terms of global structures, systems, or moments are, like Jameson's, predicated on questionable assumptions about (what is labeled) realist, modernist, and postmodernist fiction that derive either from misconceptions about the global structure, system, or moment appealed to, or from misconceptions about the implications of such a structure, system, or moment.

The shortcomings of holism are clearly exposed in the attempts of a number of contemporary theorists to cast eighteenth- and nineteenth-century fiction as a reflection of a Newtonian worldview, and early and/or late twentieth-century fiction as a reflection of an Einsteinian and post-Einsteinian worldview. In *Fiction in the Quantum Universe*, Susan Strehle, for one, argues that:

> [r]ealist fiction represented the Newtonian cosmos, in all its causal continuity. Examining the novel's origins in the eighteenth century, Ian Watt underscores its rejection of the classical and medieval

heritage of universals in favor of the position of philosophical realism, 'that truth can be discovered by the individual through his senses.' This assumption belongs, of course, as much to Newton as it does to Descartes and Locke; it has disappeared from the conception of reality in recent physics. Describing the analogies between philosophical realism and prose fiction, Watt sketches a ground mapped powerfully in classical physics. 'The methods of investigation' used in philosophical realism and the novel,' Watt says, emphasize 'the study of the particulars of experience by the individual investigator, who, ideally at least, is free from the body of past assumptions and traditional beliefs.'

(1992: 15)

The premise of Strehle's book is that while eighteenth- and nineteenth-century realist fiction reflects the 'Newtonian worldview,' reflects what she claims became 'the new universal principles relied on unawares by realistic fiction – a faith in 'absolute mathematical time and space, in causality, in objectivity and certainty' (15) – postmodernist fiction reflects a post-Einsteinian view of reality. What renders postmodernist fiction different from both eighteenth-/ nineteenth- and early twentieth-century fiction, she argues, is that it 'engage[s] the outer world,' yet reflects a view of reality as discontinuous, relative, subjective, and uncertain, thus 'neither merely repudiat[ing] nor merely imitat[ing] either [its] twentieth-century modernist parents or [its] nineteenth-century premodernist grandparents' (quoting Barth), but forging instead 'an original fusion that transforms both strands of [this] literary heritage' (6).

This pat thesis is unconvincing for a number of reasons. First of all, the theory that knowledge is primarily derived, not from innate ideas (as Descartes and other rationalists claimed), but from sense experience – did not, as Strehle suggests, produce a faith in absolute mathematical space and time, in causality, in objectivity, and certainty. On the one hand, empiricism does not entail the truth of particular theories about the nature of time and space or causality – it is not 'a conception of reality,' but a theory of knowledge. On the other, from Locke, who argued that the knowledge human beings could attain was both limited and in many cases not certain, to Hume, who maintained that what we perceive as a necessary connection between cause and effect in objects is the product of habits of mind and that we could know nothing of the ultimate nature of this relation, to the logical positivists who either claimed that causality was mere regularity in succession or viewed the question of whether there was something more to causation than this as a meaningless one, empiricism has always engendered some degree of skepticism with respect to causality, objectivity, and certainty.[1]

Second, Strehle's argument is based on the assumption that there is a causally determining relation between scientific/philosophical theories and literature. Not only is this assumption questionable in its own right; it is also at odds with her claim that one aspect of contemporary physics reflected in contemporary fiction is the rejection of causality – for if there's no such thing as causality, there can be no such thing as a causally determining relation between Newtonian physics and realist fiction. She claims, for instance, that the repudiation of causality is reflected in the fact that the episodes of Pynchon's *Gravity's Rainbow* 'cannot be said to "produce" or "cause" others, but rather to parallel each other, metaphorically' (29). But given this, how can she claim that 'changes in physical theories inspire [i.e., cause or produce] changes in a culture's general attitudes' (8)?

Whether she can or not, she does, and this is because she wants to argue that there is a fundamental difference between realist and postmodernist fiction with respect to the conception of reality reflected in each ('[a]ctualism differs from previous modes of fiction,' she asserts, 'not only in the vastly altered reality emerging at the level of content, or theme, but also in the renewal it accomplishes at the level of fictive form' (15)). Strehle could not hope to make good on such an argument by merely suggesting, for example, that some eighteenth- and nineteenth-century realist writers were interested in Newtonian physics and expressed this interest in their fiction, because such a suggestion would be too weak to support the categorical claims she needs to make about realist fiction in order to demonstrate not only that it is 'outmoded'[2] but also 'pernicious' ('[a]ctualistic texts,' she states, 'attempt to dispel the outmoded and pernicious Newtonian/realist system and to deconstruct the literary forms it has authorized' (64–5)).

So she argues instead that such principles as absolute mathematical time and space, causality, objectivity, and certainty became the new principles relied upon *unawares* by realist writers. This line of argument has the further advantage of relieving Strehle of the responsibility of having to show how and where, exactly, faith in such principles makes itself apparent in realist fiction generally – these principles underwrote the scientific and philosophical theories of the time, the story goes, and so they just *have* to be reflected in realist fiction. She attempts to bolster this crude trickle-down theory with the following:

> In a persuasive argument for the realistic novel's basis in New-tonian assumptions, Robert Nadeau writes, 'The novelist was con-fident in his ability to depict the objectively real in fiction because he implicitly assumed, as Newton did, that its essential structures were known to him. Since the conceptual forms inherent in the construction of the fictive landscape were presumed to have an actual existence in the life of nature, the objective space of the novel, to use the eighteenth-century metaphor, was regarded as the mirror held up to objective space itself.'
>
> (15–16)

Even if we grant that Newton did assume that the essential struc-tures of reality were known to him (which he didn't – 'the cause of gravity,' he wrote, 'I do not pretend to know' (quoted in Strawson, 1989: 202)), Nadeau's argument doesn't provide any evidence that realist novelists did. Nadeau merely assumes what needs to be proven. He does, unlike Strehle, acknowledge that one might object to his study on the grounds that the suggestion that 'novelists are causally influenced by ideas from physics appears specious' (1981: 15) – though it's only fair to point out that it is not clear that it is the notion that novelists are causally *determined* to reflect the assumptions of scientific theories that Nadeau is responding to in raising this possible objection. That is, the idea that novelists are influenced by scientific theories is not questionable – rather, what is questionable is the systematic way in which Strehle, in the ab-sence of providing any kind of argument for the truth of determin-ism (indeed, she appears to reject determinism) imagines all realist fiction to be reflecting *unawares* a faith in absolute space and time, causality, certainty, and objectivity, the implication being that it couldn't have done otherwise. In contrast, it seems that at least in part what Nadeau is trying to do by raising and answering the possible objection to his study that the notion that novelists are causally influenced by ideas from physics appears specious is to offer an explanation that would make plausible his premise that the effect of scientific theories is such that the 'diverse products of a given culture' are similar in form and meaning, in light of the fact that most writers don't have an intimate knowledge of scientific theories. 'I am inclined,' Nadeau explains, to view change as it is conceived in quantum physics as analogous to that form of change on the macro level called civilization. From this perspective civilization, like all processes in nature, is a complex interplay of forces within which it is impossible to isolate a particular idea and determine its fixed and final relationship to any other idea. *Intellectual climate* is that vague but useful term we normally use to denote these forces, the effects of which we witness in diverse products of a given culture that closely resemble one another in form and meaning in spite of the fact that they might be produced by individuals who had no direct contact with one another's art or ideas.

(16; emphasis in original)

'Intellectual climate' is, I agree, a vague but nonetheless useful term – Darwin's ideas, for example, contributed to the intellectual climate of the mid-nineteenth century in a way that distinguishes this epoch from other epochs, and his work certainly had an impact on many poets and novelists of the time (and continues to have an impact today). But surely no one would want to claim that Darwinianism became an implicit assumption of mid- and late nineteenth-century literature (e.g., that every novelist or poet implicitly assumed, say, the truth of natural selection). Likewise, Freud's ideas are a part of the twentieth-century intellectual climate, but it could not be argued that Freudianism is an implicit assumption of early and late twentieth-century literature (e.g., that all twentieth-century fiction implicitly assumes, say, that it is true that women suffer from penis-envy). And so it is with the ideas of Newton, Locke, Berkeley, Hume, Kant, and other important thinkers of the seventeenth and eighteenth centuries – that is to say, first of all, that there were other thinkers around at the time besides Newton, and secondly, that there's no a priori reason for assuming that eighteenth-century writers were any more the stupid and unreflective mouthpieces of some scientist's or philosopher's views (or of their popularization) than are twentieth-century writers.

There is a difference, then, on the one hand, between identifying the ideas that contribute to the intellectual climate of a historical moment (Newton's theory of gravity, Berkeley's immaterialism, Darwin's theory of natural selection, Freud's theory of the unconscious), and discussing, where relevant, the impact those ideas had or have on writers, and claiming on the other that since Berkeley, for example, was an important thinker of the eighteenth century (and friendly with Addison, Swift, Steele, and Pope), it can be assumed that eighteenth-century writers in general were immaterialists. For, among other things, artists of a given period are not all influenced, even indirectly, by the same scientific or philosophical theories, and even those who are don't necessarily read them or respond to them in the same way. So I contest Nadeau's suggestion, predicated on the assumption of a unified *Weltanschauung* rather than on the notion of direct influence, that we do witness the effects of an intellectual climate 'in the diverse products of a given culture that closely resemble one another in form and meaning' – that is, I don't see that the effects of an intellectual climate are such that the products of a given culture will necessarily closely resemble one another in form and meaning. Indeed, it's hard to see how the products of a given culture could really be said to be diverse if they all closely resembled one another in form and meaning.

Similar problems to those I have identified with Nadeau's appeal to the notion of 'intellectual climate' also beset N. Katherine Hayles's appeal to the related idea of a 'climate of opinion' in her *The Cosmic Web: Scientific Field Models and Literary Strategies in the Twentieth-Century*. 'That Saussure's proposals are remarkably similar in spirit to those occurring about the same time in physics and mathematics does not,' Hayles argues, 'require that Saussure knew of Einstein's 1905 papers or read *Principia Mathematica*':

> Indeed, to suppose that such parallels require direct lines of influence is to be wedded to the very notions of causality that a field model renders obsolete. A more accurate and appropriate model for such developments would be a field notion of culture, a societal matrix which consists (in Whitehead's phrase) of a 'climate of opinion' that makes some questions interesting to pursue and others uninteresting or irrelevant. Such a field theory of culture has yet to be definitively articulated, and it is beyond the scope of this study. But it is already possible to see some of the elements it would include. It would, for example, define more fully how a 'climate of opinion' is established, and demonstrate that it is this climate, rather than direct borrowing or transmission, that is the underlying force guiding intellectual inquiry. The climate would be, of course, as capable of influencing scientific inquiry as it is of guiding any other conceptualizations. Such a history would insist that we not be misled by a causal perspective into thinking of correspondences between disciplines as

one-way exchanges, for example, by asserting that the change in scientific paradigms *caused* a shift in literary form.

(1989: 22–3; her emphasis)

'In its treatment of the modern novel,' Hayles continues,

this history would show that the cultural matrix was so configured as to draw modern novelists to considerations similar to those Saussure entertained. It would point out, for example, that just as linguistic meaning in a field model was deemed to derive from relational exchanges within the language system, so meaning in a literary text was deemed to derive not from a mimetic relationship between the text and 'real life,' but from the internal relations of literary codes.

(23)

Like 'intellectual climate,' 'climate of opinion' seems a potentially useful conceit. However, Hayles's account of the notion of a 'climate of opinion' and of how this notion might inform the construction of a history of ideas and its relationship to twentieth-century literature is fraught. For one thing, Hayles assumes that Saussure did consider the meaning of signs to be intra-linguistic. She rightly observes that Saussure argued that language systems should be regarded as 'unified systems in which meaning *derives* from the relational exchanges' (22; my emphasis), but then commits the error commonly committed by theorists of postmodernism in their interpretation of Saussure of confusing how signs mean with what they mean by arguing that '[t]he effect of this view was to locate meaning not in a one-to-one correspondence between the sign and its external referent, but in the relations between signs' (22). Since it is questionable that Saussure was drawn to entertain the notion that the meaning of signs is located in the relations between them, Hayles's suggestion that there was a cultural matrix so configured as to draw modern novelists to entertain considerations similar to those she ascribes to Saussure is also questionable. That is to say, it may well be that a number of modern novelists *did* consider meaning to be intra-linguistic, or assume as she suggests, that 'literature, like language, is an internal system that has no necessary reference to anything outside it' (23), but if they did, the fact of their so doing would not necessarily be capable of being explained by reference to a cultural matrix of the sort she outlines. She argues that her study begins with the premise that the history she has been sketching 'would end by establishing' – namely, 'that well-known developments in the novel are part of a larger paradigm shift within the culture to the field concept' (24). But it just the premise of a larger paradigm shift – 'a revolution in world view' (15) – that is unconvincing.

It is not just unconvincing because Hayles's representation of Saussure's position is questionable. It's also that the theory that meaning is intralinguistic does not seem 'remarkably similar in spirit' to theories being proposed by Einstein or Russell at about the same time. As Paul Gross and Norman Levitt point out in a discussion of Hayles's *Chaos Bound*:

> The cultural moment, she reasons, has brought forth chaos theory simultaneously with Derrida's *Of Grammatology* and de Man's *Allegories of Reading*, and hence, some unspecified mechanism of the zeitgeist must be responsible for both developments. This is a bizarre thesis. Why should the theory of dynamical systems be more closely related to the gyrations of literary exegetes than it is to major league baseball or Jane Fonda's workout tape? Aside from the irrelevant fact that both kinds of theorizing take place, for the most part, on university campuses, there is no ground for positing any kind of conceptual relationship. Hayles's arguments, such as they are, are based on subjective and shoddy analogies, leaky metaphors, and (not unusual for work immersed in postmodern theory) flat and unsupported assertions.
>
> (1994: 99)

Hayles admits that most of the authors she is concerned with 'know little of science, and what little they know is often colored by their idiosyncratic interpretations' (24), and the remarks of a number of those authors – Pirsig, Lawrence, and Nabokov, for example – about twentieth-century science that she cites seem to bear out her observation. But Hayles is not content to argue that she is merely exploring the idiosyncratic interpretations of a handful of novelists to twentieth-century physical and mathematical theories – rather, she claims that the authors she discusses are 'not reacting to science as such, but to a more general set of ideas pervasive in the culture' (25). If indeed, however, these novelists know of little of science and what they do know is colored by their idiosyncratic interpretations of it, then Hayles's claim, for example, that Lawrence and

Nabokov, despite their being 'relatively ignorant of the new science, nevertheless participate in the cultural matrix and so, willy-nilly, encounter in some way the matrix's underlying paradigm' (26) is debatable. On the one hand, if, for example, what any number of scientists are proposing is different from what any number of novelists believe they are proposing, then the parallelism that would be required to warrant positing the existence of such an underlying paradigm does not obtain. On the other, even if some of the parallelisms Hayles argues for do obtain – and I don't deny that some of them might – they are neither pervasive enough nor specific enough to justify positing the existence of a 'revolution in world view.' Hayles argues, for example, that the new science rejects the belief 'in causality, in an objective world that exists independently of human perception, and in the universal truth of scientific law' (48). Some scientists have indeed rejected such beliefs, and it is plausible to assume that some novelists have as well. However, only some scientists have done so; many others have not. Further, the belief in causality, in an objective world that exists independently of human perception, and in the truth of scientific law have been questioned for centuries, and so it can't be that the possibility of questioning them is a specific consequence of developments in twentieth-century science, literature, or philosophy. For there to be a revolution in world view, there have to be, well, revolutionary ideas, and the idea that, say, metaphysical realism is false just wasn't revolutionary in the early twentieth century.

Even a theorist like Ihab Hassam, who acknowledges the problems involved with positing analogies between science and literature and with assuming that there is a consensus among contemporary scientists about, for instance, causality, the nature of reality, and the universal truth of scientific law, still wants to argue for the existence of a distinctive postmodern episteme in which twentieth-century science participates. 'Granting that we inhabit neither a Newtonian nor Laplacian universe,' he writes, 'how then can the new sciences contribute to a definition of postmodernism?':

> The question must be answered by admitting first its obdurancies. Scientific concepts, we are cautioned, should not be confused with cultural metaphors and literary tropes. Nor is there unanimity among scientists themselves concerning the implications of their discoveries. Against the instrumentalism of Bohr, Einstein to the end clung to his realism, while Schrödinger stood uneasily

between. We encounter another difficulty when we coerce mathematical forms to yield philosophical statements about the nature of reality; the former tend to vanish, leaving behind only an abstract grin.

(1987: 60)

'Admittedly,' he notes, 'current analogies between science, culture, and sundry artistic and spiritual phenomenon can prove too facile' (63). However, despite having made these observations, he still argues that 'Relativity, uncertainty, complementarity, and incompleteness are not simply mathematical idealizations; they are concepts that begin to constitute our cultural languages; they are a new order of knowledge founded on both indeterminacy and immanence.' (62–3). He claims that 'it is possible to be at once too rigorous and too timorous in exploring the cognitive possibilities of homologies' (63), but the problem is that since the order of knowledge in the late twentieth century doesn't partake, for example, of the relativity that Einstein's theory describes – and it doesn't even if one allows for the sake of argument that it is grounded in a widely shared belief in the truth of relativism because Einstein's theory is anti-relativistic – it's not clear that there are homologies here in which 'we may . . . discover models for our own historical moment' (63). In other words, one has to be at once both rigorous and timorous in exploring the cognitive possibility of the homologies Hassan wants to explore, for only if, among other things, the relativity that Einstein's theory describes or the uncertainty that Heisenberg's principle describes also described the order of knowledge as such in the late twentieth century would there be grounds for positing the emergence of a new episteme. To analogize from the particular kind of uncertainty, for example, that the uncertainty principle describes to an uncertainty about our knowledge in general is not only to fail to understand that the uncertainty principle itself is not uncertain, but is also to describe a kind of uncertainty that is not unique to the late twentieth century and that hence cannot be claimed as a concept in which we may discover a model for our own historical moment.

   Strehle and Nadeau also premise their arguments on a number of ideas that are too general to be called 'Newtonian' and 'post-Newtonian' – ideas that, because of this generality, fail to be of any use in delineating something like an eighteenth-, nineteenth-, or twentieth-century *Zeitgeist*. Strehle, for example, argues that Jack

Gibbs, a physics teacher in William Gaddis's *J R*, attempts, in telling his students that '[o]rder is simply a thin perilous condition we try to impose on the basic reality of chaos,' to introduce them to

> the new physical world, grounded in energy which dissipates rather in enduring, stable, predictable matter. Gibbs voices Gaddis' awareness of the pernicious hold the old, Newtonian physics continues to retain in the public curriculum and the popular imagination.
>
> (95)

Newtonian physics, however, has nothing to do with the 'pernicious hold' that a belief in determinate, stable, and enduring matter continues to retain in the 'popular' imagination – for one thing, people believed matter was stable and persistent long before Newton arrived on the scene; for another, my cat, who hasn't had the benefits of a public school education and who has no access to the imagination of the apparently misguided and unenlightened masses, is, nevertheless, repeatedly able to gauge accurately the distance between the table and the windowsill, a feat it presumably could not perform if the objects it negotiated did not appear to it to be stable, determinate, and persistent. Which is to say that interactions among individual quantum systems do yield something enduring, stable and predictable – *viz.*, macrophysical objects. In claiming that 'the new physical world [is] grounded in energy which dissipates rather than in enduring, stable, predictable matter' and that the term 'uncertain,' among others, begins 'to describe the external world as we know it in the later years of the twentieth century' (218), Strehle confuses what Michael Morton argues 'might be called spheres of relevance' (1993: 312 n.31). '[T]he mistake (repeatedly pointed out by Wittengstein),' he notes, is that of

> lifting the grammar of a given language-game out of the realm in which it is at home and seeking to apply it in another realm, to which, however, it has no connection. To conclude, for example, from the indeterminate nature of elementary particles that the phenomena of everyday life are themselves correspondingly indeterminate (and, in that sense, uncertain) would be analogous to supposing that in conversation with an acquaintance I do not really know to whom I am speaking if I am unable to specify his blood type or whether he dreams in black and white or in color.
>
> (312 n.31)

That macrophysical reality in the later years of the twentieth century is as determinate and stable as it was in the eighteenth and nineteenth centuries is not, however, in the final analysis, relevant to Strehle's argument, since, despite her claiming that actualist fiction 'departs from the stable material reality underpinning Newtonian science' and that it 'abandons and even subverts the narrative conventions of realism' not in order to 'replace reality with the purified aesthetics of self-reflexivity' but rather to 'renew art's readiness for its perennial project: the human interpretation of a nonhuman reality' (7), it becomes clear in the course of her analysis of it that her concern is not so much with its interpretation of nonhuman reality as with its interpretation of human reality. And since the uncertainties of human reality that she argues are thematized in actualist fiction are persistently thematized in realist fiction as well, her thesis that actualist fiction is original in this respect falls flat on its face. It is because Strehle wants to claim that the thematization of uncertainty is what distinguishes postmodernist fiction from realist fiction that she fails pursue what would perhaps have been a more profitable line of argument: that the difference between, say, a George Eliot and a Thomas Pynchon is not that the former represents human beings as possessing certainty in matters metaphysical, epistemological, religious, moral, or political, and that the latter does not, but that each appropriates different scientific concepts as metaphors for the uncertainties that have historically attended human beings' understanding of such matters. Quantum uncertainty is not literally figured in the fiction Strehle discusses; it has no specific bearing on the uncertainties of human reality that she focuses on, and so it can at best only be functioning metaphorically. But because Strehle appears to think it is quantum physics that gives rise to the very idea that human reality is uncertain, she is blinded to the possibility of pursuing the issue of the specific ways quantum uncertainty functions metaphorically in the fiction she has chosen to analyze. And so, as her argument stands, quantum physics is more or less superfluous to it. What Gross and Levitt identify as the tendency of a number of theorists of postmodernism to 'stud[ ] their essays with knowing references to chaos theory as a way of dressing up truisms about the complexity of life, art, and human experience' (95) fairly describes the use to which Strehle puts quantum mechanical principles in her book.

The idea that reality exists independently of mind and that our senses yield true knowledge of it is also hardly distinctive of eighteenth- and nineteenth-century thought, much less peculiarly Newtonian. At the same time, both metaphysical and epistemological realism are theses too specific to be identified as defining features of realist fiction generally. As Watt, to whom Strehle appeals, points out in his discussion of what he calls 'philosophical realism,' 'the view that the external world is real, and that our senses give us a true report of it, obviously does not in and of itself throw light on literary realism'; people in all ages, he writes, have 'in one way or another been forced to some such conclusion about the external world by [their] own experience' (1957: 12). Though Watt does seek to establish analogies between literary realism and what he calls philosophical realism, he is patently not attempting to demonstrate that eighteenth- and nineteenth-century realist fiction 'represented the Newtonian cosmos, in all its causal continuity,' or that such narrow and specific theses as metaphysical and epistemological realism are inherent components of all realist fiction. '[T]he distinctive tenets of realist epistemology,' he argues

> are for the most part too specialised in nature to have much bearing on literature. What is important to the novel in philosophical realism is much less specific; it is rather the general temper of realist thought, the methods of investigation it has used, and the kinds of problems it has raised.
>
> (12)

There are, nevertheless, problems with Watt's argument. On the one hand, the distinctive tenets of realist epistemology are not too specialized to have a bearing on literature; rather, they are too specialized to have a bearing on the definition of literary realism. On the other, what he describes as the general temper of philosophical realism ('anti-traditional and innovating'), its methods of investigation ('the study of the particulars of experience by the individual investigator, who, ideally at least, is free from the body of past assumptions'), and the kinds of problems it has raised ('the nature of the correspondence between words and reality') (12) are too general – the nature of the correspondence between words and reality, for example, has always been a concern of western philosophers – to support the claim that there are nontrivial analogies between literary and philosophical realism.

If what Watt describes as the general temper of philosophical realism, its methods of investigation, and the kinds of problems it has raised are too general to give weight to the argument that there is a nontrivial relationship between it and literary realism, Nadeau's assertion that the conceptual forms inherent in the construction of the fictive landscape in the realist novel were presumed to have had an actual existence in the life of nature, that '[t]he primary opposition within the novel itself, between the character-substance and all other external presences in the map space, clearly implies that the world is a thing apart from the people who occupy it' (187) is too specific a claim about realist fiction to be supported by the evidence he adduces for it. That is, what he describes as the 'split in the novel between consciousness and the objects of perception' (187) does not, in and of itself, necessarily imply that the objects of perception in the real world are mind-independent. Such a split is also compatible with the idea that objects are constituted out of perceptions.

It's not just Nadeau's assumption that the split between consciousness and objects of perception is evidence that the conceptual forms inherent in the construction of the fictive landscape in the realist novel were presumed to have had an actual existence in the life of nature that is problematic. It's also his assumption that the reason they were was because such was 'the idea of the time' in the eighteenth and nineteenth centuries, since, in point of fact, whatever Newton's views, realist theories no more dominated the philosophical scene then than anti-realist theories do today. Indeed, skepticism both about the existence of an independent reality and about the possibility of objective, certain knowledge of it was prevalent in eighteenth- and nineteenth-century philosophical thought. As Richard Popkin – summarizing Georgio Tonelli's 'The Weakness of Reason in the Age of Enlightenment' – remarks:

[A]s an introduction to their epistemological claims, most major eighteenth-century thinkers, far from exalting the power of reason, pointed out that it could not *know* about a real world independent of the mind. The subjectivity of all knowledge was usually alleged to have been demonstrated already by Gassendi, Locke, Fontenelle, even Pascal. Locke's denial of scientific knowledge, or knowledge that could not possibly be false, was taken as proof that we could know only about our experiences, not whether they and our knowledge about them related to independent real objects.

(1992: 285)

And any number of nineteenth-century thinkers tended, as John Passmore notes, 'toward the conclusion that both "things" and facts about things [were] dependent for their existence upon the operations of a mind' (1957: 175). Neither Mill, Green, Bradley, nor James, among others, Passmore argues, 'however near they came to this point,' was 'prepared explicitly and consistently to assert that facts are merely *recognised* by a mind, not made by it. And in this refusal they were seconded by the genetic sciences – biology, psychology, anthropology – which flourished in the nineteenth century as never before' (175). So it's not surprising to find, for example, the speaker in the young Tennyson's 'The Devil and the Lady' querying:

> Yet I know not your natures, or if that
> Which we call palpable and visible
> Is condensation of firm particles.
> O suns and spheres and stars and belts and systems,
> Are ye or are ye not?
> Are ye realities or semblances
> Of that which men call real?
> Are ye true substance? Are ye anything
> Except delusive shows and physical points
> Endowed with some repulsive potency?
> Could the Omnipotent fill all space, if ye
> Or the least atom in ye or the least
> Division of that atom (if least can dwell
> In infinite divisibility) should be impenetrable?
> I have some doubt if ye exist when none
> Are by to view ye.
>
> (1969: 29–30)

Nadeau assumes that the conceptual forms inherent in the structure of the fictive landscape in the realist novel were presumed to have had an independent existence in the life of nature because, among other things (e.g., that such a metaphysics is entailed by Newtonian physics), he assumes that metaphysical realism was generally held to be true. But if his model of the relationship between scientific-philosophical ideas and literature is valid, then, by the terms of his argument, his claim must be false, since metaphysical realism was by no means generally held to be true. Likewise if, as James Mellard claims, it is true that 'the novel has always depended upon those conceptions of nature, reality, and the world given the highest credibility in any epoch' (1980: 14) then his assertion that 'the traditional novelist seldom questions our assumptions under-lying either the reality of the world or our ability to know it' (177), must, by his own terms, be false, since it is predicated on the assumption that eighteenth- and nineteenth-century thinkers did not raise questions about the nature of reality or our ability to know it. Mellard proposes, in terms similar to those of Strehle, that the emergence of an 'adequate' postmodernist realism will be marked by a reorientation 'toward a relativism such as linguists associate with Edwin Sapir and Benjamin Whorf, and the structuralists with Saussure' (188). Adopting a thesis posited by David Goldknopf in *The Life of the Novel*, he suggests that the postmodernist novel will be called a ' "new" realism' because it will reject both of the basic conceptions of reality one finds in the 'traditional' novel, namely, 'reality as a hard-rock donnée' and 'reality as a "projection" of the imagination of the fantasist.' Either of these, according to Mellard, 'must appear too naive for any postmodernist, post-Heisenbergian mentality'; the alternative, as Goldknopf puts it, is 'the concept of reality as a communal formulation.' Like Strehle's thesis, Mellard's is reductive, historically uninformed, and disturbingly prescriptivist.

So too Betty Jean Craige's claim in *Literary Relativity* that the 'lit-erary "realism" governing the novel from the seventeenth through the nineteenth centuries' reflects a belief in a 'material world inde-pendent of [man's] consciousness' (1982: 32), reflects 'his confidence in an objectively definable external reality' and his assumption 'that the order which he sees in the world (which is the order he actually imposes upon the world, the order his culture establishes) is the order intrinsic to the world' (33–4) must be false, if, as she argues, 'a shift in a culture's paradigm makes its first appearance at the frontiers of its intellectual disciplines, and . . . gradually expresse[s] itself in the transformation of the culture's episteme' (23). If what she argues were true, then one would expect to find, for example, any number of realist novels of the eighteenth and nineteenth cen-turies reflecting not the assumption that 'the order which [man] sees in the world . . . is the order intrinsic to the world,' but Locke's belief that we cannot 'rank and sort things, and consequently (which is the end of sorting) denominate them, by their real essences; be-cause we know them not':

Our faculties carry us no further towards the knowledge and distinction of substances than a collection of sensible ideas which

we observe in them; which, however, made with the greatest dili-
gence and exactness we are capable of, yet is more remote from
the true internal constitution from which those qualities flow, than,
as I said, a countryman's idea is from the inward contrivance of
that famous clock at Strasbourg, whereof he only sees the outward figures and motions. There is not so contemptible a plant or
animal that does not confound the most enlarged understanding.
Though the familiar use of things about us take off our wonder,
yet it cures not our ignorance. When we come to examine the
stones we tread on, or the iron we daily handle, we presently find
we know not their make, and can give no reason of the different
qualities we find in them. It is evident the internal constitution,
whereon their properties depend, is unknown to us. Therefore we
pretend in vain to range things into sorts, and dispose them into
certain classes under names, by their real essences, that are so far
from our discovery or comprehension.

(1964: 287)[3]

If what Craige asserts were true, one would also expect to find
any number of early twentieth-century novels reflecting not, as she
suggests, the idea that 'external material reality [is] . . . constituted
by discourse,' but that it is mind-independent, since, as Passmore
notes, by the early years of the twentieth century, 'it could no longer
be presumed that Realism was intellectually disreputable, a mere
vulgar prejudice':

What a mind knows, Bretano and Meinong had argued, exists
independently of the act by which it is known . . . Moore, seconded by Russell, had rejected the thesis which Idealists like
Bradley and phenomenalists like Mill had united in regarding as
indisputable: that the existence of the objects of perception consists in the fact that they are perceived.

(259)

So the problem with these arguments is not just that they are all
predicated on the crude notion that literature passively reflects the
'ideas-of-the-time,' but also that their authors haven't even got the
ideas of the time right.[4] The lack of familiarity that many literary
theorists and critics demonstrate with eighteenth-, nineteenth- and
twentieth-century thought can perhaps be attributed to their pro-
vincialism, a problem that George Levine, for one, addresses in

his 'Scientific Realism and Literary Representation.' Levine, who considers himself to be 'rather sternly antifoundationalist' and who regards the 'exposure of the ideological underpinnings of ostensibly objective discourse' and the 'denaturalizing of the ideas, language and assumptions central to the way our culture thinks . . . as one of the healthiest developments in modern literature and thought' (1991: 18), nevertheless is 'interested in opening up a wider debate, one that would include the kinds of discussions that have been going on with great intensity among philosophers of science on the issue of "scientific realism"' (18):[5]

> As we press beyond the constraints of disciplinary restrictions, it seems odd that literary theorists, except for very special purposes that confirm what they already believe, have by and large refused not only to privilege science as a mode of knowledge, but even to consider it as one. . . . One can normally expect the invocation of Kuhn's *Structure of Scientific Revolutions* when theorists are at work extending the empire of language over all manifestations of culture, even though Kuhn himself is a 'realist.' Kuhn's work has been read as demonstrating that science is no more progressive and rational than any other form of knowledge, and that its developments are linked to the social community (of scientists) rather than to the internal logic and inevitability of what science discovers. But no literary theorist I have read quotes Kuhn when he calls himself and Richard Boyd 'unregenerate realists.'
>
> (18–19)

Levine's discussion is useful as corrective to literary theoretical insularism. However, I do not think it bears on the issue of literary realism. Levine argues that '[r]ealism remains a serious option in science in a way it does not in literary criticism, and it is this fact that I want to intrude into the near unanimity of attack on realism in literature' (19). In so arguing, what he seems to assume is that to take arguments for scientific realism seriously is to reopen the possibility of taking literary realism seriously – that is, what he seems to assume is that the viability of literary realism stands or falls with the viability of scientific realism. He rightly sees that it is the notion that reality does not exist independently of language that largely accounts for the 'near unanimity of attack on realism in literature'; he fails to see that the appropriate response to this attack is that whether reality exists independently of language or not is irrelevant to the viability of literary realism, as well as to the viability of literary representation as such (which he seems to conflate with literary realism – the title of his paper is 'Scientific Realism and Literary Representation'; in the paper itself, however, he speaks of 'realism in literature').

The fact is that not only is there no necessary connection between literary and metaphysical or scientific realism, but also arguments for metaphysical realism, metaphysical anti-realism, and variations thereupon (including combinations thereof – Kant's transcendental idealism, Putnam's 'realism with a human face'), as well as skepticism about the tenability of metaphysical speculation itself – the expression of which takes forms ranging from the cautious and wary (Locke, for example) to the exasperated (Hume, for example) to the hostile (Carnap, for example) – coexist throughout the eighteenth, nineteenth and twentieth centuries,[6] so that to assign a belief in metaphysical realism to the eighteenth and nineteenth centuries, calling it 'Newtonian,' and a rejection of it to the twentieth, calling it 'post-Newtonian,' and then to cast the literature of the eighteenth and nineteenth centuries as a reflection of the former, and the literature of the twentieth as reflection of the latter, is bound to result in falsification. It is impossible to link Newtonian or post-Newtonian physics with a particular metaphysics, and futile, in any event, to appeal to metaphysics as a means of defining the 'sensibility' of any of the past three centuries; from this it follows that to try to distinguish realism from 'modernism' and/or 'postmodernism' on such grounds is doomed.

As futile is the attempt to distinguish nineteenth- from early and/or late twentieth-century fiction on the grounds that the former embraces causality and determinism, while the latter embraces probability and indeterminism. Strehle, for example, argues that Tyrone Slothrop of Pynchon's *Gravity's Rainbow* 'enacts the Western view of history as realistic narrative' (30): he 'begins as a realist, chasing a deterministic version of the past' (30), and 'with expectations of linear continuity in his own and the world's history, with the realist's anticipation of causal connections' (38–9). In contrast, she argues, the 'actualists' of the novel – Tchitcherine, Geli Tripping, Roger Mexico, Enzian, Leni Pokler, Pig Bodine, among others, 'do not forge the linear, necessary, and unified plots of realism'; rather, 'they tell themselves the plural and indeterminate stories of actualism' (35). The problem here is not the suggestion that the idea that there are causal connections between events informs the construction of plots in realist fiction – certainly, many events in realist narratives 'bring about' other events, just as they do in *Gravity's Rainbow* – but rather the conflation of causality with necessity. To believe that a glass will break if one drops it on the floor by no means entails a commitment to determinism. Such a belief is perfectly compatible with the belief that things could have been otherwise. So the fact that certain events are the cause of other events coming about in a realist narrative is no evidence that realist fiction is committed to determinism.

Even if one were to admit Strehle's crude assumption that realist fiction 'represented the Newtonian cosmos is all its causal continuity,' it would not follow from this that it reflected a belief in determinism. As Elizabeth Anscombe notes, 'Newton's mechanics is a deterministic system; but this does not mean that believing them commits us to determinism':

> Let us pretend that Newton's laws were still to be accepted without qualification: no reserve in applying them in electrodynamics; no restriction to bodies travelling a good deal slower than light; and no quantum phenomena . . . We could say: of course nothing violates those axioms or the laws of the force of gravity. But animals, for example, run about the world in all sorts of paths and no path is dictated for them by those laws, as it is for planets. Thus in relation to the solar system (apart from questions like whether in the past some planet has blown up), the laws are like the rules of an infantile card game: once the cards are dealt we turn them up in turn, and make two piles each, one red, one black; the winner has the biggest pile of red ones. So once the cards are dealt the game is determined, and from any position in it you can derive all others back to the deal and forward to win or draw. But in relation to what happens on and inside a planet the laws are, rather, like the rules of chess; the play is seldom determined, though nobody breaks the rules.
>
> (1981: 143)

So a belief in causality does not commit one to determinism, and a belief in indeterminism does not commit one to the repudiation of causality – 'not being determined,' as Anscombe points out, 'does not imply not being caused' (145). Further, the fact that there are regularities in the world that, as Galen Strawson puts it, 'are correctly captured only by statistical or probabilistic formulae of the form "99 per cent (or indeed 29 per cent) of As which become B become C"' does not 'threaten the claim that it is reasonable to postulate causation in any way' (1989: 88):

> Some interpretations of quantum theory involve the claim that there is objective indeterminism in nature, and it is worth remarking that dispute about this claim has no bearing [on the question of whether there is such a thing as causation]. For whether the claim is true or false – suppose for the sake of argument that it is true – there is still (massive) regularity.
>
> (87)

Moreover, as Gross and Levitt note in the course of critiquing the work of Stanley Aronowitz, 'the view that the causal and deterministic view of things implicit in classical physics has been irrevocably banished' is 'simply wrong' (52):

> The assertion that deterministic causality is still viable within the phenomenal world of quantum mechanics may come as a surprise to people far better informed than Aronowitz, but recent work in the mathematical foundations of the subject seems to support it strongly. A beautiful result of Dür, Goldstein, and Zanghi shows that a large part of classical quantum theory emerges naturally from a dynamical model which is deterministic through and through, and in which the only 'hidden' variables are thoroughly classical variables like position and velocity.
>
> (262 n.9)

'The moral, if one must be whimsical,' they conclude, 'is that Occam's Razor may now cut through the leash that heretofore bound us to Schrödinger's Cat' (262 n.9):

> In other words, (a) Einstein was right: God does not play dice with the cosmos. (b) On the other hand, since individually and collectively we are not God, nor Laplace's Demon, nor any other demiurge of comparable intellectual power, we must inevitably regard the universe as something of a crap game. As far as (b) is concerned, note well that even if the universe were purely Newtonian in the best eighteenth-century tradition, and the perplexities of quantum mechanics entirely avoided, the crap game would still be inevitable. This follows from the work of Poincaré

on classical mechanics and from that of his latter-day disciples, which goes under the fashionable name 'chaos theory.'

(262 n.9)

The latter point – that owing to our limitations we must inevitably regard the universe of something of a crap game – is a sentiment likewise expressed by Condorcet, who came to hold such a view, as Richard Popkin explains, under the influence of the skepticism of Locke, Hume, Pascal and Bayle. 'We cannot,' writes Popkin, summarizing Condorcet's position,

> arrive at a necessary science of nature because of our limitations. We can empirically observe what happens all the time, but not why it happens. Even Newton's laws do not guarantee that nature must behave in certain ways and cannot be otherwise. . . . The world may be completely determined, but we can only begin with what we know, the empirical observations and intuitively recognized relations of ideas. From the empirical facts we can induce laws, but they are only probable, because we do not know whether nature will be uniform and hence whether the future will resemble the past.
>
> (287)

Pace Strehle, then, who argues that Robert Coover's fiction 'specifically engages the shift, crucial to recent scientific understandings of the way events occur, from causality to probability' (68), probability does not preclude causality. Coover's plots, she claims,

> often address the irruption of chance in the lives of characters who have believed in causality; a mining accident sets off *The Origin of the Brunists* (1966), and 'A Pedestrian Accident' (1969) begins, 'Paul stepped off the curb and got hit by a truck.'
>
> (69)

But whatever the odds of such events occurring, their occurrence, whether in fiction or life, does not in any way demonstrate 'the illusion of causality' (68) (and nor, for that matter, does it prove that physical determinism is false). Why should the 'irruption of chance' into the lives of characters in fiction or into that of real people undermine their belief in causation? After all, Paul's pedestrian accident is *caused* by something – namely, being hit by a truck.

The idea that there are such things as chance and accident, moreover, features largely in the plots of realist fiction. Strehle, aware, perhaps, of the futility of trying to argue otherwise, yet determined nevertheless to effect a distinction between realist and postmodernist fiction in terms of a commitment on the part of the former to determinism and a commitment to indeterminism on the part of the latter, asserts that chance and accident in realist fiction only seem to be chance and accident. Many of 'the meetings and conversations leading to important events' in *J R*, she states, 'occur by accident, like the meeting of Amy and Jack on the train at the start of their affair' (118). 'How different,' she argues, 'when, by chance, Strether takes a trip to the country, stops at a randomly chosen inn, strolls to the river, and learns the truth about Mme de Vionnet and Chad Newsome: coincidence inevitably illuminates the ends of the realistic novelist because it is never really chance, but artfully concealed intention. In Gaddis's text, by contrast, *nothing* hides behind chance' (119; her emphasis).

But how, exactly, is this different? It can't be that the difference is that Strether's chance trip to the country is, unlike Amy's and Jack's meeting, 'artfully concealed intention,' contrived by James to advance the plot of *The Ambassadors*, since the chance meeting of Amy and Jack on the train is just as much of a contrivance, devised by Gaddis to advance the plot of *J R*. That is, *something* does hide behind chance in *J R*, as in *The Ambassadors*, namely the author. Nor can it be, as Strehle claims, that 'unlike the accidents and coincidences of well-made novels, where chance always serves meaning and aesthetic unity,' the accidents in *J R* don't. Strehle claims that the accidents in *J R* 'lead only to pain and frustration, never to epiphany,' that 'Amy Joubert steps on Bast's hand, and it means nothing – except that the world is accidental' (118). But the idea that the world is accidental, and that its being so causes only pain and frustration, is meaningful, and so chance in *J R*, by her own account, does serve both meaning and aesthetic unity.

The notion that freedom is guaranteed by physical indeterminism is, furthermore, dubious. 'With linear continuity,' Strehle claims, 'the actualists [of *Gravity's Rainbow*] also reject the colonialistic conquest of the "out-of-line." They refuse to assimilate or convert the other but rather allow it to remain alien, accidental, free'; 'typically they do not fix, control, or keep the other but rather encourage change and freedom' (53). And Nadeau argues that 'in Fowles' estimation, the indeterminacy principle invalidates the notion that all events in nature are predetermined by abstract and immutable laws. Freedom of choice is, therefore, not only a possibility but also a given in nature' (73) and that Vonnegut, in *Breakfast of Champions*, affirms 'the possibility of freedom in which indeterminacy makes imaginative choice a possibility' (129). But, as Gary Watson notes, the denial of physical determinism 'does not ensure, by itself, that *we* determine anything' (1982: 9) – that is, it does not in itself indicate that we possess self-determination. Or, to put this another way, if it is true, as Anscombe suggests, that 'physical indeterminism is . . . indispensable if we are to make anything of the claim to freedom,' it is not sufficient: 'The physically undetermined in not thereby "free" . . . [f]or freedom at least involves the power of acting according to an idea, and no such thing is ascribed to whatever is the subject (what would be the relevant subject?) of unpredetermination in indeterministic physics' (146).

'The hapless theorists of the influence of Einstein'

The difficulty of attempting to define realism in terms of theories that are associated with Newton, and modernism and/or postmodernism in terms of theories that are associated with twentieth-century physicists, is also well-exemplified by the service into which postmodernist theorists have tried to press Newton's theory of absolute space and time and Einstein's theory of special relativity. Strehle argues that

> most devastating of all to the worldview of classical physics and to the parallel ontology of realistic fiction [is that] now no inertial, accurate, or absolute frame of reference exists. . . . The rejection of a privileged frame implies, for modern and postmodern artists, that narratives cannot 'frame' or enclose reality in a static picture.
>
> (129)

For one thing, however, developments within quantum mechanics as well as within astrophysics, according to David Hodgson, suggest that 'while certain aspects of [the theory of relativity] seem unlikely to be overthrown, there is now reason to question at least its assertion of the equivalence of all frames of reference' (1991: 436–7). The discovery of a universal background radiation, thought to be residue of the Big Bang, Hodgson explains, 'seems to provide a universal frame of reference [in that] this radiation appears to be isotrophic, that is, the same in all directions' (437). In quantum mechanics, both Bell's inequality theorem and a set of experiments conducted by Alain Aspect demonstrating the nonlocality of quantum systems also, Hodgson suggests, provide evidence that questions the equivalence of all frames of reference:

> It has been shown that interaction with a quantum system comprising two separated particles apparently simultaneously affects spatially separated parts of the system: quantum theory thus suggests simultaneity of distant (quantum) events, and accordingly it suggests some preferred frame of reference according to which such distant events are simultaneous.
>
> (437)

And, according to Phillip Bricker, more than three hundred years after Newton's Scholium on absolute space, time, and motion, 'the debate between absolutists and relationalists is as vigorous as ever' (1990: 77):

> Earlier in this century it was widely held that Einstein's theory showed once and for all the falsity – if not the incoherence – of Newton's absolutist position. But much progress has been made since then. We know now that Einstein and other modern relationalists tended to conflate different senses of 'absolute.' Relativity theory teaches us that space, time, and motion are not absolute only for some senses of 'absolute.' Once the different senses have been carefully distinguished, it becomes clear that philosophically important versions of absolutism can survive the advent of relativity theory (although absolute space and absolute time must be traded in for absolute space-time).
>
> (77)

The point is that twentieth-century physics and philosophy of science are not monolithic. Quantum physicists, for example, agree that quantum theory is an enormously successful predictive one (agree that it is, in fact, the most successful predictive theory there has ever been), but there is no consensus, so far as I can tell, as to the nature of the subatomic world – indeed, in *Quantum Reality*, Nick Herbert identifies eight vastly different 'quantum realities.' Theorists of postmodernism who want to see contemporary fiction as partaking in a 'paradigm shift' inaugurated by developments in science, however, assume that twentieth-century physics is a homogeneous, seamless whole, and, accordingly, render the fiction they analyze a homogeneous, seamless whole. Seventeenth-, eighteenth-, and nineteenth-century physics and philosophy of science likewise were not monolithic. Berkeley rejected the idea of absolute space, time, and motion. Leibniz attacked what he thought amounted to an admission of action-at-a-distance in Newton's theory of gravity. There were wave theories of light proposed by, *inter alia*, Hooke and Huygens, in opposition to Newton's corpuscular theory. And given this, there's no reason to assume *a priori* that seventeenth-, eighteenth- or nineteenth-century fiction that drew on scientific theories reflected only Newton's views or views ascribed to Newton.

Even a theorist like Lyotard, who, drawing on René Thom's account of catastrophe theory, suggests that 'postmodern science' is, like Thom's catastrophic model, characterized by conflict, ends up homogenizing contemporary science. 'Postmodern science – by concerning itself with such things as undecidables, the limits of precise control, conflicts characterized by incomplete information, *'fracta,'* catastrophes, and pragmatic paradoxes – is,' he claims, 'theorizing its own evolution as discontinuous, catastrophic, nonrectifiable, and paradoxical' and thus 'changing the meaning of the word *knowledge,* while expressing how such a change can take place' (1984: 60; his emphasis); it is, he argues, 'producing not the known, but the unknown' (60). Not only would one encounter dissension over the conclusions Lyotard draws from contemporary science's concern with undecidables, etc., but the idea of dissension and conflict as such is not, as Lyotard seems to want to claim, unique to 'postmodern science.' As John Neubauer remarks of Larry Laudan's rejection of Kuhn's notion of a homogeneous 'normal science':

> As Laudan puts it, 'virtually every major period in the history of science is characterized . . . by the co-existence of numerous competing paradigms.' While such battles do get resolved, they often flare up at a later date. The alternating acceptance and rejection of the corpuscular theory of light, of atomism, or of the notion of a continental drift demonstrates that scientific issues are never conclusively settled. Kuhn attributes the standards of science to a social group rather than nature, but he continues to believe that these standards are strictly enforced and universally held. It is the great merit of recent theories of science to have recognized

that inconsistencies within theories and unresolved disputes between rival paradigms are no mere revolutionary irregularities but
the normal condition of science. Newtonian science, for example,
had a formative impact on eighteenth-century research, but it
meant radically different things to different people, depending
on the texts they regarded as authoritative and the idiosyncratic
reading they gave them.

(1983: 34)

And, he continues,

this new picture of science is relevant to the historiography of
literature. . . . [T]he historicist model of *Geistesgeschichte*, with its
monolithic periods dominated by a Baroque, a Renaissance, a
Classicist, or a Romantic *Zeitgeist* is as inadequate for the comprehension of the historical profusion and interaction of styles and
forms as the Kuhnian paradigms are for the history of science.

(35)

Moreover, Newton's theory of absolute space and time and
Einstein's special theory of relativity don't have the implications
theorists of postmodernism typically ascribe to them. On the one
hand, even if, as Strehle claims, the 'ontology' of realist fiction were
grounded in Newton's theory of absolute space and time, it wouldn't
follow from this that it reflected a 'static picture' of reality, since no
such picture of reality follows from the theory of absolute space
and time. Indeed, it was Newton, R.I.G. Hughes points out, who
'originated the revolutionary proposal that every part of the material world is in continuous dynamical interaction with every other
part' (1990: 11)

On the other hand, it does not follow from the theory of relativity
that, as Mellard argues, 'our knowledge can only be relative, provisional, situational, and temporal' (37). Neither, *pace* Strehle, is it any
consequence of the theory of relativity, if, as she claims, the colloca-
tion of the characters' accounts of events in Barth's *LETTERS* 'does
not enable the reader to construct an "objective" and hence reliable
final version but reinforces the relativity of all accounts' (152). Nor is
it, as Adelaide Morris argues of H.D.'s *HERmione*, that to accept
Hermione's 'relativistic measurements' in the forest outside Gart
Grange – 'a mosquito near the ear on a hot night is as huge as a
chicken hawk, a peony petal near the eye covers the whole house'

(1991: 208) – as 'valid statements about the world' affirms 'two key postulates of relativity theory: the contention that measurements of size, distance, and duration vary from one frame of reference to another and the insistence that no one frame is inherently superior to any other' (208), affirms that there is 'no privileged position apart from or above the whirl of the wind of this world, no universal clock or ruler to provide "true" or "objective" measurements of time and space' (208). Nor, finally, is it the case, contra Craige, that the idea that 'knowledge is obtainable only subjectively and relative to a point of view' (18) owes to Heisenberg and Einstein, that '[w]hat Derrida and Foucault present is the intellectual climate of the twentieth century, the relativism to which Einstein and Heisenberg contribute fundamentally' (19).

The theory of relativity does not imply that space-time measurements are subjective, provisional, or unreliable; it is always and objectively true by the theory that, for example, less time will have elapsed on a rocket that travels at a speed closer to the speed of light relative to the earth than will have elapsed on earth. Mellard, Strehle, Craige, and Morris all appear to be assuming that the relativity of space-time measurements is a function of the subjectivity of the observer (so Morris, for example, thinks that the subjective impression that 'a mosquito near the ear on a hot night is as huge as a chicken hawk' affirms the postulates of the theory of relativity), but, if t^1 amount of time has elapsed in a rocket I'm traveling in that is moving at a speed closer to the speed of light relative to the earth, then t^2 amount of time will have elapsed on earth no matter how much time I happen to think will have elapsed on earth.

Neither does the theory of relativity entail cognitive relativism – it doesn't follow from the theory that space-time measurements are relative to motion that the truth of statements of fact are relative – nor is it itself relativistic – it doesn't posit that space-time measurements are relative to motion only for Einstein, or only for western physicists, or only for earthlings. Moreover, relativity as Craige and Strehle describe it – 'the observers in Barth's text,' Strehle argues, 'inhabit single, moving vantage points that cannot be declared "right" or "wrong"' (152); 'in a world of relativity,' Craige asserts, 'there is no correct or incorrect "reading" of reality since there is no definable reality independently of man's perception: there are as many readings as there are perceivers' (19) – not only fails to describe relativity; it also fails to describe cognitive relativism. Cognitive relativists don't deny the existence of truth; rather, they argue that the truth of judgments of fact are relative either to individuals, contexts, or conceptual schemes. And since the notion of relative truth would be meaningless if it weren't possible for individuals to have false beliefs, cognitive relativists hold that individuals can have beliefs that are false for him or her, false relative to context, or false with respect to a conceptual scheme.

Morris does point out that 'for Einstein, relativity did not mean "everything is relative"' (210) and argues further that there is an important difference between relativity theorists and quantum theorists: 'while relativity theorists aim to extend the possibility of making "true" statements about the world, quantum theorists argue that all the mind can ponder is its own cognitive constructions' (205). But what Morris says here about relativity theorists contradicts what she claims are the implications of relativity in *HERmione*; moreover, what she says about quantum theorists is false – they do not deny the possibility of making true statements about the world. As Gross and Levitt point out, the uncertainty principle, for example – which, they note, 'is undoubtedly one of the cornerstones of quantum mechanics' – is 'a tenet of physics, a predictive law about the behavior of concrete phenomena that can be tested and confirmed like other physical principles' (51–2). 'It is not,' they continue,

> some brooding metaphysical dictum about the Knower versus the Known, but rather a straightforward statement, mathematically quite simple, concerning the way in which the statistical outcomes of various phenomena must be interrelated. And, indeed, it has been triumphantly confirmed. It has been verified as fully and irrefutably as is possible for an empirical proposition. In other words, viewed as a law of physics, the uncertainty principle is a very certain item indeed. *It is an objective truth about the world.* (If that were not the case, there never would have been so much fuss about it.)
>
> (52; their emphasis)[7]

Strehle too, in a footnote, admits that (her conception of) relativism does not follow from the theory of relativity: 'Relativity must not,' she writes, 'be misconstrued to imply a relativistic equality in all outlooks and values' (248 n.20). Having made this disclaimer, however, she proceeds to ignore it altogether. For what does her talk of the relativity of all accounts in Barth's *LETTERS*, none of which she claims is right or wrong, amount to but the suggestion that relativity implies 'a relativistic equality in all outlooks and values'? And if she doesn't think that the theory of relativity implies a relativistic equality in all outlooks and values, then why does she invoke it in the first place? Why doesn't she just argue that the inability to construct an objective version of events in *LETTERS* reinforces the relativism of all accounts, and leave the theory of relativity out of it altogether? She can't, of course – given that the premise of her book is that 'actualistic fiction expresses . . . a literary version of the reality constituted by fundamentally new physical theories in the first half of the twentieth century' (7), she needs to find a way to make Einstein's relativity relevant to this fiction.

The difficulty she has doing so is not only revealed by her admission that 'relativism is not a necessary conclusion of Einstein's theories' (248 n.20), but also by her attempt to treat the subjective experience of feeling that time is dragging along slowly or passing by very quickly as an instantiation of special relativity. She claims, for example, that '[t]ime does not flow "equably without relation to anything external" in *LETTERS* but rather speeds and slows as characters perceive it in relation to events,' citing one character who writes that '[t]ime itself has gone torpid in Maryland since the solstice; summer limps like one long day,' and another who writes '[e]verything's suspended, held, and arrested, as if Time had declared time out' (154). These, however, are similes, and their power as similes, moreover, does not derive from the special theory of relativity – that is, there's nothing about them that would allow one to identify them as similes that derive from the special theory of relativity. (Strehle's suggestion that 'the end of a text like Dickens's *Hard Times*, where the omniscient narrator resolves the present action and foretells the futures of every central character' (157) reflects 'a Newtonian faith that absolute motion culminates in absolute rest' (157) is likewise, to say the least, strained.)

Strehle might, of course, have argued that although special relativity doesn't entail relativism, the authors of the novels she discusses believe it does. But this would have constituted a very different kind of argument from the one she opts to make, an argument the aim of which would not be to show that 'actualistic fiction expresses . . . a literary version of the reality constituted by fundamentally new physical theories in the first half of the twentieth century,' that would not be to demonstrate how late twentieth-century fiction participates in a paradigm shift, or a *Zeitgeist*. I don't know to what extent twentieth-century authors have fallen prey to popular literary-critical misconceptions about twentieth-century physics, but Strehle, Nadeau, Mellard, Craige, and Morris all assume that the authors they discuss understand the physics and so they never address the questions that any literary critic examining the relationship between science and literature should address: to what extent writers misinterpret science, and where they do, whether the misinterpretation is valuable or not, whether it results in what Gillian Beer has called 'creative misprision' or not. The reason they don't address these questions, I suggest, is that they are not as interested in exploring the different ways in which, and the different reasons why, authors appropriate scientific concepts as they are in positing the existence of a revolution in world view, the birth of a new episteme that early and/or late twentieth-century literature partakes in. Given their interests, they cannot allow for the possibility of dissonance between what an Einstein, a Heisenberg, a Bohr proposes and what authors who invoke their theories in their work think they are proposing. The idea of a paradigm shift in which science, literary criticism, philosophy, literature, etc. all partake ('the paradigm which underlies twentieth-century philosophy, literary criticism, sociology, science, music, and art' (26), Craige claims, is relativity) requires a fundamental conceptual consonance across these disciplines (as well as that the concept or concepts in question are new); to point out that any number of twentieth-century novelists who introduce special relativity into their work misunderstand it if they think it implies that 'everything is relative' would thus be to cast doubt on the notion that there has been a paradigm shift (that relativism is not new and that there is no consensus now, just as there never has been a consensus, as to its truth also casts doubt on the idea that we've entered a new age).

The attempt to distinguish realist from modernist and/or postmodernist fiction on the grounds that the former reflects a commitment to Newton's theory of absolute space, time, and motion and hence to the belief that all knowledge is absolute, objective and certain, and that the latter reflects a commitment to Einstein's theory of relativity and hence to the belief that all knowledge is relative, subjective, and uncertain, is spurious, then, because, among other reasons, neither theory entails those beliefs about the nature of knowledge ascribed to them by Craige, Mellard, Strehle, and Morris.

Neither do Newtonian or quantum physics have the moral and political implications that Strehle, for one, ascribes to them. She argues, for example, that Gaddis' twentieth-century Americans 'consider[ ] [value] to inhere in tangible goods, not in being and doing, but in owning, conserving, and controlling *things*' (96) and that this materialism, 'arising from and expressing generally shared Newtonian assumptions about reality . . . takes over everywhere in [*J R*], with devastating human consequences' (96). But Newtonian physics in no way 'authorizes,' as she suggests, instrumental materialism or the exploitation of nature. As Hughes notes,

> there is no connection, logical or psychological, between such attitudes and Newton's science, and hence . . . if this science has been appropriated by an ideology that seeks to exploit the natural world, then the explanation for this must lie outside the internal dynamics of intellectual history.
>
> (14)

Furthermore,

> acceptance of Newton's science and of its functional autonomy is consistent with many different kinds of attitudes concerning ethics, theology, and the natural world. It is consistent, for example, with the view that the material world is a world from which God has been banished, and within which judgments of value are irredeemably subjective, and views of this kind are typically thought of as 'Newtonian.' But it does not entail those views. Nor, interestingly, did it prompt their historical emergence in any immediate way.
>
> (12)

So even assuming realist fiction were based in Newtonianism, it wouldn't follow, as Strehle seems to think, that it necessarily gave expression to the belief that value 'inhere[s] in tangible goods, not in being and doing, but in owning, conserving, and controlling things' since Newtonianism is consistent with, though does not entail, the belief, as Hume puts it, that it is we who gild or stain objects as they stand in nature with value (whether moral, aesthetic, or monetary). On the other hand, the theory of relativity does not entail, as Craige suggests, 'the death of God' and 'therefore the death of an objective universe in which things and events and persons have significance prior to and independent of man's perception' (21), and so if any number of twentieth-century avant-garde texts give voice to such ideas, they do so for reasons other than that these notions are a consequence of the theory of relativity.

Further, there is no reason to suppose that an acceptance of quantum physics entails a rejection of materialism or any of the other evils theorists of postmodernism tend to associate with Newtonianism. That Strehle, for one, naively assumes it does is suggested by the following passages from her discussion of *Gravity's Rainbow*:

The 'un-hep' . . . persist in imagining Newtonian levers beneath experience, in Pynchon's version of the clash between the old and new realities. Like other actualists, Pynchon writes a large and public novel, with a huge cast of characters, many of whom are 'public servants.' Like Gaddis or Coover, he locates the most conservative dedication to Newton's principles in the public sector – in various governments and corporations, in the firm and the cartel. These institutions encourage and exploit popular beliefs in stability, continuity, causality, objectivity, and certainty, because Newtonian beliefs make citizens and soldiers more docile and useful for institutional work. An assumption that phenomena are causally linked, for example, can be channeled into dutiful productivity for the 'war effort' or 'the nation,' but the notion that things are accidental and mysterious creates an undependable worker.

(28)

For the good public servant like Teddy Bloat or Pirate Prentice, [the view that there are causal links between successive events] encourages submission to duty and dedication to higher causes – like Nazism, for example, which Von Braun served during the war. The faith in causal continuity, which is inscribed in the public consciousness in scientific/Newtonian, religious/Calvinist, and aesthetic/realist forms, carries with it a sinister belief that the discontinuous, the arbitrary, the aberrant, and the preterite should be either assimilated to the meaningful series – colonized, as it were – or eradicated. A seemingly innocuous notion that the world obeys Newton's laws thus becomes, for Pynchon, a commitment to the imperialist politics through which the West has fought to control life.

(30–1)

Strehle perhaps isn't aware that Heisenberg was the head of atomic research in Nazi Germany. The man who in 1930 rejected causal determinism was not thereby rendered incapable of contributing to the war effort, submitting to duty, and dedicating himself to 'higher' causes. The point is not to impugn Heisenberg – the point is rather that it's not that simple. Political or moral correctness does not follow magically from the knowledge, for example, that quantum systems behave probabilistically. Moreover, since probabilities at the microphysical level become virtual certainties at the macrophysical level, of what possible interest could the fact that the outcome of a quantum event can only be predicted within a certain range of probabilities be to western governments committed to imperialism? Such a fact has neither moral force – that is, it's not likely to convince anyone committed to imperialist politics that it is morally reprehensible – nor the pragmatic force that might at least compel a change in policy.

The upshot of the foregoing is that even if realist fiction could be regarded as 'represent[ing] the Newtonian cosmos,' and early and/or late twentieth-century fiction as representing the Einsteinian/post-Einsteinian cosmos, it would not follow that any of them could be seen as giving expression to a unified or 'totalized' set of epistemological, metaphysical, moral, and political beliefs, since both Newtonian and Einsteinian/post-Einsteinian physics are epistemologically, metaphysically, morally, and politically underdetermined. Whatever the relationship between certain so-called realist, modernist, and postmodernist novels and physical theories, the fiction of the eighteenth, nineteenth, early- and late- twentieth centuries cannot be understood in terms of the 'reflection' of a homogeneous eighteenth- and nineteenth-century or pre-WWII or post-WWII philosophical 'sensibility' to which developments in science contribute, not least of all because no such homogeneous philosophical sensibility is to be found anywhere in the eighteenth, nineteenth, or twentieth centuries.

I would note that in arguing that theorists of postmodernism tend to represent the literature of the past several centuries in just such terms, I do not mean to suggest that they deny the existence of diversity in, for example, what they identify as 'modernist' and 'postmodernist' literature. On the contrary. But the fact that they don't does not answer the charge I'm leveling, because to claim, for example, that there are myriad currents in 'modernist' and 'postmodernist' literature is, by the very invocation of the terms 'modernist' and 'postmodernist,' to imply the existence of a commonality among these currents. Any number of theorists of postmodernism have asserted that postmodernism in particular is so radically diverse that nothing unifies it, failing, in so asserting, to recognize that to subsume that diversity under the concept of postmodernism is to imply the existence of a principle or principles that unifies it. Not only does the very appeal to the term 'postmodernism' imply the existence of such a principle or principles, but theorists of postmodernism who claim that postmodernism is so radically diverse that nothing unifies it nevertheless tend, despite having claimed as much, to offer accounts of the general principles informing postmodernism. Consider, for example, M. Keith Booker's claim that

> [t]here is a reason that various theoretical explorations of postmodernist culture have tended to reach such widely different and even contradictory conclusions, and the reason is that postmodernism itself is a multifaceted and contradictory phenomenon. If there is a central thesis of postmodernist art, if there is a unifying Kuhnian paradigm of postmodernist culture, it is that there is no central thesis or unifying paradigm.
>
> (1994: 184–5)

Booker is self-conscious enough here to recognize that to subsume the multi-facetedness and contradictoriness he alludes to under the concept of postmodernism is problematic, but that self-consciousness avails him of little. For, on the one hand, in claiming that if there is a central thesis or unifying paradigm of postmodernist culture, it is that there is no central thesis or unifying paradigm, Booker implies that it is the lack of such a central thesis or unifying paradigm that distinguishes 'postmodernist' culture from preceding cultures. But since, as I've been arguing, there is no central thesis or unifying paradigm of the pre-WW II period or the eighteenth- and nineteenth-century centuries either, the claim that contemporary culture is multi-faceted not only fails to distinguish it from other cultures, but is also trite. On the other hand, despite his asserting that if there is a central thesis or underlying paradigm of postmodernist culture, it is that there is no central thesis or underlying paradigm, Booker nonetheless argues – perhaps because he is aware that the idea that there is no central thesis or underlying paradigm of postmodernism is empty, and would, if clung to, make it impossible to say anything substantive about a concept that he's clearly invested in – that, for example, 'postmodernist fiction in general' is 'informed by a skepticism toward absolutes' (183) (and he claims this only several sentences before he argues that 'if there is a central thesis or postmodernist art, if there is a unifying Kuhnian paradigm of postmodernist culture, it is that there is no central thesis or unifying paradigm'). The nods, then, that theorists of postmodernism give to the idea of plurality, difference, diversity, multifacetedness, etc., does not answer my claim that they tend to construct accounts of the history of literature that represent what they identify as realist, modernist, and postmodernist literature in terms of the reflection of a homogeneous philosophical sensibility. Indeed, my point is that they cannot do otherwise because they are committed to the idea of periodization (an issue to which I will return below).

If it is not, as I've been maintaining, tenable to represent eighteenth- and nineteenth- and early- and late twentieth-century fiction in terms of the reflection of monolithic philosophical sensibility via an appeal to the notion that it gives voice to, at the level of content, widely shared beliefs about, for example, the nature of reality, truth, knowledge, self, it also not tenable to try to effect a reduction of it to a unified set of metaphysical, epistemological, moral, and political beliefs by way of an appeal to literary forms or narrative strategies. Sensing, perhaps, the inherent difficulties in attempting to construct overarching metanarratives about the assumptions informing what they designate as realist, modernist, and/or postmodernist fiction on the basis of content, many theorists of postmodernism resort to arguing that such assumptions are 'implicit' in the literary forms and conventions common to them. Recourse to this strategy has resulted in literary forms being arbitrarily made to express whatever assumptions critics and theorists want them to express, and in literary forms being 'essentialized' or hypostatized. John Johnston, for example, argues that

> [s]elf-reflexivity in postmodern fiction almost always functions politically as a refusal of two kinds of complicity: first, with a certain *image* of society that novelistic representation automatically conveys by not admitting chaos, disorder, fragmentation, and dislocation except within the larger, rationalized frame of novelistic conventions, and second, with an *image* of language as a transparent signifying system adequate or commensurate with the expression of the needs and desires of unified subjects. In an era that witnessed the complete erosion of credibility and coherence in official discourse, and the multiplication of differences within and among subjects, self-reflexivity indeed appeared

necessary if the novel was to establish its own credibility and claim of relevance.

(1990: 188–9)

The irony is that Johnston should acknowledge the 'multiplication of differences within and among subjects' and yet claim that self-reflexivity in postmodern fiction almost always functions in the same way. To abandon the idea that self-reflexivity bears some 'fixed' meaning, as well as the idea that self-reflexivity is necessary if the contemporary novel is to be credible and relevant, would be to take one step in the direction of liberating contemporary fiction from the endless repetition of the same to which it has been condemned by many theorists of postmodernism.

Booker, for another, despite his claiming that 'Peter Bürger rightfully questions Adorno's conclusions concerning the political force of montage by pointing out that artists with a wide variety of political orientations have employed the technique' and concluding that 'we cannot assign a fixed meaning to a procedure' (17), nevertheless assumes the existence of an 'ideology of realism' (77), and asserts, for example, that '[t]he Christian sense of apocalypse' – which is, according to him, 'an especially notable feature of the mindset of nineteenth-century realistic fiction,' is reflected in 'the way that the conclusions of realistic novels typically tie together all that has come before' (83). And even though his claim that the specific nature of the goals that 'modernists' believed 'sheer artistic technique' could achieve 'can be drastically different from one text to the next, even if the techniques employed are not' (17) and that 'postmodernist skepticism toward form can be put to a range of ideological uses' (17–18) might well suggest that Booker would be unwilling to assign an ideology to modernism and postmodernism on the basis of what he identifies as their narrative strategies, it emerges that this is not the case. Not only does he argue that Vargas Llosa's *War of the End of the World* 'represents a skeptical attitude toward the apocalypse that is neither Christian nor modern, but postmodern' (7) – 'after all,' he notes, 'Vargas Llosa's book arises within an historical context that is neither Christian nor modern' – but he also claims that the 'differentiation among realism, modernism, and postmodernism goes beyond the specific case of apocalypse . . . and suggests a general difference in attitude toward the sorts of belief structures . . . that traditionally provide order and stability . . . in society' (88). 'These three different attitudes,' he concludes, 'cannot peacefully coexist, and the postmodernist approach inherently wins out, since both the realist and modernist approaches require a serious dedication to certain ideas that is radically undermined by the skepticism of postmodernism' (89).

In the end, then, Booker cannot allow the idea that writers may use the same narrative strategies to radically different purposes to stand, for if he did he would not be able to assert that realism, modernism, and postmodernism reflect, respectively, general nineteenth-, early-twentieth-, and late-twentieth-century attitudes toward belief structures. And it is just his wanting to assert that there are such general attitudes that is the problem. How, in the face of rampant millennialism of all sorts, for example, can he suggest that it just stands to reason that *The War of the End of the World* is 'characterized by the same "boredom with Apocalypse"' that Bruce Sterling notes in the work of cyberpunk science fiction writers' (87) because it arises in a historical context that is 'neither Christian nor modern, but postmodern'? Booker is free to argue that the narrative strategies of some contemporary novels imply a boredom with the idea of apocalypse, but he cannot plausibly claim that these novels exemplify a general and quintessentially late-twentieth century attitude toward apocalypse.

Especially common among theorists of postmodernism is the idea that third-person omniscient narration always 'implies' that everything is knowable and certain, and that first-person narration always 'implies' the opposite. So Linda Hutcheon argues in *A Poetics of Postmodernism*:

> Typically postmodern, [Kosinski's 'Death in Cannes'] refuses the omniscience and omnipresence of the third person and engages instead in a dialogue between a narrative voice (which both is and is not Kosinski's) and a projected reader. Its viewpoint is avowedly limited, provisional, personal.
>
> (1988: 10)

There are variations on this theme, to the effect that third-person narration always 'implies' that everything is knowable and certain only in nineteenth-century realist narratives. Ronald Sukenick claims, for example, that

> in Kafka we have omniscient narration, but it's omniscient narration in which part of the omniscience is, paradoxically, awareness

of its limits. The normal situation of the omniscient narrator is inverted. What the narrative knows is the extent of the unknown. This may be omniscient narration technically, but intellectually, spiritually, it is the reverse of the Victorian voice of authority which implies that everything, if not known, is at least knowable. . . . Realism, insofar as it is a component of Kafka's style, retains its authority only through the admission that reality is unknowable.

(1985: 69–70)

Nothing justifies Sukenick's claim that omniscient narration in Victorian fiction implies that everything, if not known, is at least knowable. He merely assumes that in the middle- to late-nineteenth century everything was thought to be knowable and that therefore omniscient narration in a Victorian novel must, as a matter of course, reflect this view. Even if it were true that everything was thought to be knowable in the middle to late nineteenth century, it wouldn't follow that that's what omniscient narration in Victorian novels 'meant.'

Strehle similarly suggests that divisions between major and minor characters, significant and insignificant information, and dominant and subordinate motifs in 'traditional' novels always 'mean' the same thing:

With binary oppositions, Pynchon rejects an insidious corollary: namely, the hierarchical categories erected to preserve systems in power. Not only does he interrogate colonialism in all its various guises, as it privileges 'civilized' over 'savage,' Western over non-Western, elect over preterite; he also undermines the hierarchies of narrative form that tacitly support colonialism in traditional narratives. Divisions like 'major' and 'minor' characters, significant and insignificant information, or dominant and subordinate motifs appear in texts reaffirming ontological and political hierarchies, whether explicitly or implicitly. Even the structural paradigm, calling after Aristotle, for a crisis and denouement implies a hierarchial arrangement of experience in which narratives valorize one event over all others.

(60)

Presumably, it also follows that novels in which there is a division between major and minor characters or in which there is a denouement, give expression, whether explicitly or implicitly, to the belief that the moon is made of green cheese. (Or perhaps it is the other sort of novel that reflects such a belief – it all depends, really, on whether, by postmodernist standards, such a belief would count as 'advanced' or 'retrograde,' and it is by no means easy to predict what sorts of beliefs theorists of postmodernism are likely to regard as 'advanced.') If hierarchies as such tacitly support colonialism, then *Gravity's Rainbow* must tacitly support colonialism, since it 'valorizes,' for instance, anti-climax and irresolution over crisis and denouement.[8] Indeed, Strehle herself must tacitly support colonialism because she 'privileges' novels without denouements and divisions between major and minor characters over novels with denouements and divisions between major and minor characters. Suffice it to say that there are novels – both realist and anti-realist – in which there are climaxes, denouements, divisions between major and minor characters and dominant and subordinate motifs, and so forth, that don't tacitly support colonialism (and that may not tacitly oppose it either – there are novels that, *mirabili dictu*, aren't about colonialism at all).[9]

Craige, for another, claims that 'if, as I believe, aesthetic form reflects the understanding of its time, we should be able to discover in the avant-garde literature the aesthetics of twentieth-century monism, the literary consequences of relativity' (26). Craige, however, doesn't discover anything: she assumes the existence of an 'understanding' of the time that is reflected in aesthetic form, and so it doesn't matter what the aesthetic forms of twentieth-century avant-garde literature are – they just have to, whatever they are, reflect 'man's advanced knowledge of evolution, relativity, and indeterminacy' (24). Not surprisingly, what she 'discovers' in the aesthetics of twentieth-century 'traditional' literature is what she takes to be the categorical opposite of what she discovers in avant-garde literature, *viz.*, man's emotional attachment to the fiction of creationism, absolutism, and determinacy. She further argues that 'the coexistence of the traditional with the avant-garde continues because man is both emotional and intellectual' (24). This *is* tidy, the emotional half of man being expressed in 'traditional' literature, and the intellectual half being expressed in 'avant-garde' literature. The problem, needless to say, is not just this pat dichotomy between twentieth-century 'traditional' and 'avant-garde' literature, but Craige's misconstrual of the theory of relativity and her assumption that there is an *a priori* connection between avant-garde literature and relativity:

because she assumes as much, she can, of course, discover in its aesthetic forms exactly the meaning she wants to. (So, for example, one finds her claiming that 'the aesthetic of unreliable narration' – 'the natural literary consequence of relativism' – signifies that 'there is no verifiable external reality' (50).) As John Limon remarks of 'the hapless theorists of the influence of Einstein':

> One finds oneself at slide shows aching with good intentions to see special relativity in the *Demoiselles d'Avignon*. It may, for all I know, be a cliché of Faulkner criticism that *The Sound and the Fury* – three parts from one time but three standpoints, one part from a different era, is modeled on space-time. I do not need to make absurdities up: critics have seen relativity in Poe.
>
> (1990: 11)

The Sound and the Fury, 'consist[ing] in the juxtaposition of four sections, three of which are first-person monologues,' Craige claims, reflects 'the relativist's shift in focus from beyond the text itself, his concern with relationships instead of with an absolute external reality, and his recognition of his own role in the production of meaning' (53–4).

Mellard likewise claims that the aspects that make the novel in this century modern

> are found . . . in novelists' expression – usually unconscious – of notions from various disciplines aggrandizing the importance of subjectivity, of consciousness, in an atomistic, indeterminate, exploding universe. As various conceptions of relativity and indeterminacy – expressed or exemplified in writers ranging from Henry Adams, John Dewey, and William James, to Joyce, Pound, Eliot, and Yeats – were gradually introduced into the novel-as-genre, either as elements of form or theme, they could only (we can see now) explode the monolithic nineteenth-century form.
>
> (40)

'Once the world had become subjective and relative,' he crudely claims, 'the novel had to become subjective and relative too, or disappear as other genres had disappeared' (55); as 'absolutes about the world began to diminish . . . the novel lost its absolute, homogeneous, monolithic aesthetic, because it could no longer presume congruent epistemological and ontological bases' (55). The fact that 'even during the critical phase of modernist consolidation we still find naturalistic novels naively projected as other than a mode [that is, projected as something in which the author believes] in, for instance, Richard Wright's *Native Son*, Norman Mailer's *The Naked and the Dead*, and James Jones's *From Here to Eternity*; and [that] in the works of Louis Auchincloss, J.P. Marquand, John O'Hara, and the novelists of manners we find a relatively naive realistic form' (17), Mellard construes as a sort of aberration, borne of nostalgia: modes, metaphors, mythoi, Mellard claims, 'may all persist after origination and, after epochal "old age" or "death," may thrust forth again, sentimentally, at any historical moment' (17).

Not only do Craige, Strehle, and Mellard all assume that literary forms carry 'static, fixed, eternal meanings' (to borrow a postmodernist cliché); they also assume that form has to reflect content. Each of these assumptions reinforces the other: the Newtonian *Weltanschauung* 'inheres' in the forms of the realist novel, and so in order for twentieth-century fiction to give expression to the post-Newtonian *Weltanschauung*, new forms must be found in which it 'inheres.' The reduction is thus complete: the new physics has demonstrated that reality is indeterminate, subjective, and relative, and so the novel, if it is to be 'adequate' to the 'new' reality, must not only be about how reality is indeterminate, subjective, and relative, but must also have an indeterminate, subjective, and relative form (which, because it is assumed a priori that the 'avant-garde' novel will 'reflect' the 'advanced' idea that reality is indeterminate, subjective, and relative, in most cases[10] just means that whatever forms and strategies it happens to use will be construed as reflecting the idea that reality is indeterminate, subjective, and relative).[11]

'The new monistic vision,' Craige pronounces, 'demands a different aesthetic expression from that appropriate to the dualistic vision' (23). 'We must be made,' Nadeau claims, 'to inhabit a fictive landscape in which the metaphysics commensurate with the new physics is pervasive and implicit throughout, a landscape in which the idea and mode of realization have achieved some final union in both narrative form and technique' – the 'brave new novelist who attempts to construct such a landscape,' he adds, 'confronts, however, a major and seemingly insurmountable difficulty – the metaphysical assumptions implicit in Newtonian physics are equally implicit in the art form that was also a product of the eighteenth century' (183). Strehle outlines her approach to the novels she discusses as involving a concern with 'both the content through which

[a] novel meditates on relativity or uncertainty [discontinuity, sub-jectivity, etc.] and the formal strategies through which it becomes, itself, relative or uncertain [discontinuous, subjective, etc., etc.]' (25–6).[12] As Tallis points out, the idea that there is and ought to be 'an isomorphism between the world at large and literature belongs to a crudity of understanding that has no place outside of the Sixth Form':

> Sensed disorder is not automatically mirrored in the order or disorder of a work. If that were the case, one would expect an artist who had lost a much loved wife to write works in which every sentence was broken off in the middle. Art is no more a simple mirror of reality, or an individual's experience of it, than is language itself.
>
> (1988b: 185)

Strehle herself asserts that in displacing 'Newton's absolute space with the interactive field theorized by Einstein, Heisenberg, and Bohr . . . [the actualist] necessarily reconceives art's relation to actuality. In the field model, art can no longer be the transparent glass or reflective mirror, and fiction cannot simply represent external reality' (18). In her attempt to back up this theoretical claim, she denies, for example, that Barth's character Ambrose in LETTERS is a mirror of either Barth or the character of the Author, arguing that

> [t]he creation of author-characters who provide a stable reflection of their creator belongs to a group of logocentric assumptions: that language mirrors reality, that the text can or should be a mirror up to nature, that the artist is an earthly allotrope of God, that good narratives reflect the cycle of fall and redemption that is, in the Western tradition, the story of life. Such assumptions characterize the metaphysical tradition in literature in its vari-ous (realist and modernist) phases. Like other actualists, Barth focuses some of the energy of his text on the disruption of this heritage and therefore demolishes the tidy system for which one thing is the same as another.
>
> (149)

However, Strehle's book is nothing if not a reflection of these so-called 'logocentric assumptions' (not to mention a veritable monu-ment to the building of tidy systems in which one thing – e.g.,

Heisenberg's uncertainty principle – is the same as another – e.g., existential uncertainty). For one thing, whether author-characters provide a stable reflection of their creator aside, Strehle certainly assumes that the novels she discusses are the stable reflection of their authors' beliefs. For another, her very premise is that contemporary fiction reflects the 'new physical reality,' so it's hard to see how it's not, on her own account, a 'mirror up to nature.' Moreover, since the 'new physical reality' in this fiction could only be given expression to through language (fiction being made, after all, out of words), language must, perforce, be the 'mirror' of this new reality in it. Finally, her interpretation of each of the novels she discusses amounts precisely to a reenactment of that story that she claims is, in the Western tradition, the story of life: characters reject the 'fallen' and 'pernicious' Newtonian view of reality and are redeemed by embracing the new physics.[13]

Strehle's contention that nineteenth-century realist forms are outmoded is likewise predicated on the idea that they do not 'reflect' reality. She claims, for instance, that '[a]ll of the artificial forms imposed on time in conventional narratives disintegrate in *J R*, leaving time flowing. Gaddis does not divide his narrative: without chapters, sections, or even open spaces in the text, time passes unclassified, unorganized, unspatialized'; 'one can,' she continues, 'further suppose that Gaddis deliberately made it impossible to "plot" his actions in chronological, objective, almanac time in order to emphasize instead the subjective, open, and "plotless" nature of lived time' (117–18). But what could it mean to suggest that novels without chapters, sections, or open spaces in the text are more 'natural' than novels with chapters, sections, or open spaces? 'Artificial' and 'natural' just aren't terms that apply to literary forms – to think that they are is to assume that there is a way in which language can be isomorphic with reality. The absence of chapters, sections, or open spaces in *J R* may well contribute to a sense of the plotless nature of lived time (though I would argue that the typographic continuity serves as a counterpoint to disconnectedness of the narrative and to its thematization of disconnectedness), but their absence in it is no more 'natural' than their presence in other novels is 'artificial.'

Since Strehle is prepared, moreover, to argue that the form of Margaret Atwood's *Cat's Eye* implies that 'the subject – even the artist – can't find an absolute frame from which to validate its perspective but floats without attainable certainty in relative spacetime' (184), and since the novel has chapters, sections, as well as open spaces, then, on her own terms, it follows that either it is possible to write a novel with chapters, sections, and open spaces that nevertheless 'fracture[s] the illusion of Newtonian absolute time' (186) or that the illusion of Newtonian absolute time does not inhere in chapter divisions.

Literary forms, conventions, and strategies have no metaphysical, epistemological, or political significance independently of the context in which they are embedded (and the context may well be such that no particular epistemological, metaphysical, or political significance can be attached to them): to assume that self-reflexivity from one contemporary novel to the next is expressive of the idea that reality is a linguistic construct, or to assume that third-person omniscient narration in realist fiction is indicative of the idea that everything is knowable and certain, or signifies an imperialist desire to control 'the Other,' is to ascribe a 'transcendental' meaning to them that they don't have.

It is worth pointing out that the idea that they do seems to owe in part to Whorf's hypothesis that the deep structure of languages implicitly reflects, e.g., metaphysical assumptions. If, however, it were true, for example, that the grammatical structure of Indo-European languages reflected a 'separate object' picture of the universe, then how could it be that 'Objects exist independently of perceptions of them' and 'Objects do not exist independently of perceptions of them' express different metaphysical beliefs? In appealing to Whorf's hypothesis on the grounds that it subverts the notion that form is merely a vehicle for content, theorists of postmodernism have failed to see that to regard a literary form or strategy as, irrespective of context, always 'meaning' x constitutes a way of looking at form that is no different from 'envelope' conceptions of it.

For real

It should be clear that, despite the frequency with which theorists of postmodernism invoke Lyotard's by now famous definition of the postmodern, they themselves, by and large, demonstrate anything but an incredulity toward metanarratives. They produce 'a discourse of legitimation,' one that seeks to justify both their theories and the literature they identify as 'postmodernist' in terms of an uncomplicated notion of progress, by recourse to the idea that they 'emancipate' us from the falsehoods systematically engendered by some univocal entity variously termed 'modernity' or 'Enlightenment thinking' or 'the western metaphysical tradition,' which falsehoods are passively 'mirrored' in both realist and modernist fiction.

That from which we have been ostensibly liberated includes not only the allegedly simplistic notions about self, reality, and truth that theorists of postmodernism attribute to 'Enlightenment'/ 'modernist' thinkers, but also what a number of them refer to as 'Enlightenment'/'modernist' beliefs in periodization and progress. The suggestion that what in part characterizes the 'postmodern' is a rejection of an 'Enlightenment'/'modernist' belief in periodization and progress is frequently made by theorists of postmodernism, especially by those who are anxious to dispel the notion that the ideas they characterize as 'postmodernist' are meant to be regarded as novel or more 'advanced' than the ideas of so-called 'modernists.'

So one finds David Couzens Hoy, for example, arguing that 'periodization is a modernist tool,' that the 'postmodern thinker challenges [the belief in periodization] by disrupting the modernist assumption that periods are self-contained unities or coherent wholes which can be clearly individuated from one another' (1988: 13), that the 'most characteristic feature of the postmodern attitude is the way it has moved beyond not only the rhetoric of progress but also the rhetoric of nostalgia' (28), and that 'since there is no necessary progress . . . the postmodern cannot imply that there is any normative advantage that comes from being either later in time or a sign of the future,' 'cannot and should not claim to be better, more advanced, or more clever than what preceded it' (38). 'That modernism does assume this superiority,' Couzens Hoy claims, 'is what distinguishes it from postmodernism' (38). The irony, of course, is that Couzens Hoy has to appeal to very notions of periodization and progress that he claims postmodernists reject in order to make these claims at all. To question such notions, Couzens Hoy would have to reject the very ideas of the 'modern' and 'postmodern' that he invokes in order to make the spurious distinctions he makes; he, however, is unable to do so because he is invested in the notion he claims postmodernist theorists reject – that is, he is invested in the notion that there *is* some identifiably 'postmodern attitude.'

Similarly, David Cowart argues in a recent essay on John Hawkes's *Whistlejacket* that literary postmodernism should not be conceived of as 'displacing modernism or realism' (1995: 100), should not be thought of in terms of a hierarchy in which 'one kind of art must be better or more advanced than another' (102), for, he claims, to 'assume a need in postmodernism to break with the past is to confuse its ends and means with those of the modernism that preceded it' (102). However, Cowart, by virtue of invoking the concept of 'postmodernism' in the first place (and a 'modernism' that preceded it), suggests that there has indeed been a break with the past, a break that he construes in terms of an opposition between the need on the part of 'modernism' to posit itself as a break with the past and the lack of such a need on the part of 'postmodernism.' Just as Couzens Hoy's claim that postmodernism challenges the 'modernist' assumptions of periodization and progress is predicated on those very same assumptions, so Cowart's claim that postmodernism rejects the 'modernist' need to see itself as a break with the past is predicated on the assumption of a break with the past, for by Cowart's unwitting account, postmodernism breaks with the past by breaking with the idea of breaking with the past.

Couzens Hoy, in contrast to Cowart, is aware of the difficulties of his position. He claims that 'the modernist may wish to rejoin that in using the prefix *post*, postmoderns are themselves invoking periodization' (13). 'The postmoderns could reply, however,' he goes on, 'that they are doing so simply because they are speaking to moderns. If postmoderns use the tools of modernity, they may do so rhetorically to subvert the progressivist assumption that modernity is the unequivocal telos of history' (13–14). This is a coy, but nevertheless inadmissible, argument, for, among other things, Couzens Hoy again has to assume the existence of some univocal entity – 'the moderns' – in order to make it, and he's just argued that the idea of periodization is problematic because it assumes the existence of self-contained or coherent wholes. If there are no such self-contained or coherent wholes (and I agree that there aren't), then the opponent to whom his postmoderns are speaking does not exist, indeed can't exist – without the existence of such self-contained or coherent wholes, there can't be any such thing as 'the moderns' or 'the modernist.' On the other hand, if Couzens Hoy wants to claim that 'the moderns' did in general assume that, for example, modernity was the unequivocal telos of history, then he needs to abandon the idea that what postmodernists demonstrate is that periodization is problematic because those who invoke it assume the existence of self-contained or coherent wholes. For if 'moderns' in general did assume as much, then periodization wouldn't be problematic. Couzens Hoy's investment in the concept of postmodernism thus puts him in a double bind.

Many theorists of postmodernism are not only committed to a

vision of the history of western thought as a simple linear one, as a march from the 'primitive' conceptions of a Plato, an Aristotle, a Descartes, to the 'advanced' thought of a Derrida, a Foucault, a Lacan – the flimsy protestations of a number of these theorists and critics to the ascription of such a belief to them notwithstanding – but are also in the thrall of the so-called 'binary thinking' they allege has been a feature of western thought since 'at least Plato.' It is indeed their wholehearted commitment to just such thinking that is in large part the source of all that is wrong with postmodernist theory and criticism. For in order to represent both postmodernist theory and fiction as transcending 'the western metaphysical tradition' and its reflection in realist and modernist fiction, postmodernists have had to flatten out the history of ideas as well as the history of literature.

Even theorists of postmodernism who are self-conscious about the problem that attends 'oppositional thinking' – *viz.*, the problem that, given the rejection of so-called 'binary thinking,' ensues from the attempt to oppose postmodernism to, for example, modernism in order to claim that postmodernism has transcended modernism – are unable to get around it, for the simple reason that, a I remarked of Couzens Hoy above, they are unwilling to abandon the concept of postmodernism itself (as well as, by extension, the concept of modernism). In *Virginia Woolf and Postmodernism*, for example, Pamela Caughie relies on what she calls 'postmodern assumptions and strategies' to challenge 'the necessity of choosing between or reconciling two alternatives, engendered by the application of dualistic distinctions' (1991: 194). 'In relying on postmodern assumptions and strategies to make my point,' she then asks, 'am I not in danger of falling back into the same kind of critical practice I take issue with, namely, setting up an opposition between two types of writing, modernism and postmodernism?' (194). In attempting to answer this question she points out quite rightly that

> [i]t does little good . . . to set up an opposition between traditional and modern novels in terms of the individual as central (nineteenth-century realism) and the individual as decentered (twentieth-century postmodernism), for as *The Voyage Out* shows, the individual is of great importance to some activities (falling in love, telling a story) and less so to others (translating Greek, writing a parody). The status of the individual changes in different contexts.
>
> (202)

Further, Caughie suggests, like Couzens Hoy, that we should refuse 'to see historical periods as coherent and self-contained' (198). If, she argues, 'we are to learn the lessons of postmodernism,' then we should resist 'seeking the "internal coherence" (as Jardine does) or the "fundamental ground" (as McHale does) of postmodernism' (206). 'To provide a coherent story of postmodernism,' she continues, 'would be to assume that diversity, difference, ambiguity, and lack of consensus are obstacles to be overcome in our critical readings rather than indications of the relational and changeable nature of the thing we are describing' (206).

In suggesting, however, that 'the reason we desire such a story . . . is that our critical practice, whether as feminists or postmodernists, is still largely based on modernist assumptions and values' (206–7), and that to get over desiring such a story would be 'to learn the lessons of postmodernism,' Caughie relies on that very 'oppositional thinking' she is so studiously trying to avoid. She not only assumes that to challenge the 'necessity' of choosing between or reconciling 'opposites' is 'postmodernist,' but also that unity, sameness, directness, and consensus are 'modernist' values and that diversity, difference, ambiguity, and lack of consensus are 'postmodernist.' In so assuming, Caughie not only sets up an absurdly reductive opposition between what 'they' believed and valued 'way back when' and what 'we' believe and value now, but also compromises her stated commitment to the idea that the status of, say, consensus or directness changes in different contexts. She argues that 'a postmodern reading based on pragmatic motives does not seek to resolve conflict or to reach consensus but to discover how to go on in the face of conflict and in the absence of consensus' (207). But there are contexts in which consensus is not only possible but desirable, and contexts in which directness can achieve a desired purpose that ambiguity might not.

For Caughie to have avoided falling 'back into the same kind of critical practice' that she takes issue with, she would have had to repudiate the very notions of 'postmodern' and 'modern' assumptions, strategies, and values. If she believes that the critics whose work she questions assume that diversity, difference, ambiguity, and lack of consensus are obstacles to be overcome, and if she finds such an assumption to be limited and narrow, then, rather than label it 'modernist,' she should just call it limited and narrow. The problem is not, as Caughie imagines, in being oppositional *per se* – in, say, taking issue with the rigor and quality of a critic's or theorist's arguments – but rather in constructing oppositions between 'then' and 'now' that, because they are grounded in notions such as that to value unity and sameness is 'modernist,' while to value diversity and difference is 'postmodernist,' cannot but be false oppositions. Caughie is unable to avoid emulating the critical practice she objects to because she is committed to the idea 'we' of the late twentieth century have radically different conceptions about such fundamental issues as difference and sameness and unity and diversity than 'they' of the eighteenth, nineteenth, or early twentieth centuries had, and that is the very sort of idea that underwrites the critical practice she finds problematic.

To abandon the 'binary thinking' that informs postmodernist theory and criticism would be to abandon all the facile and reductive oppositions theorists of postmodernism have appealed to – not least of which is the 'hierarchical' opposition of 'both/and'/'either/or' – in order to justify the claim that postmodernist theory and fiction are both intellectually and aesthetically more advanced than their predecessors. This is not to deny the existence of progress *tout court*; rather, it is to deny that one can paint the last three hundred years of the history of ideas or the history of literature in the west in the broad strokes theorists of postmodernism are wont to paint them in. I accept what I should have thought was a truism – that, as Charles Taylor puts it in a discussion of Foucault, 'the reality of history is mixed and messy':

> The problem is that Foucault tidies it up too much, makes it into a series of hermetically sealed, monolithic truth-regimes, a picture which is as far from reality as the blandest Whig perspective of smoothly broadening freedom.

(1986: 98)

Many theorists of postmodernism embrace the idea of epistemes, but, as I've been suggesting, they don't regard them as being incommensurable with one another; rather, they represent the history of ideas in terms of a progression from what they assume were widely-held false beliefs about the nature of knowledge, self, reality, truth, in the eighteenth and nineteenth centuries to what they assume have become widely-held true beliefs about the nature of knowledge, self, reality, truth in the late twentieth century. As with the history of ideas, so with the history of literature. Thus John Mepham, summarizing the characteristic postmodernist take on the progression from realism to postmodernism, writes:

Postmodernist fiction repudiates [the] impossible dream [of 'naive mimesis'] and does all that it can to advertise 'textuality.' It points toward the future because it is part of the grand narrative of emancipation from past illusions (realism, mimesis) and is based on a more sophisticated philosophical grasp of the relation between language and reality. In a way, postmodernist fictions are said to 'participate in that very general tendency in the intellectual life of our time toward viewing reality as *constructed* in and through our languages, discourses, and semiotic systems.' Their vocation is the 'project of unmasking the constructed nature of reality.'

(1991: 152; quoting Brian McHale, *Postmodernist Fiction*)

Instead of opposing so-called postmodernist fiction to so-called modernist and realist fiction in terms that cannot but result in oversimplification and falsification – e.g., the latter uncritically assumes that reality exists independently of us, while the former sophisticatedly posits reality as linguistic construct – why not trace, for example, a genealogy of the relationship between metaphysical anti-realism and fiction, investigate the various ways specific brands of metaphysical anti-realism get inscribed in certain novels of the eighteenth, nineteenth, and twentieth centuries?

If theorists who have partaken and continue to partake in the project of conceptualizing postmodernism gave up the 'binary thinking'[14] (among other things, for example, the very notion of an episteme, or paradigm, which presupposes the existence of widely-shared assumptions about such fundamental issues as the nature of reality, truth, self, knowledge) that leads them to accept uncritically a picture of the history of ideas and its relation to the history of literature that is naive and uninformed – which is to say, if they questioned the concept of postmodernism itself as they've articulated it, and the need to theorize about it – they would perhaps cease endlessly recirculating their clichés about realism, modernism, and postmodernism, cease attempting to construct tidy, schematic models of literary history, and perhaps begin to see the literature of the past three hundred years, and its relationship to the history of ideas, for the complicated, messy affair that it is.

Notes

INTRODUCTION

1. My position *vis-à-vis* 'the debate over postmodernism' is akin to the position John Ellis takes with respect to deconstruction in his *Against Deconstruction*. In the context of a discussion of the slogan 'all interpretation is misinterpretation,' he writes:

    > Viewed against [a] broader background, a reasonable judgment of the value of the recent debate over the meaning and usefulness of 'all interpretation is misinterpretation' will be obvious enough: it is not very well informed and not really very interesting. On the one hand, proponents cannot really be allowed to get away with the claim that they deserve the credit for having gotten rid of absolute truth and objective knowledge. That was really done a very long time ago, and the resulting epistemological position is not a new and provocative one but instead a commonplace. But their opponents, on the other hand, are just as guilty in unnecessarily offering them this ground to occupy, ground to which they deserve no claim.
    > (1989: 100–1)

    He further notes that in some cases the claim that 'all interpretation is misinterpretation' is glossed by proponents in such a way that, rather than rendering it merely a commonplace, renders it trite – Jonathan Culler, he notes, 'provides an example of this when he explains its meaning as . . . "Since no reading can escape correction, all readings are misreadings"' (102). 'That *any* assertion or claim to know something is open to later rethinking,' Ellis notes, 'is obvious and has long been so; it cannot be used as a new view of interpretation' (102–3).

2. See also Warren Montag, 'What is at Stake in the Debate on Postmodernism?' 'Notice,' Montag writes, 'the terms of the debate on postmodernism and the disjunctive dilemmas that it imposes':

    > (1) Marxism will be transcendental or it will not be (Jameson asserts and Lyotard is only too happy to agree); (2) works of art either represent something more real than themselves which is therefore the depth beneath their surface (making them susceptible to a hermeneutic reading) or they are absolutely autonomous, indeterminate and therefore 'unanalyzable'; (3) either the subject is master of itself, its own thoughts and actions or it has simply vanished into the pure systemacity of the historical present. In addition, the first set of alternatives (transcendality, art as representation, the subject as origin-center) is often placed in historical opposition to the second set (the absence of transcendality, the indeterminacy of art, the

death of the subject) as a once existing past that has given way to the present as one historical totality to another. So, for example, the classically conceived subject once existed but no longer does, just as art once represented reality but has somehow ceased to do so.

(1988: 88)

'These of course,' Montag notes, 'are the very dilemmas that have ordered political, philosophical and aesthetic speculations for centuries' (88–89). Yes and no. Yes, in that sense that these *sorts* of issues have dominated speculation for centuries. No, in that the subject-is-master-of-itself/the subject-is-dead and art as representation/the indeterminacy of art, for example, pose *false* dilemmas.

3. As one critic has put it,

The main alternative [to the literal interpretation of the claim that language constructs reality] that suggests itself is: Our *representations* of reality are linguistic constructs. There is, so to say, a world of difference between the first interpretation and this second one. For while the first was absurd, the second is quite true. But it is unfortunately a truth so obvious that we might wonder why anyone thought it worthwhile to direct our attention towards it. For our *representations* of reality are, characteristically, in the form of sentences, and sentences, of course, are of some language or another; they are 'linguistic constructs.' So interpreted this way, the doctrine is robbed of its blinding, revelatory force. Who (we might ask) could conceivably deny it?

(Doyle, 4–5)

CHAPTER 1

1. The dialetheist believes that there are true statements of the form (P & ~P). The term 'dialethia' owes to Graham Priest and Richard Routley. The word is not, Priest notes, a bona fide Greek one, but its Greek roots are meant to indicate the Janus-faced nature of a true contradiction: if P and ~P is a true contradiction, then P 'faces' both truth and falsity (1987: 4).

   A number of contemporary logicians have attempted to answer the dialetheist's suggestion that the only way the logical paradoxes can be resolved is by accepting that they are true contradictions – see, e.g., Keith Simmons, *Universality and the Liar: An Essay on Truth and the Diagonal Argument*, and R.M. Sainsbury, *Paradoxes*.

2. Having noted that 'our founding father, Plato, wrote nothing but dialogues,' and agreeing that they are 'a spectacular impetus for our intellectual tradition' (147), Roochnik goes on to point out that nevertheless 'it is far from clear whether Plato actually thought there could be a philosophical dialogue, that is, a dialogue between philosophers. To argue that, in fact, no one, not Socrates, the Eleatic Stranger, nor Timeaus, ever gets into a dialogue with another philosopher is possible, but beyond the scope of this paper' (163, n.3).

3. I address the question of whether or not Derrida is being misrepresented below.
4. Conjunctions are true if and only if both conjuncts are true. The 'maybe both' expressed by '∨' in the left-hand side of the conjunction is negated by the right-hand side because the disjunction that constitutes it states 'either not-P or not-Q.' So either P or Q must be false. A disjunction is true if at least one of its components is true. Since the left-hand side of the conjunction rules out the possibility that both P and Q are false, the disjunction (~P ∨ ~Q) is true. The statement thus asserts that either P is true or Q is true, but not both and not neither.
5. Schrift is referring to Derrida's discussion in 'Plato's Pharmacy' of the occurrence of the word *pharmakon* in the *Phaedo*, where Plato uses it to signify the hemlock Socrates is given to drink by his executioners.
6. It is worth noting, in passing, Shankman's assumption that if language is to be adequate to reality, it must somehow 'resemble' reality (this after he has noted with approval the fact that 'Socrates . . . gets Cratylus to agree that custom or convention does in fact contribute to our understanding of language' by getting him to admit that though 'the word *skêlros* ('hard') contains the letter lambda, which is a liquid and thus, because of its softness, contradicts the meaning of the word which it helps to constitute,' it is 'nonetheless intelligible as it is conventionally spelled' and so need not be changed, as Cratylus suggests, by adopting a letter 'more appropriate to the meaning of the word' (6)). For if reality were indeed paradoxical, the statement 'reality is paradoxical' – which is not itself paradoxical – would convey that fact. I will return to this point in my discussion of postmodernist theorists and critics who assume, for example, that in order for contemporary novels to reflect the allegedly fragmented nature of contemporary reality, they themselves must be fragmented.
7. See also Debra B. Bergoffen, 'Nietzsche's Madman: Perspectivism Without Nihilism.' Bergoffen argues that '[i]n replacing Kierkegaard's either/or with his own either . . . or, Nietzsche rejects the logic of exclusive disjunction for a logic which affirms disjointed terms' (1990: 70). She claims, for example, that 'the task the Madman tells us is to be like gods,' and that '[f]rom the Greeks we learn that gods play' and 'from the Jews and Christians we learn that they create' (71). Nietzsche, 'moving beyond the either/or of the Greek and Judaeo-Christian alternative,' she concludes, 'teaches us that to be like gods is to create in the spirit of playfulness' (71). 'Gods play or they create' is not, however, an exclusive disjunction. *Pace* Clayton Koelb, then, who, in his introduction to the volume in which Bergoffen's essay appears, writes that she 'offers a version of the postmodern Nietzsche who rejects the law of noncontradiction in favor of "a logic which affirms disjointed terms"' (1990: 10), no rejection of the law of noncontradiction is required to affirm both these disjuncts because they are neither contradictories nor contraries.
8. 'The Logic of Paradox Revisited,' (162–3). Priest notes elsewhere that in rejecting the intuitionist claim and therefore endorsing the law of the excluded middle he can be seen as espousing what might be

called 'classical dialetheism.' He says, however, that an 'intuitionist dialetheism' is possible (1987: 83).

9. It should be noted that Schrift, after having argued that 'the movement of the undecidables exhibits a different principle: the nonexclusive conjunction both A and not-A,' goes on to describe Derrida as 'highlight[ing] the oscillation between undecidable opposites' (106). One might ask what a conjunction that was an oscillation between opposites would look like.

10. See also Raymond Tallis, *Not Saussure: A Critique of Post-Saussurean Literary Theory* (1988a: 208):

    What Derrida seems unable to accept is that, in ordinary experience, presence (to) and self-presence are not absolute but matters of degree. I can be more or less present to something, more or less absent from it – in terms of the sharpness of my attention to it, the collectedness of my consciousness. For Husserl, there are no degrees of presence; one can no more be a teeny-weeny bit present to one's surroundings, say, than one can be a teeny-weeny bit pregnant. Presence for him (and consequently for Derrida whose critique takes place from within the Husserlian framework) is all-or-nothing, non-graded. And since presence is an unachievable absolute, it must be nothing. Disbelief in Husserl's presence, however, does not license dissent from belief in ordinary conceptions of presence and absence. Likewise, uncovering the paradoxes in Husserlian presence does not necessarily undermine 'the Western metaphysics of presence.' It may undermine Husserl's (or even Hegel's) metaphysics of presence but not the notion of presence implicit in everyday life.

11. See also Jeffrey Nealon, *Double Reading*, who proposes regarding professionalism as *pharmakon*: theory's professionalism is 'a cure for criticism's malaise' but 'professionalism seems also to be a poison' (1993: 16). The '"systematic" undecidability' of the *pharmakon* – 'the "cure" of knowledge also brings, at the same time and through the same word, the "poison" of writing' – resembles 'the "institutional" situation of the profession of theory: the cure of theory brings with it the poison of professionalism' (16–17). According to Nealon, this puts the 'postmodern academy' at an 'impasse': with what he refers to as 'the closure of metaphysics' – that is, with the 'withdrawal' of the category of truth – 'something comes to thought that cannot be read or understood in the terms of that thought, something such as the "perfectly logical" impasse of knowledge and its institutions, the fact that the same data can lead to two conclusions that radically exclude each other' (20). The solution, he claims, is to

    rethink the path that led to this impasse, to find some way to rethink the impasse, some way to think opposites together – theory and academy, poison and cure, thinking and acting – without falling into the spuriousness of simply neutralizing the differences within some 'beyond,' but likewise without giving in to the status quo of impasse.

    (18)

But the fact that 'theory' is a 'cure' in one sense and a 'poison' in another are not two states of affairs that 'radically exclude each other,' and so there is no 'logical impasse' that needs to be rethought.

12. See also Gordon Slethaug, *The Play of the Double in Postmodern Fiction*: '[p]oststructuralists and postmodernists do not aim to create a new kind of dialectic that recognizes and resolves contrastive dualities; instead, through an awareness of metonymical displacement, they establish a dialogue of hesitation in which irreconcilable oppositions refer to the very operation of signifying' (1993: 28). But since form and content, for example – one among the 'irreconcilable oppositions' Slethaug mentions – are not in fact anything like irreconcilably opposed, postmodernists and poststructuralists need not waste their time aiming not to create a new kind of dialectic in order to avoid reconciling what isn't irreconcilably opposed in the first place.

13. See also Charles Jencks, who in *What Is Post-Modernism?* defines postmodernism as a 'paradoxical dualism, or double coding, which its hybrid name entails: the continuation of Modernism and its transcendence' (quoted in Rose, 1991: 107).

14. See also Robert Con Davis and Ronald Schleifer, who in their foreword to *Postmodern Genres*, write that 'the constant tendency of postmodern genres [is], as Perloff explains, toward nonrationalistic and wholesale "appropriation of other genres, both high and popular . . . [in] a both/and situation rather than one of either/or"' (1988: viii). Perloff herself does not claim in the introduction to the volume she has edited that the 'longing [of postmodern genre] for a both/and situation rather than one of either/or' (8) is 'nonrationalistic,' but she does note in it that the contributors to the volume 'repeatedly use terms like *violation, disruption, dislocation, decentering, contradiction, confrontation, multiplicity and indeterminacy*' to describe 'postmodern texts' (7–8; her emphasis).

15. Hassan, too, however, argues that 'a "period" . . . must be perceived in terms *both* of continuity *and* discontinuity, the two perspectives being complementary and partial':

> The Apollonian view, rangy and abstract, discerns only historical conjunctions; the Dionysian feeling, sensuous, though nearly purblind, touches on only the disjunctive moment. Thus postmodernism, by invoking two divinities at once, engages a double view. Sameness and difference, unity and rupture, filiation and revolt, all must be honored if we are to attend to history, apprehend (perceive, understand) change as both a spatial, mental structure and as a temporal physical process, both as pattern and unique event.
> (88)

He, unlike Hutcheon and others, does not refer to this 'double view' as constituting an 'unresolvable contradiction.' But he is equivocal as to whether this 'double view' is unique to postmodernism. He says *a* period must be perceived in terms of both continuity and discontinuity, but then intimates that postmodernism, by invoking 'two divinities at once,' is special.

16. In *Five Faces of Modernity*, Matei Calinescu similarly suggests that

> [t]hinking of the Italian notion of a 'weak thought' . . . we might say that modernism argued from a position of logical certainty and 'methodological strength,' whereas postmodernism has always been aware of the advantages of a certain 'methodological weakness': the 'either/or' logic of the former gave way to the 'both/and' logic of the latter.
>
> (283–4)

He claims, for example, that postmodernist fiction is both enjoyable and complex:

> The enjoyable, deliberately excluded from the austere aesthetics of modernism, has been fully revalued by the postmoderns, not only in architecture or the arts but also in literature (as Umberto Eco, after John Barth, has insisted).
>
> (1987: 283–4)

The dubious suggestion that modernist fiction deliberately excluded the enjoyable from its aesthetics aside, what is 'weak' or logically uncertain about the idea of fiction being both enjoyable and complex?

See also Robert Venturi, who, in *Complexity and Contradiction in Architecture*, writes:

> I prefer 'both-and' to 'either-or,' black and white, and sometimes gray, to black or white. . . . An architecture of complexity and contradiction has a special obligation toward the whole: its truth must be in the totality or its implications of totality. It must embody the difficult unity of inclusion rather than the easy unity of exclusion.
>
> (Quoted in Rose, 1991: 106)

CHAPTER 2

1. See also Jerry Aline Flieger, *The Purloined Punch Line: Freud's Comic Theory and the Postmodern Text*. Flieger, discussing Beckett, asks, '[i]s the postmodern aesthetic just a new aestheticism, a veiled avatar of the modernist elitist aesthetic of art for art's sake? Does unworked textuality preclude social reference and concerns, leaving its protagonist post-man stranded in exile?' No, she answers ('[s]ome postmoderns may have it so, but I don't think we need count Beckett (nor Derrida nor Blanchot for that matter) among them' (1991: 233)): rather, she argues, the postmodern aesthetic 'posts' a 'third perspective' that transcends 'binary logic':

> It is even perhaps this erosion of the logocentric bias that is responsible for the emergence of the postmodern comic, a self-deconstructing mode that works thanks to its own contradictions (whereas earlier comic writing, conforming to binary logic, has tended to cover up the internal contradictions of the process, masquerading as *either* a referential/utilitarian process *or* as an absolute/poetic process). Indeed, the aesthetic post-comic is at once a textual phenomenon or

characteristic . . . and a reinterpretation of the comic process itself as
an effect of desire.

(251–2)

2. If indeed, as Strehle claims, realists considered the proper goal of
    art to be the 'simple reflection of a Newtonian reality,' then, since
    Newton, like many empiricists, thought secondary qualities like color,
    sound, and smell to be 'ideal,' and primary qualities like size, exten-
    sion, and shape to be 'real,' one would expect to find this conjunction
    of realism and idealism reflected in realist fiction.

3. This is not to say that paradox doesn't feature at all in *The French
    Lieutenant's Woman*. Something like the age-old problem of divine fore-
    knowledge and free will, for example, is suggested by the narrator's
    claiming that, on the one hand, the characters he has created 'never
    existed outside of my own mind,' and on the other that he has been
    merely pretending 'until now to know my characters' minds and inner-
    most thoughts' (80), a problem he attempts to resolve by defining
    God (and, by extension, himself – 'The novelist is still a god, since he
    creates'), as 'the freedom that allows other freedoms to exist' (82).

4. See also Craig Owens, 'The Allegorical Impulse: Toward a Theory of
    Postmodernism.' Discussing the question pondered in Laurie Ander-
    son's *Americans on the Move* of how an extra-terrestrial might read the
    raised-arm gesture of the male emblazoned on Appollo 10, Owens
    writes:

    Two alternatives: either the extraterrestrial recipient of this message
    will assume that it is simply a picture, that is, an analogical likeness
    of the human figure, in which case he might logically conclude that
    male inhabitants of Earth walk around with their right arms per-
    manently raised. Or he will somehow divine that this gesture is
    addressed to him and attempt to read it, in which case he will be
    stymied, since a single gesture signifies both greeting and farewell,
    and any reading of it must oscillate between these two extremes.
    The same gesture could also mean 'Halt!' or represent the taking of
    an oath, but if Anderson's text does not consider these alternatives
    that is because it is not concerned with ambiguity, with multiple
    meanings engendered by a single sign; rather, two *clearly defined but
    mutually incompatible* readings are engaged in blind confrontation in
    such a way that it is impossible to choose between them . . . and this
    works to problematize the activity of reading, which must remain
    forever suspended in its own uncertainty.

    (1984: 219–20; his emphasis)

    However, not only are these readings not necessarily mutually incom-
    patible (the gesture could mean both 'Farewell to the inhabitants of
    earth' and 'Hello to the inhabitants of other planets'), but there's also
    no reason to suppose that, even if they were, it would be in principle
    impossible to choose between them. What Owens ignores is the fact
    that the meaning of a sign with multiple meanings (even putatively
    opposed meanings) is very often determined by the context in which
    it is used (and so it is not the case that any reading of the raised-arm

gesture must oscillate between the extremes of 'hello' and 'goodbye,' since there are contexts – a courtroom, for example – in which it signifies neither 'hello' nor 'goodbye').

5.   It could be that Kuhns is conflating the statement the analysand refers to with the analysand's statement about the statement referred to. The analysand says that the statement he is referring to is not true ('I desire such-and-such' is not true); if this is true, then his statement about this statement is true ('"I desire such-and-such" is not true' is true).

6.   Paul responds to suspicions that his ministry was just a front for his own advancement in 2 Corinthians ('[I]t is not your possessions that I want,' he writes, 'but yourselves' (1990, 2 Cor. 12:14)). That at least one of the onlookers harbors such suspicions about the mute stranger is suggested by his referring to the stranger as a 'Green prophet from Utah' – as H. Bruce Franklin notes in his edition of the novel, 'Joseph Smith, the first Mormon prophet, and Brigham Young, his successor as Prophet, were subjects of raging controversy' at the time in which Melville was writing *The Confidence-Man*. 'Smith,' Franklin claims, 'was attacked as a vicious imposter or a witless enthusiast, Young as his worldly and ambitious St. Paul' (10 f.3).

7.   Paul, claiming that 'Christ's truth is in me,' also writes that 'I will go on acting as I do at present, to cut the ground from under the feet of those who are looking for a chance to be proved my equals in grounds for boasting':

> These people are counterfeit apostles, dishonest workers disguising themselves as apostles of Christ. There is nothing astonishing in this; even Satan disguises himself as an angel of light. It is nothing extraordinary, then, when his servants disguise themselves as the servants of uprightness.
>
>   (2 Cor. 11:11–15)

Yet the question raised in the opening chapters of *The Confidence-Man* is how can the onlookers know whether the stranger who writes the words of Paul is a counterfeit apostle or not? Christ said 'make a tree sound and its fruit will be sound; make a tree rotten and its fruit will be rotten. For the tree can be told by its fruit' (Matt. 12:33). In the case of the mute stranger, however, it's not clear that the tree can be told by its fruit – that the onlookers can't tell is suggested by their varied responses to him.

8.   However, because Kuhns speaks indiscriminately of 'the indeterminacy of the truth of beliefs,' it would seem that if he does think as much, he is committing himself to the idea that *all* statements are neither true nor false.

CHAPTER 3

1.   See also Susan Hekman, who in *Gender and Knowledge: Elements of a Postmodern Feminism* asserts that 'both feminism and postmodernism challenge the epistemological foundations of western thought and argue that the epistemology that is definitive of Enlightenment humanism,

if not all of western philosophy, is fundamentally misconceived' (1990: 1). The 'postmodern feminist critique' argues that

> [t]he Enlightenment/modernist epistemology that informs both liberalism and the individualistic moral code to which it is linked is inherently sexist; the gendered connotations of the rational/irrational dichotomy are not optional. Rather, they inform that epistemology in all of its dimensions. It is an epistemology that not only defines women as incapable of reason and morality, but also questions their very identity. The liberal feminists who want to retain the 'good' elements of this epistemology while rejecting its sexism misunderstand the deep-rootedness of that sexism. An epistemology that defines women as not fully rational, moral, or even human cannot be simply repaired to allow women a new status. It must be rejected outright.
>
> (59)

If the gendered connotations of the rational/irrational dichotomy were nonoptional, it would be impossible to conceive of the concepts of rationality and irrationality without associating the former with masculinity and the latter with femininity. Since, however, it is perfectly possible to conceive of these concepts in the absence of their gendered connotations, it follows that the gendered connotations of the rational/irrational dichotomy are optional.

2. One might ask how classifying, say, spaniels, mastiffs, boxers, poodles, etc., as dogs (a) reduces the differently similar to the same (since classifying them all as dogs doesn't require that one deny that they are each particular kinds of dogs, nor does it require that one deny that every dog is different from every other dog) and (b) turns the merely different – say, cats – into the absolutely other.

3. It's also not clear what to make of Yarbrough's assertion that the law *requires* the assumption of a stable, unitary self. This seems to imply that if selves were unstable and nonunitary, the law of noncontradiction would not be true, or would not be believed to be true. And, like most postmodernists (despite his distancing himself in some respects from what he regards as poststructuralist postmodernism), he does suggest that the self is indeed unstable and nonunitary. But then why aren't selves generally indifferent, for example, to what sorts of foods they ingest? Since they are not generally indifferent, then either they are in fact stable and unitary, or believing that something isn't both poisonous and not poisonous does not require the assumption of a stable and unitary self.

4. See also Herbert J. Levine, 'Beyond Negation: Paradoxical Affirmation in Whitman's Third Edition.' Levine argues that Whitman makes use of a negative analogy that takes the form of 'not the X is so any more than the Y is' in order to 'equivocate between two forms of attachment, one visible and one invisible, one bodily and one spiritual' that 'his culture sees . . . as alternatives' but to which 'he wants to maintain equal commitments' (1994: 186). 'From "Song of Myself" and onward,' Levine claims:

> Whitman consistently links religion, the soul and death as integral elements of his faith in a future of the apocalypse of spirit. In such

a future, there will be no further need to equivocate between the contradictory claims of body and soul, because all will be 'Soul.'

(187)

That future, Levine suggests, is now here: in order for his readers 'to puzzle out what he really stood for . . . each . . . had to develop a new relationship to possessive, patriarchal, hierarchial thinking: no longer "either/or," but "both/and." More than a century after his poems were published, they begin to perform their chosen cultural work' (188). By referring to the relationship between body and soul as 'contradictory,' Levine, like Nadeau, confuses the fallacy of bifurcation that he ascribes to western culture at large with a commitment to the law of the excluded middle. That is, rather than pointing out that western culture commits a fallacy if it regards the claims of body and soul as mutually exclusive, Levine, by calling these claims 'contradictory' implies that they are indeed mutually exclusive and thus commits the fallacy himself.

5. It should be noted that the suggestion that 'we become as much aware of *sameness* as we are of *differences*' not only doesn't require a rejection of the law of the excluded middle, but is positively banal. For how could we possibly become aware of sameness without being aware of differences?

6. R.M. Dancy suggests that there is a problem with Aristotle's formulation here. That is, Aristotle seems to infer from 'all predicates apply to all things' to 'all things are one' (1975: 47). Dancy notes that 'Aristotle seems to be thinking, very loosely, that [for example] "this one thing is a battleship, a wall and a man" amounts to "a battleship, a wall, and a man are all one thing," i.e., that there *is* only one thing (since the same moves work for every predicate)' (47). However, Dancy continues, 'it is worth noting that we could support him if we saddled him with the "identity of indiscernibles": with the claim that where there are two distinct things, there is a predicate true of the one but not of the other' (47). For,

if there are two distinct things, *a* and *b*, one must have a predicate, say 'F,' that the other lacks. But if one of them, say *b*, lacks 'F,' it has 'not F' (by the law of the excluded middle), and so (by the generalized denial of the law of noncontradiction), it has 'F.' Since everything both has and lacks every predicate, there are no predicates by which distinct things can be discriminated; so nothing is distinct from anything else.

(47)

CHAPTER 4

1. The proof is as follows:

Show (P & ~P) → Q
1. P & ~P   Assumption
2. P   1, Simplification

3. P ∨ Q 2, Addition
4. ~P 1, Simplification
5. Q 3, 4, Disjunctive Syllogism

2. See, for example, Stephen Read, who argues that the argument from (P & ~P) to Q equivocates on the formula P ∨ Q (the third line of the proof). In order to infer Q from ~P, he notes, the very minimum one must know is that 'if ~P, then Q' – that is for DS (disjunctive syllogism) to be valid, the major premise 'P ∨ Q' must be equivalent to 'if ~P, then Q). However, he claims, (P ∨ Q) at line 3 is inferred from P at line 2. In one sense, then, P ∨ Q follows from P alone, but then it is not equivalent to 'if ~P, then Q.' In another sense, P ∨ Q is equivalent to 'if ~P, then Q,' and with the minor premise, ~P, entails Q. These senses, Read maintains, 'cannot be the same – or at least, that they are is as contentious as the claim that *EFQ* [*ex falso quodlibet*] is a valid consequence' (1994: 60).

3. Dancy, however, does not think (or at least did not at the time he wrote his book) that any good reasons have been advanced for accepting that there are true contradictions: 'One might deny the law of noncontradiction for all sorts of reasons. None that I have seen strike me as good reasons. But neither do I see any reason for saying that there never *could* be a good reason for denying it' (142).

4. Stephen Read, however, argues that even if one can show that it is not the case that anything follows from a contradiction by showing that *ex contradictione quodlibet* fails, there is another paradox that arises if one allows that there are true contradictions, namely Curry's paradox – in Read's example, 'If this (conditional) proposition is true, then snow is black,' where 'this (conditional) proposition' refers to the whole conditional (161). If the conditional is true, then it has a true antecedent, and so by *modus ponens* (if P, and if P then Q, therefore Q), the consequent must be true. So if the conditional is true, snow is black, which is just what the conditional says. Thus we have shown that the conditional is true. But given that the conditional is true, it must have a true antecedent, and so, again, by *modus ponens*, but now not on the assumption that the conditional is true (for we have already shown that it is true), the consequent – snow is black – must be true. So we have shown that the conditional is true, and that it follows from the fact that it is true that snow is black. Thus, Read concludes, if 'we intend to stomach the paradoxes, we must reject not only the argument that shows that if any proposition is both true and false, then snow is black, but also the argument that the above conditional is true, and hence, once again, snow is black' (161).

Read notes that it has been argued that the argument about the conditional illegitimately relies on contraction – the principle that two applications of an assumption in an argument can be replaced by one. '[H]aving assumed the conditional was true,' he explains, 'we applied that assumption twice – once as the conditional premiss of *modus ponendo ponens*, secondly, as the antecedent of that conditional premiss – to infer that snow was black' (162). And yet, he continues, 'we recorded that assumption only once when we concluded that if the conditional was true, then snow is black. If we were to make explicit the double use of the assumption, we would obtain "If the conditional is true then if the conditional is true then snow is black," which is not the conditional. Hence the argument no longer goes through' (162). But if one rejects contraction to avoid the consequences of Curry's paradox, then, Read argues, the reasoning that enables the conclusion that the liar sentence, say, is both true and false is blocked. The proof of latter proceeds by *reductio* – if it is true, then it is false, but if it is false, then it is true – but *reductio*, Read argues, is closely related to contraction – its basic form is that of *consequentia mirabilis*, 'if P, then ~P, so ~P.' ~P, in turn, is equivalent to 'if P, then absurdity,' and thus *consequentia miribalis* expands into 'if P then if P then snow is black, so if P, then snow is black,' which, according to Read, is 'an instance of contraction' (162).

5.   See also Allen Thiher, who argues that Robbe-Grillet's *In the Labyrinth*

> proposes hermeneutics as a game for which the rules must be elicited from the novel's own practice of writing. Exterior rules cannot be imposed. Robbe-Grillet discards a number of familiar rules, such as the principle of noncontradiction and the rules for temporality and chronology that are dependent on this principle. It is as if we were invited to play chess in a non-Euclidean game space. Yet Robbe-Grillet's novels are systematic in a nearly Saussurean sense. They obey rules, given within the text, such as certain types of opposition and recurrence, with a quasi-mathematical rigor. If the reader is to play the game, he is obliged to accept a ludic pact that takes him into a text that seeks to invent new language games and, perhaps, new modes of articulating the world.
>
> (1984: 179)

Yet if Robbe-Grillet 'discards' the law of noncontradiction, and if the reader is expected to discard it too, how could the reader recognize certain types of opposition and recurrence as being certain types of opposition and recurrence? A language-game founded on a generalized denial of the law of noncontradiction would not be a game at all because there would be no rules – that is, all moves would be possible.

6.   Jan Łukasiewicz argues that the law of noncontradiction has 'no logical worth, since it is valid only as an assumption,' but that 'as a consequence it acquires a *practical-ethical value*, which is all the more important' (1971: 508; his emphasis):

> *The principle of contradiction is the sole weapon against error and falsehood.* Were we not to recognize this principle and hold joint assertion and denial to be possible, then we could not defend other propositions against false or deceitful propositions. One falsely accused of murder could find no means to prove his innocence before the court. At most, he could only manage to prove that he had committed no murder; this negative truth cannot, however, remove its contradictory positive from the world, if the principle of contradiction fails. If just one witness is found who (not shirking from committing

perjury) implicates the accused, his false assertion can in no way be contradicted and the defendant is irretrievably lost. From this one sees that the necessity of recognizing the principle of contradiction is a *sign of the intellectual and ethical incompleteness of man*.

(508; his emphasis)

7. Cf. Clayton Koelb, who in his introduction to *Nietzsche as Postmodernist* argues that 'perhaps the most important insight of contemporary theory is that narratives (of all kinds, including philosophical or scientific explanations) can come into being only if they leave something out,' that 'the possibility of narrative arises only as a result of acts of exclusion' (1990: 8). He accepts that one cannot not exclude, and yet argues that what this implies is that 'the allegedly philosophical law of noncontradiction ('not A and Not-A') is untenable: not only do we violate it regularly but we *must* violate it in order to think' (8).

8. And also by her claim that Picasso's bronze statue of a baboon (*Baboon with Young*, 1951), the head of which is made out of two toy cars, violates the law of noncontradiction: it is, she says, 'both a car and not a car' (149). No: it is the head of baboon made out of two toy cars, or, if one wants, both two toy cars and the head of a baboon.

See also, Richard Kearney, *The Wake of the Imagination: Toward a Postmodern Culture*:

The postmodern deconstruction of the metaphysical opposition between the imaginary and the real opens up an alternative logic – the logic of 'dream,' of the unconscious play of language which defies the logocentric principle of noncontradiction. This dream logic of 'doubling' is frequently found in literary works, e.g., Mallarmé's notion of *mimique* or Joyce's portrayal (especially in *Finnegans Wake* of 'nighttime consciousness' which permits us to have 'two thinks at a time.' It is also anticipated by Nietzsche's talk of 'truth becoming a woman' (a pure play of appearances without any reference to an underlying reality), and by Freud's description of the unconscious as a play between the strange (*unheimlich*) and the familiar (*heimlich*). Such models undermine the *either/or* logic of metaphysics in their insistence upon 'the paradoxes of the double and of repetition, the blurring of the boundary lines between *imagination* and *reality*.'

(1989: 289; quoting Derrida, 'The Double Session')

9. 'Brain-teasers' often capitalize on just such false assumptions. Consider, for example:

Richard Roe met a friend wearing a lieutenant's uniform. They shook hands and greeted each other warmly as they had not seen each other in ten years. With his friend was a little girl: 'I've been married since you saw me last to someone you don't know,' said the lieutenant. 'This girl is my daughter.' Richard asked the child's name, and she replied that it was the same as her mother's. 'So your name is Margaret!' How did he know?

(*Esquire's Handbook for Hosts*, 1953: 246)

CHAPTER 5

1.   'I am ... well aware,' Olsen notes, 'that many of the critical strateg-
     ies I employ – notions of periodization and genre, for instance – are
     "totalizing" systems that fly in the face of what it is I am trying to
     describe: postmodern humor, a detotalizing impulse that embraces
     plurality' (34). This itself is a typical 'critical strategy' of theorists
     of postmodernism: 'totalization' flies in the face of its tenets, but so
     long as one explicitly acknowledges that it does, one is then free to
     'totalize.' Further, Olsen, of course, takes it for granted that realism
     is a totalizing impulse that rejects plurality.

2.   This is true not only with respect to primary qualities, but also with
     respect to secondary qualities – one's belief that the sky is blue, that
     lava is hot, that sewage smells is compatible with both the belief that
     such qualities are 'in' objects and that they are not. Moreover, one
     might be a realist about primary qualities and an anti-realist about
     secondary qualities.

3.   See also Firdous Azim, who argues that literary '[r]ealism puts
     subject and object of representation into dichotomous positions, and
     sees "reality" as something *external* to the narrating subject' (1993: 29;
     her emphasis). The idea that there is some reality external to one's
     mind or perceptions is too fundamental to be regarded as 'realist' or
     as distinctive of literary realism.

4.   'Of course,' Graham Priest points out in defending this position, 'the
     world as such is not the *kind* of thing that can be consistent or incon-
     sistent. Consistency is a property of sentences (statements, or what-
     ever), not tables, chairs, stars and people' (1987: 200). However,

     > it might be suggested, to say that the world is consistent is to say
     > that any true purely descriptive sentence about the world is con-
     > sistent. What we are to make of the notion of a purely descript-
     > ive statement is a moot point. Still, maybe it is possible to give a
     > satisfactory sense to this notion, and to produce some transcend-
     > ental argument for the consistency of the world in this sense; but
     > I know of no way of doing this and there are persuasive argu-
     > ments against it. Certainly, Hegel, for example, took the realm
     > of dialetheias to include statements about physical change. ...
     > Perhaps he is not a good example of a philosopher who took the
     > empirical world to be inconsistent, since his absolute idealism
     > debars him from making any real distinction between the concep-
     > tual and the world. Engels is a better example for this reason.
     >   (200)

5.   See also, Gordon E. Slethaug, *The Play of the Double in Postmodern
     American Fiction*. 'Recently,' he claims, 'the double has taken on a
     new identity: moving away from a consideration of the Cartesian
     self – an indivisible, unified, continuous, and fixed identity – and
     universal absolutes, the double in postmodern fiction explores a
     divided and discontinuous self in a fragmented universe' (1993: 3).

6.   Anthony Quinton points out, however, that the fact that from an

empiricist perspective a 'spiritual substance cannot possibly be the criterion of a person's identity and that it cannot be identified with any straightforwardly observable part of a person's mental life does not mean that it does not exist' (1962: 395). Locke did not deny its existence:

> It is plain . . . that the idea of a *corporeal substance* in matter is as remote from our conceptions and apprehensions as that of a *spiritual substance*; and that therefore from our not having any notion of spirit we can no more conclude its non-existence than we can, for the same reason, deny the existence of body[.]
>
> (1964: 187)

Hume also argues that 'we have no idea of substance of any kind, since we have no idea but what is derived from sense impression, and we have no impression of any substance either material or spiritual. We know nothing but particular qualities and perceptions' (1962: 349). As Strawson suggests, Hume's 'main claim is that the mind *so far as we know* it is nothing but a bundle of perceptions – "that we have no notion of it, distinct from the particular perceptions"' (1989: 129):

> 'The uniting principle among our internal perceptions is unintelligible.' We have no notion of these things. [But] certainly there is some such 'uniting principle.' Yet we know nothing for certain about the ultimate nature of these things. All *we* know of the mind are perceptions.
>
> (129–30)

7. John Searle likewise points out that 'realism is not a theory of truth and it does not imply any theory of truth. Strictly speaking, realism is consistent with any theory of truth because it is a theory of ontology and not of the meaning of "true." It is not a semantic theory at all. It is thus possible to hold ER [external realism] and deny the correspondence theory' (1995: 154).

8. In his introduction to Locke's *Essay*, A.D. Woozley objects to this interpretation of the Lockean 'idea.' He claims that Locke 'does not seem to have thought that the terminology of ideas would cause any trouble' and that in his letters to Stillingfleet 'he frequently expresses surprise that it did' (1964: 32). Locke, he suggests, 'would probably have been a lot more careful and guarded in his use of "idea" throughout the *Essay*, if he had known what he was letting himself in for' (32). But

> the word 'idea' occurs so frequently that the reader has to work hard if he is to succeed in immunising himself against taking it to be intended as the name of some special kind of mental thing. It is easier, too, to take 'represent,' 'resemble,' 'picture' etc. literally than metaphorically but being easier does not make it to be, or more likely to be, correct. There is not one and only one relation signified by 'represent'; the travelling salesman represents his company, the Davis Cup player represents his country, the coloured

drawing pins in the police map represent the houses broken into during the last month, the minor key is used to represent sadness, Godot has been said to represent a variety of things; but in none of these cases is the relation the same.

(33)

9. Saussure did not, moreover, emphasize that the linguistic sign is differential. Having remarked that 'in language, there are only differences *without positive terms*' (1966: 120), Saussure goes on to say:

    But the statement that everything in language is negative is true only if the signifier and signified are considered separately; when we consider the sign in its totality, we have something that is positive in its own class. . . . Although both the signifier and the signified are purely differential and negative when considered separately, their combination is a positive fact; it is even the sole type of facts that language has.

    (120)

10. 'The most revolutionary aspect of Saussure's theory – and the one that has generated the most misinterpretation –' is, as Raymond Tallis explains,

    the denial of the pre-linguistic reality of the signified. The signified is not a 'thing' out there; nor is it a pre-linguistic psychological entity, a concept correlated with a sound. The signified is a purely relational entity. . . . [T]his is true also of the material side of language: a signifier is not a particular kind of sound so much as the realisation of a bundle of features contrasted with other features, a set of phonic difference from other sounds. . . . At the heart of language is not an external relationship between a particular sound and a material thing but an internal relationship between oppositions at the phonetic level and oppositions at the semantic level.

    (1988a: 67)

11. See also Michael Devitt and Kim Sterelny, who, in critiquing Jonathan Culler's claim that a person cannot be taught the meaning of 'brown' by being presented with brown objects but can only begin to understand what brown is by grasping the relation between brown and other colors, point out that 'even if it were necessary to discriminate brown to learn the reference of "brown," it would hardly follow that it had no reference' (1987: 218).

12. Tallis notes the conflation of how signs signify with what they signify in the following passage from Catherine Belsey's *Critical Practice*:

    If discourses articulate concepts through a system of signs which signify by means of their relationship to each other rather than to entities in the world, and if literature is a signifying practice, all it can reflect is the order inscribed in particular discourses, not the nature of the world.

    (1988a: 79–80)

CHAPTER 6

1. The defense against the charge of contradiction that Boyd ascribes to anti-realists, it should be noted, is no defense at all. If anti-realists claim that they know that they cannot know, then they cannot claim to know that life is a fiction (whatever that might mean).

2. See also Lyotard, who claims that the task that 'academicism had assigned to realism' was 'to preserve various consciousnesses from doubt' (74). It has to be said that if indeed this was the task assigned to realism, realism failed to heed the call.

3. In the same spirit is Stern's repudiation of the suggestion that one has to define what reality is in order to define literary realism, his claim that what one requires in order to 'say something sensible' about literary realism is 'not a "definition of reality" at all but a certain kind of description of the world' (31–2). A certain description of the world would include, for example, the fact that people throughout the ages have believed in the existence of miracles. The occurrence of an ostensible miracle in a novel, whether contemporary or not, then, would not, in itself, disqualify the novel as realist, even though many readers may not believe in miracles, since a reader does not need to believe in the existence of miracles in order for the description of such an event to be intelligible to him or her or for him or her to appreciate that it is realistic in its representing a commonly held belief.

4. See, for example, Charles Crittenden, *Unreality: The Metaphysics of Fictional Objects* (1991: 133–8). 'Suppose,' Crittenden suggests,

   > that Conan Doyle had written that Gladstone has tea with Holmes (to use John Woods's example). Does the real Gladstone appear in the stories: does the name 'Gladstone' in the text of the story refer to the actual, historical person? Considerations about background are pertinent here. Conan Doyle has taken nineteenth-century England as his setting and has created a character based on an individual, the historical Gladstone, who existed in this setting. Particular characters taken over from real life, or story locations taken over from the general background, are to be explained in terms of the principle that fiction takes place in a setting. Such figures or places appearing in a story are created by an author using the circumstances history provides to supply details. References in a literary text are governed by the 'in the story' operator and do no purport to be about the actual man but only about his conceptual counterpart. A biography of Gladstone would not mention his having tea with Holmes; at most it might note that a fictionalized Gladstone appeared in a work by Conan Doyle and was said there to have tea. On the other, a biography of Holmes, having to rely solely on the contents of stories and not reality, would include the Gladstone meeting.

   (133–4)

5. But my objection to Elam's argument would hold even if realist fiction did simply refer to reality and anti-realist fiction didn't. It wouldn't

follow from this either that realism assumed the truth of metaphysical realism or that anti-realism demonstrated the truth of metaphysical anti-realism. It does not follow from my stating that 'In 1992, Bill
Clinton was elected president of the United States,' that reality is
mind-independent or that I believe that it is; likewise, it does not
follow from my stating that 'Pegasus is a winged animal' that reality
is mind-dependent or that I believe that it is.

6.	See also, for example, John Mepham, 'Narratives of Postmodernism,'
	Postmodernism and Contemporary Fiction, who remarks that the pur-
	pose of what he calls the strategy of 'abortive mimesis' – through
	which 'possible worlds are projected at different and incompatible
	ontological levels' (as in *The French Lieutenant's Woman*, where 'the
	author joins a character on a train journey, even though he lives in
	another century and exists on a different ontological level') and the
	strategy of 'absent mimesis' (where 'the writing does not construct a
	fictional world at all,' such as in *Finnegans Wake*) is

	> usually said to be to undermine the reader's naive realism. Seeing
	> how it is possible, by means of verbal deviance and play, to pre-
	> vent a coherent fictional world from coming into (fictional) being,
	> the reader is made aware of the fact that the world is constructed
	> in and through language.
	>
	> 					(1991: 151–2)

	Such is the one of the most common *non sequiturs* of postmodernist
	theory and criticism.

7.	It is worth noting the tendency of postmodernist theorists to regard
	fiction that does not explicitly foreground its fictionality as lacking
	aesthetic form and aesthetic sophistication, as if the explicit fore-
	grounding of fictionality were what having aesthetic form or being
	aesthetically sophisticated amounted to.

8.	The truth in this case being, according to the narrator, that 'it is
	so rarely that facts hit that nice medium required by our own en-
	lightened opinions and refined taste!' (221):

	> Perhaps you will say, 'Do improve the facts a little, then; make
	> them more accordant with those correct views which it is our privil-
	> ege to possess. The world is not just what we would like; do touch
	> it up with a tasteful pencil, and make believe it is not quite such
	> a mixed, entangled affair. Let all people who hold unexception-
	> able opinions act unexceptionally. Let your most faulty characters
	> always be on the wrong side, and your virtuous ones on the right.
	> Then we shall see at a glance whom we are to condemn, and whom
	> we are to approve. Then we shall be able to admire, without the
	> slightest disturbance of our prepossessions: we shall hate and des-
	> pise with that true ruminant relish which belongs to undoubting
	> confidence.'
	>
	> 					(221–2)

9.	This is not to say, however, that human beings think exclusively
	in language. No one, to my knowledge, has definitively answered

the question of whether human beings think exclusively in language or not.

10. Allen Thiher likewise argues from the truism that 'history perforce can only be mediated by language' to the idea that this 'leads ... to an effacing of the ontological line that modernism, not to mention Aristotle, drew between literature and history' (1984: 190). What he seems to be assuming is that the fact that our access to the past is mediated by language implies that the events historical texts record did not happen (the line between literature and history in question here being, roughly speaking, between the representation of events that could happen and events that have happened).

11. See also Brian McHale, who argues that it follows from 'the theory-dependency of "facts"' that 'faithfulness to objective "truth" cannot be a criterion for evaluating versions of reality' (1992: 2). No such thing follows because the theory-dependency of facts does not disqualify them from being objectively true.

12. See also M. Keith Booker, *Vargas Llosa Among the Postmodernists*. Booker argues that Vargas Llosa, in using the Scotsman Galileo Gall in his novel *The War of the End of the World* 'as a focus for his commentary on the unreliability of historical narration,' also 'makes an important philosophical statement about epistemological access to the world, access that is also indirect and mediated through our own preconceptions and expectations, no matter what they may be' (1994: 81). 'Such notes of epistemological skepticism' he claims, 'frequently sound in both modernist and postmodernist literature, but they are very much out of place in the world of realistic fiction' (81). Not only is the idea of a character like Gall, who, according to Booker, 'writes a detailed account of his past history as a revolutionary adventurer' that is 'so colorful that many who read it seriously doubt that it could be true' (81), hardly out of place in the world of realistic fiction, but the idea that our access to the world is indirect and mediated through our own preconceptions is hardly worthy of the label 'epistemological skepticism.'

13. Zola does relent in his attack on poetry in, for example, 'Naturalism and the Theatre,' where he argues that the naturalist novel 'attempts all subjects, writes history, treats of physiology and psychology, soars to the highest poetry, studies the most varied questions: politics, the social economy, religion, manners. All of nature is its domain. It moves there freely, adopting the form which pleases it, taking the tone it judges best, no longer subject to any bounds' (1963: 207).

14. 'James is a philosopher,' Bambrough argues, 'not only in the popular sense of a seeker of wisdom and student of life.' He also 'studies minutely what more formal philosophers call cognitive states, propositional attitudes, cognitive dissonance, intellectual virtues, *akrasia*, self-deception, self-knowledge and intuition' (171).

15. There is irony in the fact that those very 'untenable assumptions' of realism that Lee derides underwrite her own project. She assumes not just that there is a common, shared sense of reality, but also that there is common, shared sense of the *nature* of reality – *viz.*, that it

is a linguistic construct. Further, she assumes that postmodern fiction 'reflects' this 'truth' and, in assuming this, assumes not only that its language is 'transparent,' but also unequivocal – that is, it unambiguously communicates the truth that reality is a linguistic construct.

16. See also Jane Flax, who claims in one moment that '[r]ecent theories of language seem to render impossible or meaningless any claim that there can be a historical or transcendental standpoint from and by which the Real can be apprehended and reported on in or by thought,' and argues in the next that '[t]he Real is unstable and perpetually in flux' (1990: 36).

17. Recall that at the same time that Lee claims that postmodernist theory *questions* 'the very nature of "reality" and "truth"', she also states that it asserts that 'these are merely linguistic constructs.' Any number of theorists of postmodernism call themselves skeptics, but they tend not to seriously question their assumption that reality is merely a linguistic construct. The fact that they are apparently unaware of the ongoing debate in philosophical circles between realists and anti-realists is a mark of both insularity and a rather profound philosophical incuriosity.

18. Hundreds of books and essays, all making the same claim – that so-and-so's novel, painting, film, building, music, theory, sculpture, posits that reality, self, etc., etc., are linguistic constructs – have been produced in the last fifteen years or so by theorists of postmodernism. A couple of notable exceptions to this monotony are Cristopher Nash's *World-Games* and Elizabeth Dipple's *The Unresolvable Plot*.

CHAPTER 7

1. See also Catherine Belsey, who argues that literary realism is based in 'empiricist-idealism,' which she defines as the assumption that 'the world of natural objects, of bare, clear, downright facts is unproblematically given, accessible to experience' (1980: 9), that there is 'an independently constituted world of things' (4). Empiricism does not assume that 'facts' are 'unproblematically given,' nor does it assume that reality is mind-independent. Further, not only does the belief that reality is mind-independent fail to describe empiricism; it also fails to describe idealism. It is, rather, the theory Belsey subscribes to – that 'it is language which offers the possibility of constructing a world of individuals and things' (4) – that describes idealism.

   Moreover, Belsey, in assuming that 'empiricist-idealism' sums up the philosophical thought of the eighteenth and nineteenth centuries, betrays an unfamiliarity with the history of philosophy. As Richard Freadman and Seumas Miller note, 'Belsey's account of the history of ideas is less a scholarly characterization than a caricature, and it should be recognized as such' (1992: 18).

2. See also Philip Kuberski, who, citing Lancelot Law Whyte's claim that 'the sciences are manifestly converging; atom, man, and universe are, in an objective and inescapable sense, deeply related,' argues that

'[t]his convergence is not only evident in the parallels between Indian and Chinese thought and quantum mechanics, but in twentieth-century works of literature that discard the linear or exclusive frameworks of "realist" literature, for the organistic synthesis of order and disorder within a thriving chaos of interfering and yet complementary causal orders' (1994: 45).

3. See Gabriele Bernhard Jackson's 'From Essence to Accident: Locke and the Language of Poetry in the Eighteenth Century' for an analysis of the impact Locke's skepticism with respect to immaterial essence had on eighteenth-century English poetry.

4. See also Jane Flax, *Thinking Fragments: Psychoanalysis, Feminism, and Postmodernism in the Contemporary West*, who would have us believe that

> Western philosophy has been under the spell of the 'metaphysics of presence' at least since Plato. Most Western philosophers took as their task the construction of a philosophic system in which something Real would and could be represented in thought. This Real is understood to be an external or universal subject or substance, existing 'out there' independent of the knower. The philosopher's desire is to 'mirror,' register, mimic, or make present the Real. Truth is understood as correspondence to it. For postmodernists this quest for the Real conceals most Western philosophers' desire, which is to master the world once and for all by enclosing it within an illusory but absolute system[.]
>
> (1990: 34)

5. See, for example, the debate between Arthur Fine and Ernan McMullin in *Philosophical Studies* 61 (1991). Fine argues that realism is dead; in 'Piecemeal Realism,' he speaks, as McMullin notes, of it as 'having gone to pieces, as having taken flight' ('Comment: Selective Antirealism,' 97). McMullin, in contrast, claims that 'realism is not only alive,' but that 'it is thriving' (97).

6. See Richard Popkin, for example, 'Berkeley and Pyrrhonism':

> At the beginning of the eighteenth century two types of theories were current, one advocating that some sort of material reality existed (Descartes, Locke, and Malebranche), the other doubting whether anything outside the mind really existed (Baylean Pyrrhonism). Malebranche's 'seeing all things in God' tended in the direction of ignoring rather than denying materialism, and making the real world one of essences in God's Mind. Berkeley's immaterialism is a radical innovation in this battle of ideas, based on the Malebranchian theory that God's Mind is the source of all that exists, and the Pyrrhonian insistence that we only know appearances. The innovation is that the real world, produced and sustained by some spiritual substance or substances, is the world of appearance.
>
> (1983: 388–9)

7. See also Thomas P. Weissert, 'Representation and Bifurcation: Borges's Garden of Chaos Dynamics.' Weissert claims that 'as science entered

the twentieth century, its theories came to reflect the impossibility of achieving objectivity absolutely. The two great physical theories of the century – relativity and quantum mechanics – emphasize the position of the subject (or instrument) making the observations' (229). However, not only did Einstein consider the theory of relativity to be absolutely objectively true, but quantum physicists consider it to be absolutely objectively true, for example, that no measuring apparatus can record simultaneously with precision the position and momentum of a subatomic entity.

8. The 'corollary,' Tallis remarks, 'of the belief that realism is a) politically conservative and b) non-experimental, is the notion that experimental non-realism is associated with progressive, even revolutionary, politics while (inevitably) non-experimental realism is associated with reactionary postures' (1988b: 184). So deeply ingrained is the assumption that experimental form goes hand-in-hand with radical politics that one finds Steven Connor remarking on 'the peculiar *contradiction*, which is nowhere so sharp as in literary modernism, between radical disruption of form and traditionalism of content and ideology – in the work, for instance, of Pound, Eliot, Woolf and Yeats' (1989: 104; my emphasis). He not only assumes that a 'radical disruption of form' ought to 'mean' a commitment on the part of authors to a radical politics, but also that it ought to entail non-traditional content (whatever *that* might be). See also Catherine Belsey, who in *Desire: Love Stories in Western Culture* claims that she 'shares [Barthes's] perception that, in so far as it offers the reader specific knowledges, certain noncontradictory ways of understanding the world, at the level of content classic realism is politically reactionary' (though, she says, she 'no longer believe[s] [as she suggested in *Critical Practice*] that only the avant-garde is capable of precipitating a crisis in the relationship between the subject and language') (1994: 38). Aside from the generalization itself, one might ask, returning to the concerns of Part I, what exactly would be 'politically reactionary' about a 'classic realist' novel that began, say, with 'It was a dark and stormy night' (thereby implying that it was not *not* a dark and stormy night)? Or, to put this another way, what would necessarily be politically progressive about understanding the world in contradictory ways?

9. See also Thomas Docherty, 'Postmodern Characterization: The Ethics of Alterity.' The mode of characterization in realist narratives, Docherty claims, offers 'the illusion of a control over the characters, whereby the reader can place or locate them in the plot not only in relation to each other, but also in relation to the reader's own position, a position which, in transcending the hypothetical world of the characters, offers the illusion of omniscience and its corollary, omnipotence' (1991: 176):

> The situation is precisely akin to a mode of imperialist control of the Other in which, by pretending to 'know' the Other fully and comprehensibly, a Self can assure itself of its own truth and status. To this extent, 'reasonable' characters in the paradigmatic plot of enlightenment share that eighteenth-century predilection for the

imperialist or colonialist control not only of other places, but also of other 'positions'; in novelistic terms, this translates into control of other 'points of view' or, in short, of other characters.

(176–7)

'It is this imperialism of reading character which the more radical problematization of the ontological status of the reader, such as we have it in postmodern fiction, begins to challenge' (177).

10. Nadeau is an exception here because he believes that contemporary novelists have not yet found the forms that would be 'adequate' to expressing the 'new' reality.

11. It is hard to find a postmodernist critic who, in asserting that some technique or strategy is typically postmodern, doesn't argue that what the strategy or technique signifies is that reality is indeterminate, discontinuous, fragmentary, etc. See also Ellen E. Berry, 'Modernism/ Mass Culture/Postmodernism: The Case of Gertrude Stein.' Berry, discussing the so-called 'closing of the gap' between high and popular culture in contemporary art, claims that

> postmodern art more and more frequently incorporates popular and vernacular forms, and mass culture itself increasingly reflects a discontinuity generally attributed only to experimental art, evidence of a postmodern eclecticism and hybridization that reflects the fragmented and conflictual nature of contemporary culture.
>
> (1992: 170)

How exactly does the incorporation of popular and vernacular forms in 'postmodern art' as such reflect the fragmented and conflictual nature of contemporary culture? One might just as well argue that it reflects an idealized holistic transcendence of the conflictual and fragmented nature of contemporary culture. Which is to say that we ought to abandon the idea that artistic forms and strategies have a general meaning that extends to all manifestations of them.

12. See also John Johnston, 'Representation and Multiplicity in Four Postmodern American Novels,' in which he claims that

> [a]lthough the status of representation remains ambiguous in [Gaddis's] *The Recognitions*, representation becomes an obviously inadequate tool for dealing with later, more explicitly, postmodernist works. For the latter, the world is no longer simply 'out there' waiting to be registered first hand; instead, for the postmodern novelist, experience seems always already framed, multiply mediated, and only available through a set of competing and often contradictory representations. It therefore becomes necessary for the novelist to register this new difficulty, and to make the form of his or her novel an adequate reflection of it.
>
> (1995: 174–5)

Note that, in addition to giving voice to the dubious idea that form has to be made an adequate reflection of reality, Johnston also posits a distinction without a difference between postmodernist novels and (one presumes) nineteenth- and early/mid-twentieth-century novels in claiming that for the former, 'the world is no longer simply "out there" waiting to be registered first hand.' Whether the world is 'simply "out there,"' capable of being registered 'first hand' or not (or whether nineteenth and early/mid-twentieth century novelists in general believed it was) is beside the point because Johnston implies that there are true and false ways of representing reality. To put this another way, Johnston might as well have claimed that for postmodernist novelists the world is 'simply "out there," waiting to be registered first hand,' since he represents them as reflecting in their work the truth about the nature of reality and the truth about the nature of the knowledge we come to have about that reality.

13.   Such 'logocentric' assumptions inform many postmodernist accounts of contemporary fiction, from the idea that it not only reflects reality but also the truth about the nature of reality, to the idea that in representing things as they are it liberates us from the putative 'illusions' of realism, to the idea that it is a mark of the novel's intellectual and aesthetic progress from its slow, stupid infancy to its enlightened coming-of-age.

14.   This would involve regarding the manifestos of writers themselves with skepticism where skepticism is warranted – one should be as suspicious of Zola's rhetoric in 'The Experimental Novel,' or Barth's in 'The Literature of Replenishment,' as one should be of Couzens Hoy's or Caughie's.

Works Cited

Anscombe, Elizabeth. 'Causality and Determination,' in *The Collected Philosophical Papers of G.E.M. Anscombe: Metaphysics and the Philosophy of Mind*, pp. 133–47. Minneapolis: University of Minnesota Press, 1981.

Aristotle. *Metaphysics*, trans. Richard Hope. Ann Arbor: University of Michigan Press, 1952.

Ayer, A.J. *Language, Truth and Logic*. New York: Dover Publications, 1952.

Azim, Firdous. *The Colonial Rise of the Novel*. London: Routledge, 1993.

Bambrough, Renford. 'Ounces of Example: Henry James, Philosopher,' in *Realism in European Literature*, eds Nicholas Boyle and Martin Swales, pp. 169–202. Cambridge: Cambridge University Press, 1986.

Barth, John. 'The Literature of Replenishment,' in *The Friday Book: Essays and Other Nonfiction*, pp. 193–206. New York: G.P. Putnam's Sons, 1984.

Barwise, Jon and John Etchemendy. *The Liar: An Essay on Truth and Circularity*. Oxford: Oxford University Press, 1987.

Baudelaire, Charles. *The Mirror of Art*, trans. and ed. Jonathan Mayne. Garden City, NY: Doubleday, 1956.

Becker, George. 'Introduction: Modern Realism as Literary Movement,' in *Documents of Modern Literary Realism*, pp. 3–38. Princeton, NJ: Princeton University Press, 1963.

Belsey, Catherine. *Critical Practice*. London: Methuen, 1980.

Belsey, Catherine. *Desire: Love Stories in Western Culture*. London: Blackwell, 1994.

Bergoffen, Debra B. 'Nietzsche's Madman: Perspectivism Without Nihilism,' in *Nietzsche as Postmodernist: Essays Pro and Contra*, ed. Clayton Koelb, pp. 57–71. Albany: State University Press of New York, 1990.

Berry, Ellen E. 'Modernism/Mass Culture/Postmodernism: The Case of Gertrude Stein,' in *Rereading the New*, ed. Kevin J.H. Dettmar, pp. 167–89. Ann Arbor: University of Michigan Press, 1992.

Bertens, Hans. *The Idea of the Postmodern*. London: Routledge, 1995.

Best, Stephen and Douglas Kellner. *Postmodern Theory*. London: Macmillan, 1991.

Booker, M. Keith. 'What We Have Instead of God: Sexuality, Textuality and Infinity in *The French Lieutenant's Woman*,' *Novel* 24 (Winter 1991): 178–97.

Booker, M. Keith. *Vargas Llosa among the Postmodernists*. Gainesville: University Press of Florida, 1994.

Bricker, Phillip. 'Absolute Time versus Absolute Motion: Comments on Lawrence Skar,' in *Philosophical Perspectives on Newtonian Science*, eds Phillip Bricker and R.I.G. Hughes, pp. 77–89. Cambridge, Mass.: MIT Press, 1990.

Boyd, Michael. *The Reflexive Novel: Fiction as Critique*. Lewisburg, Pa.: Bucknell University Press, 1983.

Butler, Judith. 'Contigent Foundations: Feminism and the Question of

Postmodernism,' in *Critical Encounters*, eds Cathy Caruth and Deborah Esch, pp. 213–32. New Brunswick, NJ: Rutgers University Press, 1995.

Butler, Judith. *Gender Trouble: Feminism and the Subversion of Identity*. New York: Routledge, 1990.

Calinescu, Matei. *Five Faces of Modernity*. Durham, NC: Duke University Press, 1987.

Calvino, Italo. 'Levels of Reality in Literature,' in *The Uses of Literature*, trans. Patrick Creagh, pp. 101–21. San Diego, Calif.: Harvester/HBJ, 1986.

Caraher, Brian. 'Introduction: Intimate Conflict,' in *Intimate Conflict: Contradiction in Literary and Philosophical Discourse*, ed. Brian Caraher, pp. 1–33. Albany: State University Press of New York, 1992.

Caughie, Pamela. *Virginia Woolf and Postmodernism*. Urbana: University of Illinois Press, 1991.

Centore, F.F. *Being and Becoming: A Critique of Post-Modernism*. New York: Greenwood Press, 1991.

Cheney, Lynn. *Telling the Truth*. New York: Simon & Schuster, 1995.

Con Davis, Robert and Ronald Schleifer. 'Foreword,' in *Postmodern Genres*, ed. Marjorie Perloff, pp. vii–ix. Norman: University of Oklahoma Press, 1988.

Connor, Stephen. *Postmodernist Culture*. Oxford: Basil Blackwell, 1989.

Cooke, Philip. *Back to the Future*. London: Unwin Hyman, 1990.

Cowart, David. ' "Signifiant, insignificant": Realist and Postmodernist Art in Hawkes's *WhistleJacket*,' *Modern Fiction Studies* 41 (Spring 1995): 99–116.

Craige, Betty Jean. *Literary Relativity*. Lewisburg, Pa.: Bucknell University Press, 1982.

Crittenden, Charles. *Unreality: The Metaphysics of Fictional Objects*. Ithaca: Cornell University Press, 1991.

Cunningham, Valentine. *In the Reading Gaol: Postmodernity, Texts, and History*. Oxford: Basil Blackwell, 1994.

Currie, Peter. 'The Eccentric Self: Anti-Characterization and the Problem of the Subject in American Postmodern Fiction,' in *Contemporary American Fiction*, eds Malcolm Bradbury and Sigmund Ro, pp. 53–69. London: Edward Arnold, 1987.

Dancy, R.M. *Sense and Contradiction: A Study in Aristotle*. Dordrecht: D. Reidel, 1975.

de Man, Paul. *Allegories of Reading*. New Haven, Conn.: Yale University Press, 1979.

Derrida, Jacques. *Dissemination*, trans. Barbara Johnson. Chicago: University of Chicago Press, 1981a.

Derrida, Jacques. *Limited Inc.*, trans. Samuel Weber, ed. Gerald Graff. Evanston, Ill.: Northwestern University Press, 1988.

Derrida, Jacques. 'Positions,' in *Positions*, trans. and anntd. by Alan Bass, pp. 37–96. Chicago: University of Chicago Press, 1981b.

Desnoyers, Fernand. 'On Realism,' in *Documents of Modern Literary Realism*, ed. George J. Becker, pp. 80–88. Princeton, NJ: Princeton University Press, 1963.

Devitt, Michael. 'Aberrations of the Realism Debate,' *Philosophical Studies* 61 (1991): 43–63.

Devitt, Michael. *Language and Truth*. Oxford: Basil Blackwell, 2nd edn, 1991.
Devitt, Michael. 'Rorty's Mirrorless World,' in *Midwest Studies in Philosophy* XII, eds Peter A. French, Theodore E. Uehling, Jr, and Howard K. Wettstein, pp. 157–177. Minneapolis: University of Minnesota Press, 1988.
Devitt, Michael and Kim Sterelny. *Language and Reality*. Cambridge, Mass.: MIT Press, 1987.
Dipple, Elizabeth. *The Unresolvable Plot: Reading Contemporary Fiction*. New York: Routledge, 1988.
Docherty, Thomas. *After Theory: Postmodernism/Postmarxism*. London: Routledge, 1990.
Docherty, Thomas. 'Postmodern Characterization: The Ethics of Alterity,' *Postmodernism and Contemporary Fiction*, ed. Edmund Smyth, pp. 169–188. London: B.T. Batsford, 1991.
Doyle, J.A. 'Why I am so Bored with Postmodernism.' Unpublished paper.
Dummett, Michael. *Elements of Intuitionism*. Oxford: Clarendon Press, 1977.
Dummett, Michael. 'Truth,' in *Truth and Other Enigmas*, pp. 1–24. Cambridge, Mass.: Harvard University Press, 1978.
Eagleton, Terry. *Literary Theory*. Minneapolis: University of Minnesota Press, 1983.
Elam, Diane. *Romancing the Postmodern*. London: Routledge, 1992.
Eliot, George. *Adam Bede*, ed. Stephen Gill. Harmondsworth: Penguin, 1985.
Ellis, John. *Against Deconstruction*. Princeton, NJ: Princeton University Press, 1989.
Engel, S. Morris. *With Good Reason*. New York: St. Martin's Press, 1986.
Ermarth, Elizabeth. *Sequel to History: Postmodernism and the Crisis of Representational Time*. Princeton, NJ: Princeton University Press, 1992.
Esquire's Handbook for Hosts. New York: Grossnet and Dunlap, 1953.
Fine, Arthur. 'Piecemeal Realism.' *Philosophical Studies* 61 (1991): 76–96.
Flax, Jane. *Thinking Fragments: Psychoanalysis, Feminism, and Postmodernism in the Contemporary West*. Berkeley: University of California Press, 1990.
Flieger, Jerry Aline. *The Purloined Punch Line: Freud's Comic Theory and the Postmodern Text*. Baltimore, Md.: The Johns Hopkins University Press, 1991.
Fowles, John. *The French Lieutenant's Woman*. Boston, Mass.: Little, Brown, 1969; Penguin reprint, 1981.
Freadman, Richard and Lloyd Reinhardt. 'Introduction,' in *On Literary Theory and Philosophy: A Cross-disciplinary Encounter*, eds Richard Freadman and Lloyd Reinhardt, pp. 1–12. New York: St Martin's Press, 1991.
Freadman, Richard and Seumas Miller. *Re-thinking Theory: A Critique of Contemporary Literary Theory and an Alternative Account*. Cambridge: Cambridge University Press, 1992.
Frye, Northrop, Sheridan Baker, and George Perkins, eds *The Harper Handbook to Literature*. New York: Harper & Row, 1985.
Goldknopf, David. *The Life of the Novel*. Chicago: University of Chicago Press, 1972.
Gąsiorek, Andrzej. *Post-War British Fiction: Realism and After*. London: Edward Arnold, 1995.
Grant, Damien. *Realism*. London: Methuen, 1970.
Gross, Paul and Norman Levitt. *Higher Superstition: The Academic Left and Its*

Quarrels with Science. Baltimore, Md.: The Johns Hopkins University Press, 1994.

Grube, G.M.A. *Five Dialogues*. Indianapolis, Ind.: Hackett, 1981.

Harris, Wendell V. 'The Complexities of Contradiction,' *Philosophy and Literature* 17 (1993): 333–42.

Hassan, Ihab. *The Postmodern Turn: Essays in Postmodern Theory and Culture*. Columbus: Ohio State University Press, 1987.

Hayles, N. Katherine. *The Cosmic Web: Scientific Field Models and Literary Strategies in the Twentieth-Century*. Ithaca, NY: Cornell University Press, 1984.

Hekman, Susan. *Gender and Knowledge: Elements of a Postmodern Feminism*. Boston, Mass.: Northeastern University Press, 1990.

Herbert, Nick. *Quantum Reality*. New York: Doubleday, 1985.

Hodgson, David. *The Mind Matters: Consciousness and Choice in a Quantum World*. Oxford: Clarendon Press, 1991.

Hoesterey, Ingeborg. 'Postmodernism as Discursive Event,' in *Zeitgeist in Babel: The Postmodernist Controversy*, ed. Ingeborg Hoesterey, pp. ix–xv. Bloomington: Indiana University Press, 1991.

Holub, Robert. *Reflections of Realism: Paradox, Norm, and Ideology in Nineteenth-Century German Prose*. Detroit, Mich.: Wayne State University Press, 1991.

Hoy, David Couzens. 'Foucault: Modern or Postmodern?' in *After Foucault, Humanistic Knowledge, Postmodern Challenges*, ed. Jonathan Arac, pp. 12–41. New Brunswick, NJ: Rutgers University Press, 1988.

Hughes, R.I.G. 'Philosophical Perspectives on Newtonian Science,' *Philosophical Perspectives on Newtonian Science*, eds Phillip Bricker and R.I.G. Hughes, pp. 1–16. Cambridge, Mass.: MIT Press, 1990.

Hume, David. *An Enquiry Concerning the Principles of Morals*, ed. L.A. Selby-Bigge, rev. P.H. Nidditich. Oxford: Clarendon, 1988.

Hume, David. *A Treatise of Human Nature* I, ed. D.G.C. Macnabb. Glasgow: Collins, 1962.

Hutcheon, Linda. *A Poetics of Postmodernism*. London: Routledge, 1988.

Jackson, Gabriele Bernhard. 'From Essence to Accident: Locke and the Language of Poetry in the Eighteenth Century,' *Criticism* XXIX (1987): 27–66.

James, Henry. 'Nana,' in *Documents of Modern Literary Realism*, ed. George J. Becker, pp. 236–43. Princeton, NJ: Princeton University Press, 1963.

Jameson, Fredric. *Postmodernism, or the Cultural Logic of Late Capitalism*. Durham, NC: Duke University Press, 1991.

Jameson, Fredric. *Signatures of the Visible*. London: Routledge, 1992.

Johnston, John. *Carnival of Repetition: Gaddis' 'The Recognitions' and Postmodern Theory*. Philadelphia: University of Pennsylvania Press, 1990.

Johnston, John. 'Representation and Multiplicity in Four Postmodern American Novels,' in *Critical Essays on American Postmodernism*, ed. Stanley Trachtenberg, pp. 169–81. New York: G.K. Hall, 1995.

Kearney, Richard. *The Wake of the Imagination: Toward a Postmodern Culture*. Minneapolis: University of Minnesota Press, 1989.

Kiely, Robert. *Reverse Tradition: Postmodern Fictions and the Nineteenth Century Novel*. Cambridge, Mass.: Harvard University Press, 1993.

Koelb, Clayton. 'Introduction,' in *Nietzsche as Postmodernist: Essays Pro and*

Contra, ed. Clayton Koelb, pp. 1–18. Albany: State University Press of New York, 1990.

Kuberski, Philip. *Chaosmos: Literature, Science, and Theory*. Albany: State University of New York Press, 1994.

Kuhns, Richard. 'Contradiction and Repression: Paradox in Fictional Form,' in *Intimate Conflict: Contradiction in Literary and Philosophical Discourse*, ed. Brian Caraher, pp. 181–98. Albany: State University of New York Press, 1992.

Kvale, Steinar. 'Themes of Postmodernity,' in *The Truth about the Truth: De-confusing and Re-constructing the Postmodern World*, ed. Walter Truett Anderson, pp. 18–25. New York: G.P. Putnam's Son, 1995.

Lawson, Hilary. *Reflexivity: The Post-Modern Predicament*. La Salle, Ill.: Open Court, 1985.

Lee, Alison. *Realism and Power: Postmodern British Fiction*. London: Routledge, 1990.

Levine, George. 'Scientific Realism and Literary Representation,' *Raritan* 10 (Spring 1991): 18–39.

Levine, Herbert J. 'Beyond Negation: Paradoxical Affirmation in Whitman's Third Edition,' in *Negation, Critical Theory, and Postmodern Texuality*, ed. Daniel Fischlin, pp. 175–90. Dordrecht: Kluwer Academic, 1994.

Lilly, W.S. 'The New Naturalism,' in *Documents of Modern Literary Realism*, ed. George J. Becker, pp. 274–95. Princeton, NJ: Princeton University Press, 1963.

Limon, John. *The Place of Fiction in the Time of Science*. Cambridge: Cambridge University Press, 1990.

Livingston, Paisley. 'Why Realism Matters: Literary Knowledge and the Philosophy of Science,' in *Realism and Representation*, ed. George Levine, pp. 134–54. Madison: University of Wisconsin Press, 1993.

Locke, John. *An Essay Concerning Human Understanding*, ed. and with an introduction by A.D. Woozley. New York: New American Library, 1964.

Loomis, Roger Sherman. 'A Defense of Naturalism,' in *Documents of Modern Literary Realism*, ed. George J. Becker, pp. 535–48. Princeton, NJ: Princeton University Press, 1963.

Łukasiewicz, Jan. 'Über den Satz des Widerspruchs bei Aristoteles.' *Bulletin Interne de l'Académie des Sciences de Cracovie*, Cl. d'histoire et de philosophie, 1910. 'On the Principle of Contradiction in Aristotle,' trans. Vernon Wedin, *Review of Metaphysics* 24 (1971): 485–509.

Lyotard, Jean François. *The Postmodern Condition*, trans. Geoff Bennington and Brian Massumi. Minneapolis: University of Minnesota Press, 1984.

McGowan, John. *Postmodernism and Its Critics*. Ithaca, NY: Cornell University Press, 1991.

McHale, Brian. *Constructing Postmodernism*. London: Routledge, 1992.

McHale, Brian. *Postmodernist Fiction*. New York: Methuen, 1987.

McMullin, Ernan. 'Comment: Selective Anti-realism,' *Philosophical Studies* 61 (1991): 97–108.

Mellard, James. *The Exploded Form: The Modernist Novel in America*. Urbana: University of Illinois Press, 1980.

Melville, Herman. *The Confidence-Man*, ed. and anntd. by H. Bruce Frankin. Indianapolis, Ind.: Bobbs-Merrill, 1967.

Mepham, John. 'Narratives of Postmodernism,' in *Postmodernism and Contemporary Fiction*, ed. Edmund Smyth, pp. 138–55. London: B.T. Batsford, 1991.

Miller, J. Hillis. 'Presidential Address 1986,' *PMLA* 102 (May 1987): 281–91.

Montag, Warren. 'What is at Stake in the Debate on Postmodernism?' in *Postmodernism and Its Discontents*, ed. E. Ann Kaplan, pp. 88–103. London: Verso, 1988.

Morris, Adelaide. 'Science and the Mythopoeic Mind: The Case of H.D.,' in *Chaos and Order: Complex Dynamics in Literature and Science*, ed. N. Katherine Hayles, pp. 195–220. Chicago: The University of Chicago Press, 1991.

Morton, Michael. *The Critical Turn: Studies in Kant, Herder, Wittgenstein, and Contemporary Theory*. Detroit, Mich.: Wayne State University Press, 1993.

Nadeau, Robert. *Readings from the New Book on Nature*. Amherst: University of Massachusetts Press, 1981.

Nash, Cristopher. *World-Games*. New York: Methuen, 1987.

Nealon, Jeffrey. *Double Reading*. Ithaca, NY: Cornell University Press, 1993.

Neubauer, John. 'Models for the History of Science and Literature, *Science and Literature*, eds Harry Garvin and James M. Heath, pp. 17–37. Lewisburg, Pa.: Bucknell University Press, 1983.

New Jersalem Bible. New York: Doubleday, 1990.

Norman, Jean and Richard Sylvan. 'Conclusion: Further Directions in Relevant Logic,' in *Directions in Relevant Logic*, eds Jean Norman and Richard Sylvan, pp. 399–437. Dordrecht: Kluwer Academic, 1989.

Olsen, Lance. *The Circus of the Mind in Motion: Postmodernism and the Comic Vision*. Detroit, Mich.: Wayne State University Press, 1990.

Owens, Craig. 'The Allegorical Impulse: Toward a Theory of Postmodernism,' in *Art After Modernism*, ed. Brian Wallis, pp. 203–235. New York: The New Museum of Contemporary Art, 1984.

Pagels, Heinz. *The Cosmic Code: Quantum Physics as the Language of Nature*. Toronto: Bantam Books, 1984 (3rd printing).

Passmore, John. *A Hundred Years of Philosophy*. London: Duckworth, 1957.

Perloff, Marjorie. 'Introduction,' in *Postmodern Genres*, ed. Marjorie Perloff, pp. 3–10. Norman: University of Oklahoma Press, 1988.

Peterson, Nancy J. 'History, Postmodernism, and Louise Erdrich's *Tracks*,' *PMLA* (October 1994): 982–994.

Plato. *The Republic*, trans. W.H.D. Rouse. New York: New American Library, 1956.

Plotkin, Cary. *The Tenth Muse: Victorian Philology and the Genesis of the Poetic Language of Gerard Manley Hopkins*. Carbondale: Southern Illinois University Press, 1989.

Polka, Brayon. 'Tragedy is – Scription Contradiction,' in *Postmodernism, Literature, and the Future of Theology*, ed. David Jasper, pp. 21–59. New York: St. Martin's Press, 1993.

Popkin, Richard. 'Berkeley and Pyrrhonism,' in *The Skeptical Tradition*, ed. Miles Burnyeat, pp. 377–96. Berkeley: University of California Press, 1983.

Popkin, Richard. 'New Views on the Role of Skepticism in the Enlightenment,' *Modern Language Quarterly* 53 (September 1992): 272–98.

Prendergast, Christopher. *The Order of Mimesis*. Cambridge: Cambridge University Press, 1986.

Priest, Graham. *In Contradiction: A Study of the Transconsistent*. Dordrecht: Martinas Nijhoff, 1987.

Priest, Graham. 'The Logic of Paradox Revisited,' *Journal of Philosophical Logic* 13 (1984): 153–79.

Quinton, Anthony. 'The Soul,' *The Journal of Philosophy* 59 (1962): 393–409.

Read, Stephen. *Thinking about Logic*. Oxford: Oxford University Press, 1994.

Reed, T.V. *Fifteen Jugglers, Five Believers: Literary Politics and the Poetics of American Social Movements*. Berkeley: University of California Press, 1992.

Robbe-Grillet, Alain. *Two Novels by Robbe-Grillet*, trans. Richard Howard. New York: Grove Press, 1965.

Robbins, Bruce. 'Modernism and Literary Realism: Response,' in *Realism and Representation*, ed. George Levine, pp. 225–31. Madison: University of Wisconsin Press, 1993.

Roemer, Michael. *Telling Stories: Postmodernism and the Invalidation of Traditional Narrative*. Lanham, Md.: Rowman & Littlefield, 1995.

Roochnik, David L. 'The Impossibility of Philosophical Dialogue,' *Philosophy and Rhetoric* 19 (1986): 147–65.

Rose, Margaret. *The Post-Modern and the Post-Industrial*. Cambridge: Cambridge University Press, 1991.

Sainsbury, R.M. *Paradoxes*. Cambridge: Cambridge University Press, 1988.

Saussure, Ferdinand de. *Course in General Linguistics*, eds Charles Bally and Albert Sechehaye in collaboration with Albert Riedlinger, trans. Wade Baskin. New York: McGraw-Hill, 1966.

Schleifer, Ronald. *Rhetoric and Death: The Language of Modernism and Postmodern Discourse Theory*. Urbana: University of Illinois Press, 1990.

Schrift, Alan. 'The Becoming-Postmodern of Philosophy,' in *After the Future: Postmodern Times and Places*, ed. Gary Shapiro, pp. 99–113. Albany: State University Press of New York, 1990.

Searle, John. *The Construction of Social Reality*. New York: The Free Press, 1995.

Searle, John. 'The World Turned Upside Down,' *The New York Review of Books* (27 October 1983): 74–9.

Shankman, Steve. 'Plato and Postmodernism,' in *Plato and Postmodernism*, ed. Steve Shankman, pp. 3–28. Glenside, Pa.: Aldine Press, 1994.

Sidney, Philip. 'Astrophil and Stella 89,' in *The Norton Anthology of Literature* I, 5th edn, eds M.H. Abrams et al., p. 496. New York: W.W. Norton, 1986.

Simmons, Keith. *Universality and the Liar: An Essay on Truth and the Diagonal Argument*. Cambridge: Cambridge University Press, 1993.

Slethaug, Gordon. *The Play of the Double in Postmodern Fiction*. Carbondale: Southern Illinois University Press, 1993.

Smyth, Edmund. 'Introduction,' in *Postmodernism and Contemporary Fiction*, ed. Edmund Smyth, pp. 11–15. London: B.T. Batsford, 1991.

Stern, J.P. *On Realism*. London: Routledge, Kegan & Paul, 1973.

Stove, David. *The Plato Cult and Other Philosophical Follies*. Oxford: Basil Blackwell, 1991.

Strawson, Galen. *The Secret Connexion: Causation, Realism and David Hume*. Oxford: Clarendon Press, 1989.

Strehle, Susan. *Fiction in the Quantum Universe*. Chapel Hill: University of North Carolina Press, 1992.

Sukenick, Ronald. *In Form: Digressions on the Act of Fiction*. Carbondale: Southern Illinois University, 1985.

Suleiman, Susan R. *Risking Who One Is: Encounters with Contemporary Art and Literature*. Cambridge: Harvard University Press, 1994.

Tallis, Raymond. *Not Saussure: A Critique of Post-Saussurean Literary Theory*. London: Macmillan, 1988a.

Tallis, Raymond. *In Defence of Realism*. London: Edward Arnold, 1988b.

Tarski, Alfred. 'Truth and Proof,' *Scientific American* 194 (1969): 63–77.

Taylor, Charles. 'Foucault on Freedom and Truth,' in *Foucault: A Critical Reader*, ed. David Couzens Hoy, pp. 69–102. Oxford: Basil Blackwell, 1986.

Tennyson, Lord Alfred. *Poems*, ed. Christopher Ricks. London: Longman, 1969.

Thiher, Allen. *Words in Reflection: Modern Language Theory and Postmodern Fiction*. Chicago: University of Chicago Press, 1984.

Watson, Gary. 'Introduction,' *Free Will*, ed. Gary Watson, pp. 1–14. Oxford: Oxford University Press, 1982.

Watt, Ian. *The Rise of the Novel*. Berkeley: University of California Press, 1957.

Waugh, Linda. 'Against Arbitrariness: Imitatation and Motivation Revived,' *Diacritics* (Summer 1993): 71–87.

Waugh, Patricia. *Practising Postmodernism/Reading Modernism*. London: Edward Arnold, 1992.

Weissert, Thomas P. 'Representation and Bifurcation: Borges's Garden of Chaos Dynamics,' in *Chaos and Order: Complex Dynamics in Literature and Science*, ed. N. Katherine Hayles, pp. 223–43. Chicago: University of Chicago Press, 1991.

Wiggins, David. *Needs, Values, Truth*. Oxford: Basil Blackwell, 2nd edn, 1991.

Yarbrough, Stephen. *Deliberate Criticism: Towards a Postmodern Humanism*. Athens: University of Georgia Press, 1992.

Young, Iris Marion. *Justice and the Politics of Difference*. Princeton, NJ: Princeton University Press, 1990.

Zelechow, Bernard. 'Nietzsche's Theology of History and the Redemption of Postmodernism,' in *Postmodernism, Literature, and the Future of Theology*, ed. David Jasper, pp. 120–42. New York: St. Martin's Press, 1993.

Zola, Emile. 'The Experimental Novel,' in *Documents of Modern Literary Realism*, ed. George J. Becker, pp. 161–96. Princeton, NJ: Princeton University Press, 1963.

Zola, Emile. 'Naturalism and the Theatre,' in *Documents of Modern Literary Realism*, ed. George J. Becker, pp. 197–229. Princeton, NJ: Princeton University Press, 1963.

Index